I0114686

THE GYPSIES

BY

CHARLES G. LELAND

© 2010 Benediction Classics

PREFACE.

———

THE reader will find in this book sketches of experiences among gypsies of different nations by one
who speaks their language and is conversant with
their ways. These embrace descriptions of the justly
famed musical gypsies of St. Petersburg and Moscow, by whom the writer was received literally as
a brother; of the Austrian gypsies, especially those
composing the first Romany orchestra of that country,
selected by Liszt, and who played for their friend as
they declared they had never played before for any
man; and also of the English, Welsh, Oriental, and
American brethren of the dark blood and the tents.
I believe that the account of interviews with American gypsies will possess at least the charm of novelty, but little having as yet been written on this
extensive and very interesting branch of our nomadic
population. To these I have added a characteristic
letter in the gypsy language, with translation by a
lady, legendary stories, poems, and finally the substance of two papers, one of which I read before the
British Philological Society, and the other before

the Oriental Congress at Florence, in 1878. Those
who study ethnology will be interested to learn from
these papers, subsequently combined in an article in
the " Saturday Review," that I have definitely determined the existence in India of a peculiar tribe of
gypsies, who are *par eminence* the Romanys of the
East, and whose language is there what it is in England, the same in vocabulary, and the chief slang of
the roads. This I claim as a discovery, having learned
it from a Hindoo who had been himself a gypsy in
his native land. Many writers have suggested the
Jats, Banjars, and others as probable ancestors or
type-givers of the race ; but the existence of the *Rom
himself* in India, bearing the distinctive name of Rom,
has never before been set forth in any book or by
any other writer. I have also given what may in
reason be regarded as settling the immensely disputed origin of the word "Zingan," by the gypsies'
own account of its etymology, which was beyond all
question brought by them from India.

In addition to this I have given in a chapter certain conversations with men of note, such as Thomas
Carlyle, Lord Lytton, Mr. Roebuck, and others, on
gypsies; an account of the first and family names
and personal characteristics of English and American
Romanys, prepared for me by a very famous old
gypsy; and finally a chapter on the " Shelta Thari,"
or Tinkers' Language, a very curious jargon or language, never mentioned before by any writer except
Shakespeare. What this tongue may be, beyond the

fact that it is purely Celtic, and that it does not seem to be identical with any other Celtic dialect, is unknown to me. I class it with the gypsy, because all who speak it are also acquainted with Romany.

For an attempt to set forth the tone or feeling in which the sketches are conceived, I refer the reader to the Introduction.

When I published my " English Gypsies and their Language," a reviewer declared that I " had added nothing to our " (that is, his) " knowledge on the subject." As it is always pleasant to meet with a man of superior information, I said nothing. And as I had carefully read everything ever printed on the Romany, and had given a very respectable collection of what was new to me as well as to all my Romany rye colleagues in Europe, I could only grieve to think that such treasures of learning should thus remain hidden in the brain of one who had never at any time or in any other way manifested the possession of any remarkable knowledge. Nobody can tell in this world what others may know, but I modestly suggest that what I have set forth in this work, on the origin of the gypsies, though it may be known to the reviewer in question, has at least never been set before the public by anybody but myself, and that it deserves further investigation. No account of the tribes of the East mentions the Rom or Trablûs, and yet I have personally met with and thoroughly examined one of them. In like manner, the " Shelta Thari " has remained till the present day entirely unknown to all writers on either the languages or the nomadic people of Great Britain. If we are so ignorant of the wanderers among us, and at our very doors, it is not remarkable that we should be ignorant of those of India.

CONTENTS.

CONTENTS.

INTRODUCTION.

I HAVE frequently been asked, "Why do you take an interest in gypsies?"

And it is not so easy to answer. Why, indeed? In Spain one who has been fascinated by them is called one of the *aficion*, or affection, or "fancy;" he is an *aficionado*, or affected unto them, and people there know perfectly what it means, for every Spaniard is at heart a Bohemian. He feels what a charm there is in a wandering life, in camping in lonely places, under old chestnut-trees, near towering cliffs, *al pasar del arroyo*, by the rivulets among the rocks. He thinks of the wine skin and wheaten cake when one was hungry on the road, of the mules and tinkling bells, the fire by night, and the *cigarito*, smoked till he fell asleep. Then he remembers the gypsies who came to the camp, and the black-eyed girl who told him his fortune, and all that followed in the rosy dawn and ever onward into starry night.

> "Y se alegre el alma llena
> De la luz de esos luceros."

> And his heart is filled with rapture
> At the light of those lights above.

This man understands it. So, too, does many an Englishman. But I cannot tell you why. Why do I love to wander on the roads to hear the birds; to see old church towers afar, rising over fringes of forest, a river and a bridge in the foreground, and an ancient castle beyond, with a modern village springing up about it, just as at the foot of the burg there lies the falling trunk of an old tree, around which weeds and flowers are springing up, nourished by its decay? Why love these better than pictures, and with a more than fine-art feeling? Because on the roads, among such scenes, between the hedge-rows and by the river, I find the wanderers who properly inhabit not the houses but the scene, not a part but the whole. These are the gypsies, who live like the birds and hares, not of the house-born or the town-bred, but free and at home only with nature.

I am at some pleasant watering-place, no matter where. Let it be Torquay, or Ilfracombe, or Aberystwith, or Bath, or Bournemouth, or Hastings. I find out what old churches, castles, towns, towers, manors, lakes, forests, fairy-wells, or other charms of England lie within twenty miles. Then I take my staff and sketch-book, and set out on my day's pilgrimage. In the distance lie the lines of the shining sea, with ships sailing to unknown lands. Those who live in them are the Bohemians of the sea, homing while roaming, sleeping as they go, even as gypsies dwell on wheels. And if you look wistfully at these ships far off and out at sea with the sun upon their sails, and wonder what quaint mysteries of life they hide, verily you are not far from being affected or elected unto the Romany. And if, when you see the wild birds on the wing, wending their way to the South, and wish that you could fly with them, — anywhere, anywhere over the world and into adventure, — then you are not far in spirit from the kingdom of Bohemia and its seven castles, in the deep windows of which Æolian wind-harps sing forever.

Now, as you wander along, it may be that in the wood and by some grassy nook you will hear voices, and see the gleam of a red garment, and then find a man of the roads, with dusky wife and child. You speak one word, " Sarishan !" and you are introduced. These people are like birds and bees, they belong to out-of-doors and nature. If you can chirp or buzz a little in their language and know their ways, you will find out, as you sit in the forest, why he who loves green bushes and mossy rocks is glad to fly from cities, and likes to be free of the joyous citizenship of the roads, and everywhere at home in such boon company.

When I have been a stranger in a strange town, I have never gone out for a long walk without knowing that the chances were that I should meet within an hour some wanderer with whom I should have in common certain acquaintances. These be indeed humble folk, but with nature and summer walks they make me at home. In merrie England I could nowhere be a stranger if I would, and that with people who cannot read ; and the English-born Romany rye, or gentleman speaking gypsy, would in like manner be everywhere at home in America. There was a gypsy family always roaming between Windsor and London, and the first words taught to their youngest child were " Romany rye !" and these it was trained to address to me. The little tot came up to me, — I had never heard her speak before, — a little brown-faced, black-eyed thing, and said, " How-do, Omany 'eye ?" and great was the triumph and rejoicing and laughter

of the mother and father and all the little tribe. To
be familiar with these wanderers, who live by dale
and down, is like having the bees come to you, as
they did to the Dacian damsel, whose death they
mourned ; it is like the attraction of the wild deer to
the fair Genevieve; or if you know them to be dangerous outlaws, as some are, it is like the affection of
serpents and other wild things for those whom nature
has made their friends, and who handle them without fear. They are human, but in their lives they
are between man as he lives in houses and the bee
and bird and fox, and I cannot help believing that
those who have no sympathy with them have none
for the forest and road, and cannot be rightly familiar
with the witchery of wood and wold. There are
many ladies and gentlemen who can well-nigh die of
a sunset, and be enraptured with " bits " of color,
and captured with scenes, and to whom all out-of-
doors is as perfect as though it were painted by
Millais, yet to whom the bee and bird and gypsy
and red Indian ever remain in their true inner life
strangers. And just as strange to them, in one sense,
are the scenes in which these creatures dwell ; for
those who see in them only pictures, though they be
by Claude and Turner, can never behold in them
the fairy-land of childhood. Only in Ruysdael and
Salvator Rosa and the great unconscious artists
lurks the spell of the Romany, and this spell is un-
felt by Mr. Cimabue Brown. The child and the
gypsy have no words in which to express their sense
of nature and its charm, but they have this sense,
and there are very, very few who, acquiring culture,
retain it. And it is gradually disappearing from the
world, just as the old delicately sensuous, naïve, pic-

turesque type of woman's beauty — the perfection of natural beauty — is rapidly vanishing in every country, and being replaced by the mingled real and unreal attractiveness of " cleverness," intellect, and fashion. No doubt the newer tend to higher forms of culture, but it is not without pain that he who has been " in the spirit" in the old Sabbath of the soul, and in its quiet, solemn sunset, sees it all vanishing. It will all be gone in a few years. I doubt very much whether it will be possible for the most unaffectedly natural writer to preserve any of its hieroglyphics for future Champollions of sentiment to interpret. In the coming days, when man shall have developed new senses, and when the blessed sun himself shall perhaps have been supplanted by some tremendous electrical light, and the moon be expunged altogether as interfering with the new arrangements for gravity, there will doubtless be a new poetry, and art become to the very last degree self-conscious of its cleverness, artificial and impressional; yet even then weary scholars will sigh from time to time, as they read in our books of the ancient purple seas, and how the sun went down of old into cloud-land, gorgeous land, and then how all dreamed away into night!

Gypsies are the human types of this vanishing, direct love of nature, of this mute sense of rural romance, and of *al fresco* life, and he who does not recognize it in them, despite their rags and dishonesty, need not pretend to appreciate anything more in Callot's etchings than the skillful management of the needle and the acids. Truly they are but rags themselves; the last rags of the old romance which connected man with nature. Once romance was a splendid mediæval drama, colored and gemmed with chivalry, minnesong, bandit-flashes, and waving plumes; now there remain but a few tatters. Yes, we were young and foolish then, but there are perishing with the wretched fragments of the red Indian tribes mythologies as beautiful as those of the Greek or Norseman; and there is also vanishing with the gypsy an unexpressed mythology, which those who are to come after us would gladly recover. Would we not have been pleased if one of the thousand Latin men of letters whose works have been preserved had told us how the old Etruscans, then still living in mountain villages, spoke and habited and customed? But oh that there had ever lived of old one man who, noting how feelings and sentiments changed, tried to so set forth the souls of his time that after-comers might understand what it was which inspired their art!

In the Sanskrit humorous romance of " Baital Pachisi," or King Vikram and the Vampire, twenty-five different and disconnected trifling stories serve collectively to illustrate in the most pointed manner the highest lesson of wisdom. In this book the gypsies, and the scenes which surround them, are intended to teach the lesson of freedom and nature. Never were such lessons more needed than at present. I do not say that culture is opposed to the perception of nature; I would show with all my power that the higher our culture the more we are really qualified to appreciate beauty and freedom. But gates must be opened for this, and unfortunately the gates as yet are very few, while Philistinism in every form makes it a business of closing every opening to the true fairy-land of delight.

The gypsy is one of many links which connect the

simple feeling of nature with romance. During the
Middle Ages thousands of such links and symbols
united nature with religion. Thus Conrad von
Würtzburg tells in his " Goldene Schmiede " that the
parrot which shines in fairest grass-green hue, and
yet like common grass is never wet, sets forth the Virgin, who bestowed on man an endless spring, and yet
remained unchanged. So the parrot and grass and
green and shimmering light all blended in the ideal
of the immortal Maid-Mother, and so the bird appears in pictures by Van Eyck and Dürer. To me
the gypsy-parrot and green grass in lonely lanes and
the rain and sunshine all mingle to set forth the inexpressible purity and sweetness of the virgin parent,
Nature. For the gypsy is parrot-like, a quaint pil-
ferer, a rogue in grain as in green ; for green was
his favorite garb in olden time in England, as it is
to-day in Germany, where he who breaks the Romany law may never dare on heath to wear that fatal
fairy color.

These words are the key to the following book, in
which I shall set forth a few sketches taken during
my rambles among the Romany. The day is coming
when there will be no more wild parrots nor wild
wanderers, no wild nature, and certainly no gypsies.
Within a very few years in the city of Philadelphia,
the English sparrow, the very cit and cad of birds,
has driven from the gardens all the wild, beautiful
feathered creatures whom, as a boy, I knew. The
fire-flashing scarlet tanager and the humming-bird,
the yellow-bird, blue-bird, and golden oriole, are
now almost forgotten, or unknown to city children.
So the people of self-conscious culture and the mart
and factory are banishing the wilder sort, and it

is all right, and so it must be, and therewith *basta!* But as a London reviewer said when I asserted in a book that the child was perhaps born who would see the last gypsy, "Somehow we feel sorry for that child."

THE RUSSIAN GYPSIES.

———◆———

IT is, I believe, seldom observed that the world is so far from having quitted the romantic or sentimental for the purely scientific that, even in science itself, whatever is best set forth owes half its charm to something delicately and distantly reflected from the forbidden land of fancy. The greatest reasoners and writers on the driest topics are still " genial," because no man ever yet had true genius who did not feel the inspiration of poetry, or mystery, or at least of the unusual. We are not rid of the marvelous or curious, and, if we have not yet a science of curiosities, it is apparently because it lies for the present distributed about among the other sciences, just as in small museums illuminated manuscripts are to be found in happy family union with stuffed birds or minerals, and with watches and snuff-boxes, once the property of their late majesties the Georges. Until such a science is formed, the new one of ethnology may appropriately serve for it, since it of all presents most attraction to him who is politely called the general reader, but who should in truth be called the man who reads the most for mere amusement. For Ethnology deals with such delightful material as primeval kumbo-cephalic skulls, and appears to her votaries arrayed, not in silk attire, but in strange frag-

2

ments of leather from ancient Irish graves, or in cloth from Lacustrine villages. She glitters with the quaint jewelry of the first Italian race, whose ghosts, if they wail over the " find," " speak in a language man knows no more." She charms us with etchings or scratchings of mammoths on mammoth-bone, and invites us to explore mysterious caves, to picnic among megalithic monuments, and speculate on pictured Scottish stones. In short, she engages man to investigate his ancestry, a pursuit which presents charms even to the illiterate, and asks us to find out facts concerning works of art which have interested everybody in every age.

Ad interim, before the science of curiosities is segregated from that of ethnology, I may observe that one of the marvels in the latter is that, among all the subdivisions of the human race, there are only two which have been, apparently from their beginning, set apart, marked and cosmopolite, ever living among others, and yet reserved unto themselves. These are the Jew and the gypsy. From time whereof history hath naught to the contrary, the Jew was, as he himself holds in simple faith, the first man. Red Earth, Adam, was a Jew, and the old claim to be a peculiar people has been curiously confirmed by the extraordinary genius and influence of the race, and by their boundless wanderings. Go where we may, we find the Jew — has any other wandered so far ?

Yes, one. For wherever Jew has gone, there, too, we find the gypsy. The Jew may be more ancient, but even the authentic origin of the Romany is lost in ancient Aryan record, and, strictly speaking, his is a prehistoric caste. Among the hundred and fifty wan-

dering tribes of India and Persia, some of them Tu-
ranian, some Aryan, and others mixed, it is of course
difficult to identify the exact origin of the European
gypsy. One thing we know: that from the tenth to
the twelfth century, and probably much later on,
India threw out from her northern half a vast multitude of very troublesome indwellers. What with
Buddhist, Brahman, and Mohammedan wars, — in-
vaders outlawing invaded, — the number of out-*castes*
became alarmingly great. To these the Jats, who,
according to Captain Burton, constituted the main
stock of our gypsies, contributed perhaps half their
entire nation. Excommunication among the Indian
professors of transcendental benevolence meant social
death and inconceivable cruelty. Now there are
many historical indications that these outcasts, before
leaving India, became gypsies, which was the most
natural thing in a country where such classes had
already existed in very great numbers from early
times. And from one of the lowest castes, which
still exists in India, and is known as the Dom,[1] the
emigrants to the West probably derived their name
and several characteristics. The Dom burns the
dead, handles corpses, skins beasts, and performs
other functions, all of which were appropriated by,
and became peculiar to, gypsies in several countries
in Europe, notably in Denmark and Holland, for
several centuries after their arrival there. The Dom

[1] From the observations of Frederic Drew (*The Northern Barrier
of India*, London, 1877) there can be little doubt that the Dom, or
Dûm, belong to the pre-Aryan race or races of India. "They are
described in the Shastras as Sopukh, or Dog-Eaters" (*Types of India*). I have somewhere met with the statement that the Dom was
pre-Aryan, but allowed to rank as Hindoo on account of services rendered to the early conquerors.

of the present day also sells baskets, and wanders
with a tent; he is altogether gypsy. It is remarkable that he, living in a hot climate, drinks ardent
spirits to excess, being by no means a " temperate
Hindoo," and that even in extreme old age his hair
seldom turns white, which is a noted peculiarity
among our own gypsies of pure blood. I know and
have often seen a gypsy woman, nearly a hundred
years old, whose curling hair is black, or hardly per-
ceptibly changed. It is extremely probable that the
Dom, mentioned as a caste even in the Shastras, gave
the name to the Rom. The Dom calls his wife a
Domni, and being a Dom is " Domnipana." In English gypsy, the same words are expressed by *Rom*,
romni, and *romnipen*. D, be it observed, very often
changes to *r* in its transfer from Hindoo to Romany.
Thus *doi*, "a wooden spoon," becomes in gypsy *roi*,
a term known to every tinker in London. But,
while this was probably the origin of the word Rom,
there were subsequent reasons for its continuance.
Among the Cophts, who were more abundant in
Egypt when the first gypsies went there, the word
for man is *romi*, and after leaving Greece and the
Levant, or *Rum*, it would be natural for the wanderers to be called *Rumi*. But the Dom was in all probability the parent stock of the gypsy race, though
the latter received vast accessions from many other
sources. I call attention to this, since it has always
been held, and sensibly enough, that the mere fact
of the gypsies speaking Hindi-Persian, or the oldest
type of Urdu, including many Sanskrit terms, does
not prove an Indian or Aryan origin, any more than
the English spoken by American negroes proves a
Saxon descent. But if the Rom can be identified

with the Dom — and the circumstantial evidence, it
must be admitted, is very strong — but little remains
to seek, since, according to the Shastras, the Doms
are Hindoo.

Among the tribes whose union formed the European gypsy was, in all probability, that of the *Nats,*
consisting of singing and dancing girls and male musicians and acrobats. Of these, we are told that not
less than ten thousand lute-players and minstrels, under the name of *Luri,* were once sent to Persia as a
present to a king, whose land was then without music or song. This word *Luri* is still preserved. The
saddle-makers and leather-workers of Persia are called
Tsingani; they are, in their way, low caste, and a
kind of gypsy, and it is supposed that from them are
possibly derived the names Zingan, Zigeunner, Zin-
garo, etc., by which gypsies are known in so many
lands. From Mr. Arnold's late work on " Persia,"
the reader may learn that the *Eeli,* who constitute
the majority of the inhabitants of the southern portion of that country, are Aryan nomads, and apparently gypsies. There are also in India the Banjari,
or wandering merchants, and many other tribes, all
spoken of as gypsies by those who know them.

As regards the great admixture of Persian with
Hindi in good Romany, it is quite unmistakable,
though I can recall no writer who has attached sufficient importance to a fact which identifies gypsies
with what is almost preëminently the land of gypsies. I once had the pleasure of taking a Nile
journey in company with Prince S——, a Persian,
and in most cases, when I asked my friend what this
or that gypsy word meant, he gave me its correct
meaning, after a little thought, and then added, in
his imperfect English, " What for you want to know

such word? — that *old* word — that no more used. Only common people — old peasant-woman — use that word — *gentleman* no want to know him." But I did want to know " him " very much. I can remember that one night, when our *bon prince* had thus held forth, we had dancing girls, or Almeh, on board, and one was very young and pretty. I was told that she was gypsy, but she spoke no Romany. Yet her panther eyes and serpent smile and *beauté du diable* were not Egyptian, but of the Indian, *kalo-ratt*, — the dark blood, which, once known, is known forever. I forgot her, however, for a long time, until I went to Moscow, when she was recalled by dancing and smiles, of which I will speak anon.

I was sitting one day by the Thames, in a gypsy tent, when its master, Joshua Cooper, now dead, pointing to a swan, asked me for its name in gypsy. I replied, " *Boro pappin.*"

" No, *rya. Boro pappin* is ' a big goose.' *Sákkú* is the real gypsy word. It is very old, and very few Romany know it."

A few days after, when my Persian friend was dining with me at the Langham Hotel, I asked him if he knew what Sákkú meant. By way of reply, he, not being able to recall the English word, waved his arms in wonderful pantomime, indicating some enormous winged creature ; and then, looking into the distance, and pointing as if to some far-vanishing object, as boys do when they declaim Bryant's address " To a Water-Fowl," said, —

" Sákkú — one ver' big bird, like one *swen* — but he *not* swen. He like the man who carry too much water up-stairs[1] his head in Constantinople. That

---

[1] Up-stairs in this gentleman's dialect signified up or upon, like *top-side* in Pidgin-English.

bird all same that man. He *sakkia* all same wheel
that you see get water up-stairs in Egypt."

This was explanatory, but far from satisfactory.
The prince, however, was mindful of me, and the
next day I received from the Persian embassy the
word elegantly written in Persian, with the translation, " *a pelican.*" Then it was all clear enough, for
the pelican bears water in the bag under its bill.
When the gypsies came to Europe they named animals after those which resembled them in Asia. A
dog they called *juckal*, from a jackal, and a swan
sákkú, or pelican, because it so greatly resembles it.
The Hindoo *bandarus*, or monkey, they have changed
to *bombaros*, but why Tom Cooper should declare that
it is *pugasah*, or *pukkus-asa*, I do not know.[1] As
little can I conjecture the meaning of the prefix *mod*,
or *mode*, which I learned on the road near Weymouth
from a very ancient tinker, a man so battered, tattered,
seamed, riven, and wrinkled that he looked like a pet-
rifaction. He had so bad a barrow, or wheel, that
I wondered what he could do with it, and regarded
him as the very poorest man I had ever seen in England, until his mate came up, an *alter ego*, so excellent in antiquity, wrinkles, knobbiness, and rags that
he surpassed the vagabond pictures not only of Callot, Doré, and Goya, but even the unknown Spanish
maker of a picture which I met with not long since
for sale, and which for infinite poverty defied anything I ever saw on canvas. These poor men, who
seemed at first amazed that I should speak to them
at all, when I spoke Romany at once called me
" brother." When I asked the younger his name,

[1] *Puccasa,* Sanskrit. Low, inferior. Given by Pliny E. Chase in his
Sanskrit Analogues as the root-word for several inferior animals.

he sank his voice to a whisper, and, with a furtive air, said, —

"*Kámlo,* — Lovel, you know."

"What do you call yourself in the way of business?" I asked. "*Katsamengro,* I suppose."

Now *Katsamengro* means scissors-master.

"That is a very good word. But *chivó* is deeper."

"*Chivó* means a knife-man?"

"Yes. But the deepest of all, master, is *Modangaréngro.* For you see that the right word for coals is n't *wongur,* as Romanys generally say, but *Angára.*"

Now *angára,* as Pott and Benfey indicate, is pure Sanskrit for coals, and *angaréngro* is a worker in coals, but what *mod* means I know not, and should be glad to be told.

I think it will be found difficult to identify the European gypsy with any one stock of the wandering races of India. Among those who left that country were men of different castes and different color, varying from the pure northern invader to the negro-like southern Indian. In the Danubian principalities there are at the present day three kinds of gypsies: one very dark and barbarous, another light brown and more intelligent, and the third, or *élite,* of yellow-pine complexion, as American boys characterize the hue of quadroons. Even in England there are straight-haired and curly-haired Romanys, the two indicating not a difference resulting from white admixture, but entirely different original stocks.

It will, I trust, be admitted, even from these remarks, that Romanology, or that subdivision of ethnology which treats of gypsies, is both practical and curious. It deals with the only race except the Jew, which has penetrated into every village which European civilization has ever touched. He who speaks Romany need be a stranger in few lands, for on every road in Europe and America, in Western Asia, and even in Northern Africa, he will meet those with whom a very few words may at once establish a peculiar understanding. For, of all things believed in by this widely spread brotherhood, the chief is this, — that he who knows the *jib*, or language, knows the ways, and that no one ever attained these without treading strange paths, and threading mysteries unknown to the Gorgios, or Philistines. And if he who speaks wears a good coat, and appears a gentleman, let him rest assured that he will receive the greeting which all poor relations in all lands extend to those of their kin who have risen in life. Some of them, it is true, manifest the winsome affection which is based on great expectations, a sentiment largely developed among British gypsies ; but others are honestly proud that a gentleman is not ashamed of them. Of this latter class were the musical gypsies, whom I met in Russia during the winter of 1876 and 1877, and some of them again in Paris during the Exposition of 1878.

ST. PETERSBURG.

There are gypsies and gypsies in the world, for there are the wanderers on the roads and the secret dwellers in towns ; but even among the *aficionados*, or Romany ryes, by whom I mean those scholars who are fond of studying life and language from the people themselves, very few have dreamed that there exist communities of gentlemanly and lady-like gyp-

sies of art, like the Bohemians of Murger and George
Sand, but differing from them in being real "Bohemians" by race. I confess that it had never occurred
to me that there was anywhere in Europe, at the present day, least of all in the heart of great and wealthy
cities, a class or caste devoted entirely to art, well-to-
do or even rich, refined in manners, living in comfortable homes, the women dressing elegantly ; and yet
with all this obliged to live by law, as did the Jews
once, in Ghettos or in a certain street, and regarded
as outcasts and *cagôts.* I had heard there were gypsies in Russian cities, and expected to find them like
the *kérengri* of England or Germany, — house-dwellers
somewhat reformed from vagabondage, but still reckless semi-outlaws, full of tricks and lies ; in a word,
gypsies, as the world understands the term. And I
certainly anticipated in Russia something *queer,* — the
gentleman who speaks Romany seldom fails to achieve
at least that, whenever he gets into an unbroken
haunt, an unhunted forest, where the Romany rye
is unknown, — but nothing like what I really found.
A recent writer on Russia[1] speaks with great contempt of these musical Romanys, their girls attired in dresses by Worth, as compared with the free
wild outlaws of the steppes, who, with dark, ineffable
glances, meaning nothing more than a wild-cat's,
steal poultry, and who, wrapped in dirty sheep-skins,
proudly call themselves *Mi dvorane Polaivii,* Lords
of the Waste. The gypsies of Moscow, who appeared to me the most interesting I have ever met,
because most remote from the Surrey ideal, seemed
to Mr. Johnstone to be a kind of second-rate Rom-

---

[1] *A Trip up the Volga to the Fair of Nijni-Novgorod.* By H. A.
Munro Butler Johnstone. 1875.

anys or gypsies, gypsified for exhibition, like Mr.
Barnum's negro minstrel, who, though black as a
coal by nature, was requested to put on burnt cork
and a wig, that the audience might realize that they
were getting a thoroughly good imitation. Mr. Johnstone's own words are that a gypsy maiden in a long
queue, "which perhaps came from Worth," is "hor-
rible," "*corruptio optimi pessima est;*" and he further compares such a damsel to a negro with a cocked
hat and spurs. As the only negro thus arrayed who
presents himself to my memory was one who lay
dead on the battle-field in Tennessee, after one of the
bravest resistances in history, and in which he and
his men, not having moved, were extended in "stark,
serried lines" ("ten cart-loads of dead niggers,"
said a man to me who helped to bury them), I
may be excused for not seeing the wit of the com-
parison. As for the gypsies of Moscow, I can only
say that, after meeting them in public, and pene-
trating to their homes, where I was received as one
of themselves, even as a Romany, I found that this
opinion of them was erroneous, and that they were
altogether original in spite of being clean, deeply
interesting although honest, and a quite attractive
class in most respects, notwithstanding their ability
to read and write. Against Mr. Johnstone's impressions, I may set the straightforward and simple result
of the experiences of Mr. W. R. Ralston. "The
gypsies of Moscow," he says, "are justly celebrated
for their picturesqueness and for their wonderful capacity for music. All who have heard their women
sing are enthusiastic about the weird witchery of the
performance."

When I arrived in St. Petersburg, one of my first

inquiries was for gypsies. To my astonishment, they were hard to find. They are not allowed to live in the city ; and I was told that the correct and proper way to see them would be to go at night to certain *cafés*, half an hour's sleigh-ride from the town, and listen to their concerts. What I wanted, however, was not a concert, but a conversation ; not gypsies on exhibition, but gypsies at home, — and everybody seemed to be of the opinion that those of " Samarcand " and " Dorot " were entirely got up for effect. In fact, I heard the opinion hazarded that, even if they spoke Romany, I might depend upon it they had acquired it simply to deceive. One gentleman, who had, however, been much with them in other days, assured me that they were of pure blood, and had an inherited language of their own. " But," he added, " I am sure you will not understand it. You may be able to talk with those in England, but not with ours, because there is not a single word in their language which resembles anything in English, German, French, Latin, Greek, or Italian. I can only recall," he added, " one phrase. I don't know what it means, and I think it will puzzle you. It is *me kamáva tut.*"

If I experienced internal laughter at hearing this it was for a good reason, which I can illustrate by an anecdote : " I have often observed, when I lived in China," said Mr. Hoffman Atkinson, author of " A Vocabulary of the Yokohama Dialect," " that most young men, particularly the gay and handsome ones, generally asked me, about the third day after their arrival in the country, the meaning of the Pidgin-English phrase, ' You makee too muchee lov-lov-pidgin.' Investigation always established the fact that

the inquirer had heard it from ' a pretty China girl.'
Now *lov-pidgin* means love, and *me kamáva tut* is
perfectly good gypsy anywhere for ' I love you ; ' and
a very soft expression it is, recalling *kama-deva*, the
Indian Cupid, whose bow is strung with bees, and
whose name has two strings to it, since it means, both
in gypsy and Sanskrit, Love-God, or the god of love.
' It 's *kāma-duvel*, you know, *rya*, if you put it as it
ought to be,' said Old Windsor Froggie to me once ;
' but I think that Kāma-*devil* would by rights come
nearer to it, if Cupid is what you mean.' "

I referred the gypsy difficulty to a Russian gentleman of high position, to whose kindness I had
been greatly indebted while in St. Petersburg. He
laughed.

" Come with me to-morrow night to the *cafés*, and
see the gypsies ; I know them well, and can promise
that you shall talk with them as much as you like.
Once, in Moscow, I got together all in the town —
perhaps a hundred and fifty — to entertain the American minister, Curtin. That was a very hard thing
to do, — there was so much professional jealousy
among them, and so many quarrels. Would you have
believed it ? "

I thought of the feuds between sundry sturdy
Romanys in England, and felt that I could suppose
such a thing, without dangerously stretching my
faith, and I began to believe in Russian gypsies.

" Well, then, I shall call for you to-morrow night
with a *troika ;* I will come early, — at ten. They
never begin to sing before company arrive at eleven,
so that you will have half an hour to talk to them."

It is on record that the day on which the general
gave me this kind invitation was the coldest known

in St. Petersburg for thirty years, the thermometer having stood, or rather having lain down and groveled that morning at 40° below zero, Fahr. At the appointed hour the *troika*, or three-horse sleigh, was before the Hôtel d'Europe. It was, indeed, an arctic night, but, well wrapped in fur-lined *shubas*, with immense capes which fall to the elbow or rise far above the head, as required, and wearing fur caps and fur-lined gloves, we felt no cold. The beard of our *istvostshik*, or driver, was a great mass of ice, giving him the appearance of an exceedingly hoary youth, and his small horses, being very shaggy and thoroughly frosted, looked in the darkness like immense polar bears. If the general and myself could only have been considered as gifts of the slightest value to anybody, I should have regarded our turn-out, with the driver in his sheep-skin coat, as coming within a miracle of resemblance to that of Santa Claus, the American Father Christmas.

On, at a tremendous pace, over the snow, which gave out under our runners that crunching, iron sound only heard when the thermometer touches zero. There is a peculiar fascination about the *troika*, and the sweetest, saddest melody and most plaintive song of Russia belong to it.

THE TROIKA.

Vot y'dit troika udalaiya.

Hear ye the troika-bell a-ringing,
And see the peasant driver there?
Hear ye the mournful song he's singing,
Like distant tolling through the air?

" O eyes, blue eyes, to me so lonely,
O eyes — alas! — ye give me pain;

O eyes, that once looked at me only,
    I ne'er shall see your like again.

"Farewell, my darling, now in heaven,
    And still the heaven of my soul;
Farewell, thou father town, O Moscow,
    Where I have left my life, my all!"

And ever at the rein still straining,
    One backward glance the driver gave;
Sees but once more a green low hillock,
    Sees but once more his loved one's grave.

"*Stoi!*"—Halt! We stopped at a stylish-looking building, entered a hall, left our *shubas*, and I heard the general ask, "Are the gypsies here?" An affirmative being given, we entered a large room, and there, sure enough, stood six or eight girls and two men, all very well dressed, and all unmistakably Romany, though smaller and of much slighter or more delicate frame than the powerful gypsy "travelers" of England. In an instant every pair of great, wild eyes was fixed on me. The general was in every way a more striking figure, but I was manifestly a fresh stranger, who knew nothing of the country, and certainly nothing of gypsies or gypsydom. Such a verdant visitor is always most interesting. It was not by any means my first reception of the kind, and, as I reviewed at a glance the whole party, I said within myself: —

"Wait an instant, you black snakes, and I will give you something to make you stare."

This promise I kept, when a young man, who looked like a handsome light Hindoo, stepped up and addressed me in Russian. I looked long and steadily at him before I spoke, and then said: —

"*Latcho divvus prala!*" (Good day, brother.)

"What is *that?*" he exclaimed, startled.

" *Tu jines latcho adosta.*" (You know very well.)
And then, with the expression in his face of a man
who has been familiarly addressed by a brazen statue,
or asked by a new-born babe, " What o'clock is it?"
but with great joy, he cried : —

' *Romanichal !*' "

In an instant they were all around me, marveling
greatly, and earnestly expressing their marvel, at what
new species of gypsy I might be ; being in this quite
unlike those of England, who, even when they are
astonished " out of their senses " at being addressed
in Romany by a gentleman, make the most red-Indian
efforts to conceal their amazement. But I speedily
found that these Russian gypsies were as unaffected
and child-like as they were gentle in manner, and that
they compared with our own prize-fighting, sturdy-
begging, always-suspecting Romany roughs and *rufi-
anas* as a delicate greyhound might compare with a
very shrewd old bull-dog, trained by an unusually
" fly " tramp.

That the girls were first to the fore in questioning
me will be doubted by no one. But we had great
trouble in effecting a mutual understanding. Their
Romany was full of Russian ; their pronunciation
puzzled me ; they " bit off their words," and used
many in a strange or false sense. Yet, notwithstanding this, I contrived to converse pretty readily with
the men, — very readily with the captain, a man as
dark as Ben Lee, to those who know Benjamin, or
as mahogany, to those who know him not. But with
the women it was very difficult to converse. There
is a theory current that women have a specialty of
tact and readiness in understanding a foreigner, or in
making themselves understood ; it may be so with

cultivated ladies, but it is my experience that, among the uneducated, men have a monopoly of such quick intelligence. In order fully to convince them that we really had a tongue in common, I repeated perhaps a hundred nouns, giving, for instance, the names cf various parts of the body, of articles of apparel and objects in the room, and I believe that we did not find a single word which, when pronounced distinctly by itself, was not intelligible to us all. I had left in London a Russo-Romany vocabulary, once published in " The Asiatic Magazine," and I had met with Böhtlinghk's article on the dialect, as well as specimens of it in the works of Pott and Miklosich, but had unfortunately learned nothing of it from them. I soon found, however, that I knew a great many more gypsy words than did my new friends, and that our English Romany far excels the Russian in *copia verborum.*

"But I must sit down." I observed on this and other occasions that Russian gypsies are very naïf. And as it is in human nature to prefer sitting by a pretty girl, these Slavonian Romanys so arrange it according to the principles of natural selection — or natural politeness — that, when a stranger is in their gates, the two prettiest girls in their possession sit at his right and left, the two less attractive next again, *et seriatim.* So at once a damsel of comely mien, arrayed in black silk attire, of faultless elegance, cried to me, pointing to a chair by her side, " *Bersh tu alay, rya!* " (Sit down, sir), — a phrase which would be perfectly intelligible to any Romany in England. I admit that there was another damsel, who is generally regarded by most people as the true gypsy belle of the party. who did not sit by me.

But, as the one who had "voted herself into the chair," by my side, was more to my liking, being the most intelligent and most gypsy, I had good cause to rejoice.

I was astonished at the sensible curiosity as to gypsy life in other lands which was displayed, and at the questions asked. I really doubt if I ever met with an English gypsy who cared a farthing to know anything about his race as it exists in foreign countries, or whence it came. Once, and once only, I thought I had interested White George, at East Moulsey, in an account of Egypt, and the small number of Romanys there; but his only question was to the effect that, if there were so few gypsies in Egypt, would n't it be a good place for him to go to sell baskets? These of Russia, however, asked all kinds of questions about the manners and customs of their congeners, and were pleased when they recognized familiar traits. And every gypsyism, whether of word or way, was greeted with delighted laughter. In one thing I noted a radical difference between these gypsies and those of the rest of Europe and of America. There was none of that continually assumed mystery and Romany freemasonry, of superior occult knowledge and "deep" information, which is often carried to the depths of absurdity and to the height of humbug. I say this advisedly, since, however much it may give charm to a novel or play, it is a serious impediment to a philologist. Let me give an illustration.

Once, during the evening, these Russian gypsies were anxious to know if there were any books in their language. Now I have no doubt that Dr. Bath Smart, or Prof. E. H. Palmer, or any other of the initiated, will perfectly understand when I say that by mere force of habit I shivered and evaded the question. When a gentleman who manifests a knowledge of Romany among gypsies in England is suspected of " dixonary " studies, it amounts to *lasciate ogni speranza*, — give up all hope of learning any more.

" I 'm glad to see you here, *rya*, in my tent," said the before-mentioned Ben Lee to me one night, in camp near Weybridge, " because I 've heard, and I know, ·you did n't pick up *your* Romany out of books."

The silly dread, the hatred, the childish antipathy, real or affected, but always ridiculous, which is felt in England, not only among gypsies, but even by many gentlemen scholars, to having the Romany language published is indescribable. Vambéry was not more averse to show a lead pencil among Tartars than I am to take notes of words among strange English gypsies. I might have spared myself any annoyance from such a source among the Russian Romanys. They had not heard of Mr. George Borrow ; nor were there ugly stories current among them to the effect that Dr. Smart and Prof. E. H. Palmer had published works, the direct result of which would be to facilitate their little paths to the jail, the gallows, and the grave.

" Would we hear some singing ? " We were ready, and for the first time in my life I listened to the long-anticipated, far-famed magical melody of Russian gypsies. And what was it like ? May I preface my reply to the reader with the remark that there are, roughly speaking, two kinds of music in the world, — the wild and the tame, — and the rarest of human beings is he who, can appreciate both. Only one such man ever wrote a book, and his *nomen et omen* is Engel, like that of the little English slaves who were *non Angli, sed angeli.* I have in my time been deeply moved by the choruses of Nubian boatmen; I have listened with great pleasure to Chinese and Japanese music, — Ole Bull once told me he had done the same; I have delighted by the hour in Arab songs; and I have felt the charm of our red-Indian music. If this seems absurd to those who characterize all such sound and song as "caterwauling,' let me remind the reader that in all Europe there is not one man fonder of music than an average Arab, a Chinese, or a red Indian; for any of these people, as I have seen and know, will sit twelve or fifteen hours, without the least weariness, listening to what cultivated Europeans all consider as a mere charivari. When London gladly endures fifteen-hour concerts, composed of *morceaux* by Wagner, Chopin, and Liszt, I will believe that art can charm as much as nature.

The medium point of intelligence in this puzzle may be found in the extraordinary fascination which many find in the monotonous tum-tum of the banjo, and which reappears, somewhat refined, or at least somewhat Frenchified, in the *Bamboula* and other Creole airs. Thence, in an ascending series, but connected with it, we have old Spanish melodies, then the Arabic, and here we finally cross the threshold into mystery, midnight, and "caterwauling." I do not know that I can explain the fact why the more "barbarous" music is, the more it is beloved of man; but I think that the principle of the *refrain*, or repetition in music, which as yet governs all decorative art, and which Mr. Whistler and others are endeavoring desperately to destroy, acts in music as a sort of animal magnetism or abstraction, ending in an *extase.* As for the fascination which such wild melodies exert, it is beyond description. The most enraptured audience I ever saw in my life was at a Coptic wedding in Cairo, where one hundred and fifty guests listened, from seven P. M. till three A. M., and Heaven knows how much later, to what a European would call absolute jangling, yelping, and howling.

The real medium, however, between what I have, for want of better words, called wild and tame music exists only in that of the Russian gypsies. These artists, with wonderful tact and untaught skill, have succeeded, in all their songs, in combining the mysterious and maddening charm of the true, wild Eastern music with that of regular and simple melody, intelligible to every Western ear. I have never listened to the singing or playing of any distinguished artist — and certainly never of any far-famed amateur — without realizing that neither words nor melody was of the least importance, but that the man's manner of performance or display was everything. Now, in enjoying gypsy singing, one feels at once as if the vocalists had entirely forgotten self, and were carried away by the bewildering beauty of the air and the charm of the words. There is no self-consciousness, no vanity, — all is real. The listener feels as if he were a performer; the performer is an enraptured listener. There is no soulless "art for the sake of art," but art for direct pleasure.

"We intend to sing only Romany for *you, rya,*" said the young lady to my left, "and you will hear our real gypsy airs. The *Gaji* [Russians] often ask for songs in our language, and don't get them. But you are a Romanichal, and when you go home, far over the *baro kālo pāni* [the broad black water, that is, the ocean], you shall tell the Romany how we can sing. Listen!"

And I listened to the strangest, wildest, and sweetest singing I ever had heard, — the singing of Lurleis, of sirens, of witches. First, one damsel, with an exquisitely clear, firm voice, began to sing a verse of a love-ballad, and as it approached the end the chorus stole in, softly and unperceived, but with exquisite skill, until, in a few seconds, the summer breeze, murmuring melody over a rippling lake, seemed changed to a midnight tempest, roaring over a stormy sea, in which the *basso* of the *kālo shureskro* (the black captain) pealed like thunder. Just as it died away a second girl took up the melody, very sweetly, but with a little more excitement, — it was like a gleam of moonlight on the still agitated waters, a strange contralto witch-gleam; and then again the chorus and the storm; and then another solo yet sweeter, sadder, and stranger, — the movement continually increasing, until all was fast, and wild, and mad, — a locomotive quickstep, and then a sudden silence — sunlight — the storm had blown away.

Nothing on earth is so like magic and elfin-work as when women burst forth into improvised melody. The bird only "sings as his bill grew," or what he learned from the elders; yet when you hear birds singing in woodland green, throwing out to God or the fairies irrepressible floods of what seems like audible sunshine, so well does it match with summer's light, you think it is wonderful. It is mostly when you forget the long training of the prima donna, in her ease and apparent naturalness, that her song is

sweetest. But there is a charm, which was well
known of old, though we know it not to-day, which
was practiced by the bards and believed in by their
historians. It was the feeling that the song was born
of the moment; that it came with the air, gushing
and fresh from the soul. In reading the strange
stories of the professional bards and scalds and minstrels of the early Middle Age, one is constantly bewildered at the feats of off-hand composition which
were exacted of the poets among Celts or Norse-
men. And it is evident enough that in some mysterious way these singers knew how to put strange
pressure on the Muse, and squeeze strains out of her
in a manner which would have been impossible at
present.

Yet it lingers here and there on earth among wild,
strange people, — this art of making melody at will.
I first heard it among Nubian boatmen on the Nile.
It was as manifest that it was composed during the
making as that the singers were unconscious of their
power. One sung at first what may have been a well-
known verse. While singing, another voice stole in,
and yet another, softly as shadows steal into twilight;
and ere I knew it all were in a great chorus, which
fell away as mysteriously, to become duos, trios, —
changing in melody in strange, sweet, fitful wise, as
the faces seen in the golden cloud in the visioned
aureole of God blend, separate, burn, and fade away
ever into fresher glory and tints incarnadined.

Miss C. F. Gordon Cumming, after informing us
that " it is utterly impossible to give you the faintest
shadow of an idea of the fascination of Tahitian
himénes," proceeds, as men in general and women
in particular invariably do, to give what the writer

really believes is a very good description indeed.
'T is ever thus, and thus 't will ever be, and the description of these songs is so good that any person
gifted with imagination or poetry cannot fail to smile
at the preceding disavowal of her ability to give an
idea.

These *himénes* are not — and here such of my too
expectant young lady-readers as are careless in spell-
ing will be sadly disappointed — in any way connected with weddings. They are simply the natural
music of Tahiti, or strange and beautiful part-songs.
" Nothing you have ever heard in any other country,"
says our writer, " bears the slightest resemblance to
these wild, exquisite glees, faultless in time and harmony, though apparently each singer introduces any
variations which may occur to him or to her. Very
often there is no leader, and apparently all sing according to their own sweet will. One voice com-
mences ; it may be that of an old native, with genuine native words (the meaning of which we had better not inquire), or it may be with a Scriptural story,
versified and sung to an air originally from Europe,
but so completely Tahitianized that no mortal could
recognize it, which is all in its favor, for the wild
melodies of this isle are beyond measure fascinating.

" After one clause of solo, another strikes in —
here, there, everywhere — in harmonious chorus.
It seems as if one section devoted themselves to pour-
ing forth a rippling torrent of ' Ra, ra, ra — ra — ra !'
while others burst into a flood of ' La, la — la — la —
la !' Some confine their care to sound a deep, boom-
ing bass in a long-continued drone, somewhat suggestive (to my appreciative Highland ear) of our
own bagpipes. Here and there high falsetto notes

strike in, varied from verse to verse, and then the choruses of La and Ra come bubbling in liquid melody, while the voices of the principal singers now join in unison, now diverge as widely as it is possible for them to do, but all combine to produce the quaintest, most melodious, rippling glee that ever was heard."

This is the *himéne ;* such the singing which I heard in Egypt in a more regular form ; but it was exactly as the writer so admirably sets it forth (and your description, my lady traveler, is, despite your disavowal, quite perfect and a *himéne* of itself) that I heard the gypsy girls of St. Petersburg and of Moscow sing. For, after a time, becoming jolly as flies, first one voice began with "La, la, la — la — la !" to an unnamed, unnamable, charming melody, into which went and came other voices, some bringing one verse or no verse, in unison or alone, the least expected doing what was most awaited, which was to surprise us and call forth gay peals of happy laughter, while the "La, la, la — la — la !" was kept up continuously, like an accompaniment. And still the voices, basso, soprano, tenor, baritone, contralto, rose and fell, the moment's inspiration telling how, till at last all blended in a locomotive-paced La, and in a final roar of laughter it ended.

I could not realize at the time how much this exquisite part-singing was extemporized. The sound of it rung in my head — I assure you, reader, it rings there yet when I think of it — like a magic bell. Another day, however, when I begged for a repetition of it, the girls could recall nothing of it. They could start it again on any air to the unending strain of "La — la — la ;" but *the* "La — la — la" of the previous evening was *avec les neiges d'antan,* with the smoke of yesterday's fire, with the perfume and bird-songs. " La, la, la — la — la ! "

In Arab singing, such effects are applied simply to set forth erotomania ; in negro minstrelsy, they are degraded to the lowest humor ; in higher European music, when employed, they simply illustrate the skill of composer and musician. The spirit of gypsy singing recalled by its method and sweetness that of the Nubian boatmen, but in its *general* effect I could think only of those strange fits of excitement which thrill the red Indian and make him burst into song. The Abbé Domenech [1] has observed that the American savage pays attention to every sound that strikes upon his ear when the leaves, softly shaken by the evening breeze, seem to sigh through the air, or when the tempest, bursting forth with fury, shakes the gigantic trees that crack like reeds. " The chirping of the birds, the cry of the wild beasts, in a word, all those sweet, grave, or imposing voices that animate the wilderness, are so many musical lessons, which he easily remembers." In illustration of this, the missionary describes the singing of a Chippewa chief, and its wild inspiration, in a manner which vividly illustrates all music of the class of which I write.

"It was," he says, " during one of those long winter nights, so monotonous and so wearisome in the woods. We were in a wigwam, which afforded us but miserable shelter from the inclemency of the season. The storm raged without ; the tempest roared in the open country ; the wind blew with violence, and whistled through the fissures of the cabin ; the rain fell in torrents, and prevented us from continu·

[1] *Seven Years in the Deserts of America.*

ing our route. Our host was an Indian, with sparkling and intelligent eyes, clad with a certain elegance,
and wrapped majestically in a large fur cloak. Seated
close to the fire, which cast a reddish gleam through
the interior of his wigwam, he felt himself all at once
seized with an irresistible desire to imitate the con-
vulsions of nature, and to sing his impressions. So,
taking hold of a drum which hung near his bed, he
beat a slight rolling, resembling the distant sounds
of an approaching storm ; then, raising his voice to a
shrill treble, which he knew how to soften when he
pleased, he imitated the whistling of the air, the
creaking of the branches dashing against one another,
and the particular noise produced by dead leaves
when accumulated in compact masses on the ground.
By degrees the rollings of the drum became more
frequent and louder, the chants more sonorous and
shrill, and at last our Indian shrieked, howled, and
roared in a most frightful manner ; he struggled and
struck his instrument with extraordinary rapidity. It
was a real tempest, to which nothing was wanting,
not even the distant howling of the dogs, nor the bel-
lowing of the affrighted buffaloes."

I have observed the same musical inspiration of a
storm upon Arabs, who, during their singing, also accompanied themselves on a drum. I once spent two
weeks in a Mediterranean steamboat, on board of
which were more than two hundred pilgrims, for the
greater part wild Bedouins, going to Mecca. They
had a minstrel who sang and played on the *darabuka*,
or earthenware drum, and he was aided by another
with a simple *nai*, or reed-whistle ; the same orchestra,
in fact, which is in universal use among all red Indians. To these performers the pilgrims listened

with indescribable pleasure; and I soon found that they regarded me favorably because I did the same, being, of course, the only Frank on board who paid any attention to the singing — or any money for it. But it was at night and during storms that the spirit of music always seemed to be strongest on the Arabs, and then, amid roaring of wild waters and thundering, and in dense darkness, the rolling of the drum and the strange, bewildering ballads never ceased. It was the very counterpart, in all respects, of the Chippewa storm song.

After the first gypsy lyric there came another, to which the captain especially directed my attention as being what Sam Petulengro calls " reg'lar Romany." It was *I rakli adro o lolo gad* (The girl in the red chemise), as well as I can recall his words, — a very sweet song, with a simple but spirited chorus; and as the sympathetic electricity of excitement seized the performers we were all in a minute " going down the rapids in a spring freshet."

" *Bagan tu rya, bagan!* " (Sing, sir, — sing) cried my handsome neighbor, with her black gypsy eyes sparkling fire. " *Jines hi bagan eto — eto latcho Romanes.*" (You can sing that, — it's real Romany.) It was evident that she and all were singing with thorough enjoyment, and with a full and realizing consciousness of gypsyism, being greatly stimulated by my presence and sympathy. I felt that the gypsies were taking unusual pains to please the Romany rye from the *dur' tem,* or far country, and they had attained the acme of success by being thoroughly delighted with themselves, which is all that can be hoped for in art, where the aim is pleasure and not criticism.

There was a pause in the performance, but none
in the chattering of the young ladies, and during this
a curious little incident occurred. Wishing to know
if my pretty friend could understand an English
gypsy lyric, I sang in an undertone a ballad, taken
from George Borrow's "Lavengro," and which begins with these words : —

> "Pende Romani chai ke laki dye ;
> 'Miri diri dye, mi shom kāmeli.' "

I never knew whether this was really an old gypsy
poem or one written by Mr. Borrow. Once, when I
repeated it to old Henry James, as he sat making
baskets, I was silenced by being told, "That ain't
no real gypsy *gilli*. That's one of the kind made
up by gentlemen and ladies." However, as soon as
I repeated it, the Russian gypsy girl cried eagerly,
"I know that song!" and actually sang me a ballad
which was essentially the same, in which a damsel
describes her fall, owing to a Gajo (Gorgio, a Gentile,
— not gypsy) lover, and her final expulsion from the
tent. It was adapted to a very pretty melody, and
as soon as she had sung it, *sotto voce*, my pretty friend
exclaimed to another girl, "Only think, the *rye* from
America knows *that* song!" Now, as many centuries must have passed since the English and Russian
gypsies parted from the parent stock, the preserva-
tion of this song is very remarkable, and its antiquity must be very great. I did not take it down, but
any resident in St. Petersburg can, if so inclined,
do so among the gypsies at Dorat, and verify my
statement.

Then there was a pretty dance, of a modified Oriental character, by one of the damsels. For this, as
for the singing, the only musical instrument used was

a guitar, which had seven strings, tuned in Spanish
fashion, and was rather weak in tone. I wished it
had been a powerful Panormo, which would have exactly suited the *timbre* of these voices. The gypsies
were honestly interested in all I could tell them
about their kind in other lands; while the girls were
professionally desirous to hear more Anglo-Romany
songs, and were particularly pleased with one beginning with the words : —

> "'Me shom akonyo,' gildas yoi,
>   Men būti ruzhior,
> Te sār i chiriclia adoi
>   Pen mengy gilior.'"

Though we " got on " after a manner in our Romany talk, I was often obliged to have recourse to my
friend the general to translate long sentences into
Russian, especially when some sand-bar of a verb
or some log of a noun impeded the current of our
conversation. Finally, a formal request was made
by the captain that I would, as one deep beyond all
their experience in Romany matters, kindly tell them
what kind of people they really were, and whence
they came. With this demand I cheerfully complied,
every word being listened to with breathless interest.
So I told them what I knew or had conjectured relative to their Indian origin : how their fathers had
wandered forth through Persia ; how their travels
could be traced by the Persian, Greek, or Roumanian
words in the language ; how in 1417 a band of them
appeared in Europe, led by a few men of great dip-
lomatic skill, who, by crafty dealing, obtained from
the Pope, the Emperor of Germany, and all the kings
of Europe, except that of England, permission to
wander for fifty years as pilgrims, declaring that they

had been Christians, but, having become renegades, the King of Hungary had imposed a penance on them of half a century's exile. Then I informed them that precisely the same story had been told by them to the rulers in Syria and Egypt, only that in the Mohammedan countries they pretended to be good followers of Islam. I said there was reason to believe that some of their people had been in Poland and the other Slavonic countries ever since the eleventh century, but that those of England must have gone directly from Eastern Europe to Great Britain; for, although they had many Slavic words, such as *krallis* (king) and *shuba*, there were no French terms, and very few traces of German or Italian, in the English dialect. I observed that the men all understood the geographical allusions which I made, knowing apparently where India, Persia, and Egypt were situated — a remarkable contrast to our own English " travelers," one of whom once informed me that he would like to go " on the road " in America, " because you know, sir, as America lays along into France, we could get our French baskets cheaper there."

I found, on inquiry, that the Russian gypsies profess Christianity ; but, as the religion of the Greek church, as I saw it, appears to be practically something very little better than fetich-worship, I cannot exalt them as models of evangelical piety. They are, however, according to a popular proverb, not far from godliness in being very clean in their persons ; and not only did they appear so to me, but I was assured by several Russians that, as regarded these singing gypsies, it was invariably the case. As for morality in gypsy girls, their principles are very po-

culiar.   Not a whisper of scandal attaches to these
Russian Romany women as regards transient amours.
But if a wealthy Russian gentleman falls in love
with one, and will have and hold her permanently,
or for a durable connection, he may take her to his
home if she likes him, but must pay monthly a sum
into the gypsy treasury; for these people apparently
form an *artel*, or society-union, like all other classes
of Russians.   It may be suggested, as an explanation
of this apparent incongruity, that gypsies all the
world over regard steady cohabitation, or agreement,
as marriage, binding themselves, as it were, by *Gand-
harbavivaha*, as the saint married Vasantasena, which
is an old Sanskrit way of wedding.   And let me remark that if one tenth of what I heard in Russia
about " morals " in the highest or lowest or any other
class be true, the gypsies of that country are shining
lights and brilliant exemplars of morality to all by
whom they are surrounded.   Let me also add that
never on any occasion did I hear or see among them
anything in the slightest degree improper or unre-
fined.   I knew very well that I could, if I chose, talk
to such *naïve* people about subjects which would
shock an English lady, and, as the reader may remember, I did quote Mr. Borrow's song, which he has
not translated.   But a European girl who would have
endured allusions to tabooed subjects would have at
all times shown vulgarity or coarseness, while these
Russian Romany girls were invariably lady-like.   It
is true that the St. Petersburg party had a dissipated
air; three or four of them looked like second-class
French or Italian theatrical artistes, and I should not
be astonished to learn that very late hours and cham-
pagne were familiar to them as cigarettes, or that

their flirtations among their own people were neither faint, nor few, nor far between. But their conduct in my presence was irreproachable. Those of Moscow, in fact, had not even the apparent defects of their St. Petersburg sisters and brothers, and when among them it always seemed to me as if I were simply with nice gentle creoles or Cubans, the gypsy manner being tamed down to the Spanish level, their great black eyes and their guitars increasing the resemblance.

The indescribably wild and thrilling character of gypsy music is thoroughly appreciated by the Russians, who pay very high prices for Romany performances. From five to eight or ten pounds sterling is usually given to a dozen gypsies for singing an hour or two to a special party, and this is sometimes repeated twice or thrice of an evening. " A Russian gentleman, when he is in funds," said the clerk of the Slavansky Bazaar in Moscow to me, " will make nothing of giving the Zigani a hundred-ruble note," the ruble rating at half a crown. The result is that good singers among these lucky Romanys are well to do, and lead soft lives, for Russia.

MOSCOW.

I had no friends in Moscow to direct me where to find gypsies *en famille*, and the inquiries which I made of chance acquaintances simply convinced me that the world at large was as ignorant of their ways as it was prejudiced against them. At last the good-natured old porter of our hotel told me, in his rough Baltic German, how to meet these mysterious minstrels to advantage. " You must take a sleigh," he said, " and go out to Petrovka. That is a place in

4

the country, where there are grand *cafés* at considerable distances one from the other. Pay the driver
three rubles for four hours. Enter a *café*, call for
something to drink, listen to the gypsies singing, and
when they pass round a plate put some money in it.
That's all." This was explicit, and at ten o'clock
in the evening I hired a sleigh and went.

If the cold which I had experienced in the general's troika in St. Petersburg might be compared
to a moderate rheumatism, that which I encountered
in the sleigh outside the walls of Moscow, on Christmas Eve, 1876, was like a fierce gout. The ride was
in all conscience Russian enough to have its ending
among gypsies, Tartars, or Cossacks. To go at a
headlong pace over the creaking snow behind an *istvostshik*, named Vassili, the round, cold moon over-
head, church-spires tipped with great inverted golden
turnips in the distance, and this on a night when the
frost seemed almost to scream in its intensity, is as
much of a sensation in the suburbs of Moscow as it
could be out on the steppes. A few wolves, more
or less, make no difference, — and even they come
sometimes within three hours' walk of the Kremlin.
Et ego inter lupos, — I too have been among wolves
in my time by night, in Kansas, and thought nothing
of such rides compared to the one I had when I went
gypsying from Moscow.

In half an hour Vassili brought me to a house,
which I entered. A " proud porter," a vast creature,
in uniform suggestive of embassies and kings' palaces,
relieved me of my *shuba*, and I found my way into a
very large and high hall, brilliantly lighted as if for
a thousand guests, while the only occupants were four
couples, " spooning " *sans gêne*, one in each corner,

and a small party of men and girls drinking in the middle. I called a waiter; he spoke nothing but Russian, and Russian is of all languages the most useless to him who only talks it "a little." A little Arabic, or even a little Chippewa, I have found of great service, but a fair vocabulary and weeks of study of the grammar are of no avail in a country where even men of gentlemanly appearance turn away with childish *ennui* the instant they detect the foreigner, resolving apparently that they cannot and *will not* understand him. In matters like this the ordinary Russian is more impatient and less intelligent than any Oriental or even red Indian. The result of my interview with the waiter was that we were soon involved in the completest misunderstanding on the subject of gypsies. The question was settled by reference to a fat and fair damsel, one of the "spoons" already referred to, who spoke German. She explained to me that as it was Christmas Eve no gypsies would be there, or at any other *café*. This was disappointing. I called Vassili, and he drove on to another "garden," deeply buried in snow.

When I entered the rooms at this place, I perceived at a glance that matters had mended. There was the hum of many voices, and a perfume like that of tea and many *papiross*, or cigarettes, with a prompt sense of society and of enjoyment. I was dazzled at first by the glare of the lights, and could distinguish nothing, unless it was that the numerous company regarded me with utter amazement; for it was an "off night," when no business was expected, — few were there save " professionals " and their friends, — and I was manifestly an unexpected intruder on Bohemia.

As luck would have it, that which I believed was the one worst night in the year to find the gypsy minstrels proved to be the exceptional occasion when they were all assembled, and I had hit upon it. Of course this struck me pleasantly enough as I looked around, for I knew that at a touch the spell would be broken, and with one word I should have the warmest welcome from all. I had literally not a single speaking acquaintance within a thousand miles, and yet here was a room crowded with gay and festive strangers, whom the slightest utterance would convert into friends.

I was not disappointed. Seeking for an opportunity, I saw a young man of gentlemanly appearance, well dressed, and with a mild and amiable air. Speaking to him in German, I asked the very needless question if there were any gypsies present.

"You wish to hear them sing?" he inquired.

"I do not. I only want to talk with one, — with *any* one."

He appeared to be astonished, but, pointing to a handsome, slender young lady, a very dark brunette, elegantly attired in black silk, said, —

"There is one."

I stepped across to the girl, who rose to meet me. I said nothing for a few seconds, but looked at her intently, and then asked, —

"*Rakessa tu Romanes, miri pen?*" (Do you talk Romany, my sister?)

She gave one deep, long glance of utter astonishment, drew one long breath, and, with a cry of delight and wonder, said, —

"*Romanichal!*"

That word awoke the entire company, and with it

they found out who the intruder was. "Then might you hear them cry aloud, 'The Moringer is here!'" for I began to feel like the long-lost lord returned, so warm was my welcome. They flocked around me; they cried aloud in Romany, and one good-natured, smiling man, who looked like a German gypsy, mounting a chair, waved a guitar by its neck high in the air as a signal of discovery of a great prize to those at a distance, repeating rapidly, —

"*Av'akai, ava'kai, Romanichal!*" (Come here; here's a gypsy!)

And they came, dark and light, great and small, and got round me, and shook hands, and held to my arms, and asked where I came from, and how I did, and if it was n't jolly, and what would I take to drink, and said how glad they were to see me; and when conversation flagged for an instant, somebody said to his next neighbor, with an air of wisdom, " American Romany," and everybody repeated it with delight. Then it occurred to the guitarist and the young lady that we had better sit down. So my first acquaintance and discoverer, whose name was Liubasha, was placed, in right of preëmption, at my right hand, the *belle des belles*, Miss Sarsha, at my left, a number of damsels all around these, and then three or four circles of gypsies, of different ages and tints, standing up, surrounded us all. In the outer ring were several fast-looking and pretty Russian or German blonde girls, whose mission it is, I believe, to dance — and flirt — with visitors, and a few gentlemanly-looking Russians, *vieux garçons*, evidently of the kind who are at home behind the scenes, and who knew where to come to enjoy themselves. Altogether there must have been about fifty present, and I soon observed that every word I uttered was promptly repeated, while every eye was fixed on me.

I could converse in Romany with the guitarist, and without much difficulty; but with the charming, heedless young ladies I had as much trouble to talk as with their sisters in St. Petersburg. The young gentleman already referred to, to whom in my fancy I promptly gave the Offenbachian name of Prince Paul, translated whenever there was a misunderstanding, and in a few minutes we were all intimate. Miss Sarsha, who had a slight cast in one of her wild black eyes, which added something to the gypsiness and roguery of her smiles, and who wore in a ring a large diamond, which seemed as if it might be the right eye in the wrong place, was what is called an earnest young lady, with plenty to say and great energy wherewith to say it. What with her eyes, her diamond, her smiles, and her tongue, she constituted altogether a fine specimen of irrepressible fireworks, and Prince Paul had enough to do in facilitating conversation. There was no end to his politeness, but it was an impossible task for him now and then promptly to carry over a long sentence from German to Russian, and he would give it up like an invincible conundrum, with the patient smile and head-wag and hand-wave of an amiable Dundreary. Yet I began to surmise a mystery even in him. More than once he inadvertently betrayed a knowledge of Romany, though he invariably spoke of his friends around in a patronizing manner as "these gypsies." This was very odd, for in appearance he was a Gorgio of the Gorgios, and did not seem, despite any talent for languages which he might possess, likely to trouble himself to acquire Romany while Russian would answer every purpose of conversation. All of this was, however, explained to me afterward.

Prince Paul again asked me if I had come out to hear a concert. I said, "No; that I had simply come out to see my brothers and sisters and talk with them, just as I hoped they would come to see me if I were in my own country." This speech produced a most favorable impression, and there was, in a quiet way, a little private conversation among the leaders, after which Prince Paul said to me, in a very pleasant manner, that "these gypsies," being delighted at the visit from the gentleman from a distant country, would like to offer me a song in token of welcome. To this I answered, with many thanks, that such kindness was more than I had expected, for I was well aware of the great value of such a compliment from singers whose fame had reached me even in America. It was evident that my grain of a reply did not fall upon stony ground, for I never was among people who seemed to be so quickly impressed by any act of politeness, however trifling. A bow, a grasp of the hand, a smile, or a glance would gratify them, and this gratification their lively black eyes expressed in the most unmistakable manner.

So we had the song, wild and wonderful like all of its kind, given with that delightful *abandon* which attains perfection only among gypsies. I had enjoyed the singing in St. Petersburg, but there was a *laisser aller*, a completely gay spirit, in this Christmas-Eve gypsy party in Moscow which was much more " whirling away." For at Dorot the gypsies had been on exhibition; here at Petrovka they were frolicking *en*

famille with a favored guest, — a Romany rye from
a far land to astonish and delight, — and he took good
care to let them feel that they were achieving a splendid success, for I declared many times that it was
būtsi shūkár, or very beautiful. Then I called for
tea and lemon, and after that the gypsies sang for
their own amusement, Miss Sarsha, as the incarna-
tion of fun and jollity, taking the lead, and making me join in. Then the crowd made way, and in
the space appeared a very pretty little girl, in the
graceful old gypsy Oriental dress. This child danced
charmingly indeed, in a style strikingly like that of
the Almeh of Egypt, but without any of the erotic expressions which abound in Eastern pantomime. This
little Romany girl was to me enchanting, being altogether unaffected and graceful. It was evident that
her dancing, like the singing of her elder sisters, was
not an art which had been drilled in by instruction.
They had come into it in infancy, and perfected
themselves by such continual practice that what they
did was as natural as walking or talking. When the
dancing was over, I begged that the little girl would
come to me, and, kissing her tiny gypsy hand, I said,
" *Spassibo tute kamli, eto hi būtsi shūkár* " (Thank
you, dear; that is very pretty), with which the rest
were evidently pleased. I had observed among the
singers, at a little distance, a very remarkable and
rather handsome old woman, — a good study for an
artist, — and she, as I also noticed, had sung with a
powerful and clear voice. "She is our grandmother,"
said one of the girls. Now, as every student of gypsies knows, the first thing to do in England or Germany, on entering a tent-gypsy encampment, is to
be polite to " the old woman." Unless you can win

her good opinion you had better be gone. The Russian city Roms have apparently no such fancies. On the road, however, life is patriarchal, and the grandmother is a power to be feared. As a fortune-teller she is a witch, ever at warfare with the police world ; she has a bitter tongue, and is quick to wrath. This was not the style or fashion of the old gypsy singer ; but, as soon as I saw the *puri babali dye*, I requested that she would shake hand with me, and by the impression which this created I saw that the Romany of the city had not lost all the feelings of the road.

I spoke of Waramoff's beautiful song of the "Krasneya Sarafan," which Sarsha began at once to warble. The characteristic of Russian gypsy-girl voices is a peculiarly delicate metallic tone, — like that of the two silver bells of the Tower of Ivan Velikoi when heard from afar, — yet always marked with fineness and strength. This is sometimes startling in the wilder effects, but it is always agreeable. These Moscow gypsy girls have a great name in their art, and it was round the shoulders of one of them — for aught I know it may have been Sarsha's great-grandmother — that Catalani threw the cashmere shawl which had been given to her by the Pope as " to the best singer in the world." " It is not mine by right," said the generous Italian ; " it belongs to the gypsy."

The gypsies were desirous of learning something about the songs of their kindred in distant lands, and, though no singer, I did my best to please them, the guitarist easily improvising accompaniments, while the girls joined in. As all were in a gay mood, faults were easily excused, and the airs were much liked, — one lyric, set by Virginia Gabriel, being even more admired in Moscow than in St. Petersburg ; apropos of which I may mention that, when I afterward visited the gypsy family in their own home, the first request from Sarsha was, "*Eto gilyo, rya!*" (*That* song, sir), referring to "Romany," which has been heard at several concerts in London. And so, after much discussion of the affairs of Egypt, I took my leave amid a chorus of kind farewells. Then Vassili, loudly called for, reappeared from some nook with his elegantly frosted horse, and in a few minutes we were dashing homeward. Cold! It was as severe as in Western New York or Minnesota, where the thermometer for many days every winter sinks lower than in St. Petersburg, but where there are no such incredible precautions taken as in the land of double windows cemented down, and fur-lined *shubas*. It is remarkable that the gypsies, although of Oriental origin, are said to surpass the Russians in enduring cold ; and there is a marvelous story told about a Romany who, for a wager, undertook to sleep naked against a clothed Muscovite on the ice of a river during an unusually cold night. In the morning the Russian was found frozen stiff, while the gypsy was snoring away unharmed. As we returned, I saw in the town something which recalled this story in more than one *moujik*, who, well wrapped up, lay sleeping in the open air, under the lee of a house. Passing through silent Moscow on the early Christmas morn, under the stars, as I gazed at the marvelous city, which yields neither to Edinburgh, Cairo, nor Prague in picturesqueness, and thought over the strange evening I had spent among the gypsies, I felt as if I were in a melodrama with striking scenery. The pleasing *finale* was the utter amazement and almost speechless gratitude of Vassili at getting an extra half-ruble as an early Christmas gift.

As I had received a pressing invitation from the gypsies to come again, I resolved to pay them a visit on Christmas afternoon in their own house, if I could find it. Having ascertained that the gypsy street was in a distant quarter, called the *Grouszini*, I engaged a sleigh, standing before the door of the Slavanski-Bazaar Hotel, and the usual close bargain with the driver was effected with the aid of a Russian gentleman, a stranger passing by, who reduced the ruble (one hundred kopecks) at first demanded to seventy kopecks. After a very long drive we found ourselves in the gypsy street, and the *istvostshik* asked me, "To what house?"

"I don't know," I replied. "Gypsies live here, don't they?"

"Gypsies, and no others."

"Well, I want to find a gypsy."

The driver laughed, and just at that instant I saw, as if awaiting me on the sidewalk, Sarsha, Liubasha, and another young lady, with a good-looking youth, their brother.

"This will do," I said to the driver, who appeared utterly amazed at seeing me greeted like an old friend by the Zigani, but who grinned with delight, as all Russians of the lower class invariably do at anything like sociability and fraternity. The damsels were faultlessly attired in Russian style, with full fur-lined, glossy black-satin cloaks and fine Orenberg scarfs, which are, I believe, the finest woolen fabrics in the world. The party were particularly anxious to know if I had come specially to visit *them*, for I have passed over the fact that I had also made the acquaintance of another very large family of gypsies, who sang at a rival *café*, and who had also treated me very kindly. I was at once conducted to a house, which we entered in a rather gypsy way, not in front, but through a court, a back door, and up a staircase, very much in the style of certain dwellings in the Potteries in London. But, having entered, I was led through one or two neat rooms, where I saw lying sound asleep on beds, but dressed, one or two very dark Romanys, whose faces I remembered. Then we passed into a sitting-room, which was very well furnished. I observed hanging up over the chimney-piece a good collection of photographs, nearly all of gypsies, and indicating that close resemblance to Hindoos which comes out so strongly in such pictures, being, in fact, more apparent in the pictures than in the faces ; just as the photographs of the old Ulfilas manuscript revealed alterations not visible in the original. In the centre of the group was a cabinet-size portrait of Sarsha, and by it another of an Englishman of *very* high rank. I thought this odd, but asked no questions.

My hosts were very kind, offering me promptly a rich kind of Russian cake, begging to know what else I would like to eat or drink, and apparently deeply concerned that I could really partake of nothing, as I had just come from luncheon. They were all light-hearted and gay, so that the music began at once, as wild and as bewitching as ever. And here I observed, even more than before, how thoroughly sincere these gypsies were in their art, and to what a degree they enjoyed and were excited by their own singing. Here in their own home, warbling like birds and frolicking like children, their performance was even more delightful than it had been in the concert-room. There was evidently a great source of excitement in the fact that I must enjoy it far more than an ordinary stranger, because I understood Romany, and sympathized with gypsy ways, and regarded them not as the *Gaji* or Gentiles do, but as brothers and sisters. I confess that I was indeed moved by the simple kindness with which I was treated, and I knew that, with the wonderfully keen perception of character in which gypsies excel, they perfectly understood my liking for them. It is this ready intuition of feelings which, when it is raised from an instinct to an art by practice, enables shrewd old women to tell fortunes with so much skill.

I was here introduced to the mother of the girls. She was a neat, pleasant-looking woman, of perhaps forty years, in appearance and manners irresistibly reminding me of some respectable Cuban lady. Like the others, she displayed an intelligent curiosity as to my knowledge of Romany, and I was pleased at finding that she knew much more of the language than her children did. Then there entered a young Russian gentleman, but not "Prince Paul." He was, however, a very agreeable person, as all Russians can be when so minded; and they are always so minded when they gather, from information or conjecture, the fact that the stranger whom they meet is one of education or position. This young gentleman spoke French, and undertook the part of occasional translator.

I asked Liubasha if any of them understood fortune-telling.

"No; we have quite lost the art of *dorriki*.[1] None

---

[1] In Old English Romany this is called *dorrikin;* in common parlance, *dukkerin.* Both forms are really old.

of us know anything about it. But we hear that
you Romanichals over the Black Water understand
it. Oh, *rya*," she cried, eagerly, "you know so
much, — you 're such a deep Romany, — can't *you*
tell fortunes ?"

"I should indeed know very little about Romany
ways," I replied, gravely, "if I could not *pen dorriki.*
But I tell you beforehand, *terni pen, ' dorrikipen hi
hokanipen,*' little sister, fortune-telling is deceiving.
Yet what the lines say I can read."

In an instant six as pretty little gypsy hands as I
ever beheld were thrust before me, and I heard as
many cries of delight. "Tell *my* fortune, *rya!* tell
mine! and *mine!*" exclaimed the damsels, and I
complied. It was all very well to tell them there
was nothing in it; they knew a trick worth two
of that. I perceived at once that the faith which
endures beyond its own knowledge was placed in all
I said. In England the gypsy woman, who at home
ridicules her own fortune-telling and her dupes, still
puts faith in a *gusveri mush,* or some "wise man,"
who with crystal or magical apparatus professes occult knowledge ; for she thinks that her own false art
is an imitation of a true one. It is really amusing to
see the reverence with which an old gypsy will look
at the awful hieroglyphics in Cornelius Agrippa's
"Occult Philosophy," or, better still, "Trithemius,"
and, as a gift, any ordinary fortune-telling book is
esteemed by them beyond rubies. It is true that
they cannot read it, but the precious volume is treas-
ured like a fetich, and the owner is happy in the
thought of at least possessing darksome and forbidden
lore, though it be of no earthly use to her. After
all the kindness they had shown me, I could not find

it in my heart to refuse to tell these gentle Zingari their little fortunes. It is not, I admit, exactly in the order of things that the chicken should dress the cook, or the Gorgio tell fortunes to gypsies ; but he who wanders in strange lands meets with strange adventures. So, with a full knowledge of the legal penalties attached in England to palmistry and other conjuration, and with the then pending Slade case knocking heavily on my conscience, I proceeded to examine and predict. When I afterward narrated this incident to the late G. H. Lewes, he expressed himself to the effect that to tell fortunes to gypsies struck him as the very *ne plus ultra* of cheek, — which shows how extremes meet ; for verily it was with great modesty and proper diffidence that I ventured to foretell the lives of these little ladies, having an antipathy to the practice of chiromancing as to other romancing.

I have observed that as among men of great and varied culture, and of extensive experience, there are more complex and delicate shades and half-shades of light in the face, so in the palm the lines are correspondingly varied and broken. Take a man of intellect and a peasant, of equal excellence of figure according to the literal rules of art or of anatomy, and this subtile multiplicity of variety shows itself in the whole body in favor of the "gentleman," so that it would almost seem as if every book we read is republished in the person. The first thing that struck me in these gypsy hands was the fewness of the lines, their clearly defined sweep, and their simplicity. In every one the line of life was unbroken, and, in fine, one might think from a drawing of the hand, and without knowing who its owner might be, that he or she was of a type of character unknown in most great European cities, — a being gifted with special culture, and in a certain simple sense refined, but not endowed with experience in a thousand confused phases of life. The hands of a true genius, who has passed through life earnestly devoted to a single art, however, are on the whole like these of the gypsies. Such, for example, are the hands of Fanny Janauschek, the lines of which agree to perfection with the laws of chiromancy. The art reminds one of Cervantes's ape, who told the past and present, but not the future. And here " tell me what thou hast been, and I will tell what thou wilt be " gives a fine opportunity to the soothsayer.

To avoid mistakes I told the fortunes in French, which was translated into Russian. I need not say that every word was listened to with earnest attention, or that the group of dark but young and comely faces, as they gathered around and bent over, would have made a good subject for a picture. After the girls, the mother must needs hear her *dorriki* also, and last of all the young Russian gentleman, who seemed to take as earnest an interest in his future as even the gypsies. As he alone understood French, and as he appeared to be *un peu gaillard*, and, finally, as the lines of his hand said nothing to the contrary, I predicted for him in detail a fortune in which *bonnes fortunes* were not at all wanting. I think he was pleased, but when I asked him if he would translate what I had said of his future into Russian, he replied with a slight wink and a scarcely perceptible negative. I suppose he had his reasons for declining.

Then we had singing again, and Christopher, the brother, a wild and gay young gypsy, became so excited that while playing the guitar he also danced and caroled, and the sweet voices of the girls rose in chorus, and I was again importuned for the *Romany* song, and we had altogether a very Bohemian frolic. .I was sorry when the early twilight faded into night, and I was obliged, notwithstanding many entreaties to the contrary, to take my leave. These gypsies had been very friendly and kind to me in a strange city, where I had not an acquaintance, and where I had expected none. They had given me of their very best; for they gave me songs which I can never forget, and which were better to me than all the opera could bestow. The young Russian, polite to the last, went bareheaded with me into the street, and, hailing a sleigh-driver, began to bargain for me. In Moscow, as in other places, it makes a great difference in the fare whether one takes a public conveyance from before the first hotel or from a house in the gypsy quarter. I had paid seventy kopecks to come, and I at once found that my new friend and the driver were engaged in wild and fierce dispute whether I should pay twenty or thirty to return.

" Oh, give him thirty ! " I exclaimed. " It's little enough."

" *Non*," replied the Russian, with the air of a man of principles. " *Il ne faut pas gâter ces gens-la.*" But I gave the driver thirty, all the same, when we got home, and thereby earned the usual shower of blessings.

A few days afterward, while going from Moscow to St. Petersburg, I made the acquaintance of a young Russian noble and diplomat, who was well informed on all current gossip, and learned from him some curious facts. The first young gentleman whom I

5

had seen among the Romanys of Moscow was the son of a Russian prince by a gypsy mother, and the very noble Englishman whose photograph I had seen in Sarsha's collection had not long ago (as rumor averred) paid desperate attentions to the belle of the. Romanys without obtaining the least success. My informant did not know her name. Putting this and that together, I think it highly probable that Sarsha was the young lady, and that the *latcho bar*, or diamond, which sparkled on her finger had been paid for with British gold, while the donor had gained the same " unluck" which befell one of his type in the Spanish gypsy song as given by George Borrow : —

> " Loud sang the Spanish cavalier,
>   And thus his ditty ran :
> ' God send the gypsy maiden here,
>   But not the gypsy man.'

> " On high arose the moon so bright,
>   The gypsy 'gan to sing,
> ' I see a Spaniard coming here,
>   I must be on the wing.' "

AUSTRIAN GYPSIES.

I.

In June, 1878, I went to Paris, during the great Exhibition. I had been invited by Monsieur Edmond About to attend as a delegate the Congrès Internationale Littéraire, which was about to be held in the great city. How we assembled, how M. About distinguished himself as one of the most practical and common-sensible of men of genius, and how we were all finally harangued by M. Victor Hugo with the most extraordinary display of oratorical sky-rockets, Catherine-wheels, blue-lights, fire-crackers, and pinwheels by which it was ever my luck to be amused, is matter of history. But this chapter is only autobiographical, and we will pass over the history. As an Anglo-American delegate, I was introduced to several great men gratis; to the greatest of all I introduced myself at the expense of half a franc. This was to the Chinese giant, Chang, who was on exhibition at a small café garden near the Trocadero. There were no other visitors in his pavilion when I entered. He received me with politeness, and we began to converse in fourth-story English, but gradually went down-stairs into Pidgin, until we found ourselves fairly in the kitchen of that humble but entertaining dialect. It is a remarkable sensation to sit alone with a mild monster, and feel like a little boy. I do not distinctly remember whether Chang is eight, or ten, or twelve feet high ; I only know that, though I am, as he said, "one velly big piecee man," I sat and lifted my eyes from time to time at the usual level, forgetfully expecting to meet his eyes, and beheld instead the buttons on his breast. Then I looked up — like Daruma to Buddha — and up, and saw far above me his "lights of the soul" gleaming down on me as it were from the top of a lofty beacon.

I soon found that Chang, regarding all things from a giant's point of view, esteemed mankind by their size and looks. Therefore, as he had complimented me according to his lights, I replied that he was a " numpa one too muchee glanti handsome man, first chop big."

Then he added, " You belongy Inklis man ? "

" No. My one piecee *fa-ke-kwok ;* [1] my Melican, galaw. You dlinkee ale some-tim ? "

The giant replied that *pay-wine,* which is Pidgin for beer, was not ungrateful to his palate or foreign to his habits. So we had a quart of Alsopp between us, and drank to better acquaintance. I found that the giant had exhibited himself in many lands, and taken great pains to learn the language of each, so that he spoke German, Italian, and Spanish well enough. He had been at a mission-school when he used to " stop China-side," or was in his native land. I assured him that I had perceived it from the first, because he evidently " talked ink," as his countrymen say of words which are uttered by a scholar, and I greatly gratified him by citing some of my own " beautiful verses," which are reversed from a Chinese original : —

---

[1] Flower-flag-nation man ; that is, American.

" One man who never leadee [1]
Like one dly [2] inkstan be :
You turn he up-side downy,
No ink lun [3] outside he."

So we parted with mutual esteem. This was the
second man by the name of Chang whom I had
known, and singularly enough they were both exhibited as curiosities. The other made a living as a
Siamese twin, and his brother was named Eng. They
wrote their autographs for me, and put them wisely
at the very top of the page, lest I should write a
promise to pay an immense sum of money, or forge a
free pass to come into the exhibition gratis over their
signatures.

Having seen Chang, I returned to the Hôtel de
Louvre, dined, and then went forth with friends to
the Orangerie. This immense garden, devoted to
concerts, beer, and cigars, is said to be capable of
containing three thousand people ; before I left it
it held about five thousand. I knew not why this
unwonted crowd had assembled ; when I found the
cause I was astonished, with reason. At the gate
was a bill, on which I read " Les Bohemiennes de
Moscow."

" Some small musical comedy, I suppose," I said to
myself. " But let us see it." We pressed on.

" Look there ! " said my companion. " Those are
certainly gypsies."

Sure enough, a procession of men and women,
strangely dressed in gayly colored Oriental garments,
was entering the gates. But I replied, " Impossible.
Not here in Paris. Probably they are performers."

" But see. They notice you. That girl certainly

---

[1] *Leadee,* reads.   [2] *Dly,* dry.   [3] *Lun,* run.

knows you. She's turning her head. There, — I
heard her say O Romany rye!"

I was bewildered. The crowd was dense, but as
the procession passed me at a second turn I saw
they were indeed gypsies, and I was grasped by the
hand by more than one. They were my old friends
from Moscow. This explained the immense multitude. There was during the Exhibition a great *furor*
as regarded *les zigains*. The gypsy orchestra which
performed in the Hungarian café was so beset by
visitors that a comic paper represented them as cov-
ering the roofs of the adjacent houses so as to hear
something. This evening the Russian gypsies were
to make their début in the Orangerie, and they were
frightened at their own success. They sang, but
their voices were inaudible to two thirds of the audience, and those who could not hear roared, " Louder ! "
Then they adjourned to the open air, where the voices
were lost altogether on a crowd calling, " *Garçon —
vite — une tasse café !* " or applauding. In the intervals scores of young Russian gentlemen, golden
swells, who had known the girls of old, gathered
round the fair ones like moths around tapers. The
singing was not the same as it had been ; the voices
were the same, but the sweet wild charm of the
Romany caroling, bird-like, for pleasure was gone.

But I found by themselves and unnoticed two of
the troupe, whom I shall not soon forget. They were
two very handsome youths, — one of sixteen years,
the other twenty. And with the first words in Romany they fairly jumped for joy, and the artist who
could have caught their picture then would have
made a brave one. ˙ They were clad in blouses of
colored silk, which, with their fine dark complexions

and great black eyes, gave them a very picturesque
air. These had not seen me in Russia, nor had they
heard of me; they were probably from Novogorod.
Like the girls they were children, but in a greater
degree, for they had not been flattered, and kind
words delighted them so that they clapped their
hands. They began to hum gypsy songs, and had I
not prevented it they would have run at once and
brought a guitar, and improvised a small concert for
me *al fresco*. I objected to this, not wishing to take
part any longer in such a very public exhibition.
For the *gobe-mouches* and starers, noticing a stranger
talking with *ces zigains*, had begun to gather in a
dense crowd around us, and the two ladies and the
gentleman who were with us were seriously incon-
venienced. We endeavored to step aside, but the
multitude stepped aside also, and would not let us
alone. They were French, but they might have
been polite. As it was, they broke our merry conference up effectively, and put us to flight.

"Do let us come and see you, *rya*," said the
younger boy. "We will sing, for I can really sing
beautifully, and we like you so much. Where do
you live?"

I could not invite them, for I was about to leave
Paris, as I then supposed. I have never seen them
since, and there was no adventure and no strange
scenery beyond the thousands of lights and guests
and trees and voices speaking French. Yet to this
day the gay boyishness, the merry laughter, and the
child-like *naïveté* of the promptly-formed liking of
those gypsy youths remains impressed on my mind
with all the color and warmth of an adventure or a
living poem. Can you recall no child by any way-

side of life to whom you have given a chance smile
or a kind word, and been repaid with artless sudden
attraction ? For to all of us, — yes, to the coldest and
worst, — there are such memories of young people, of
children, and I pity him who, remembering them,
does not feel the touch of a vanished hand and hear
a chord which is still. There are adventures which
we can tell to others as stories, but the best have no
story; they may be only the memory of a strange
dog which followed us, and I have one such of a cat
who, without any introduction, leaped wildly towards
me, "and would not thence away." It is a good life
which has many such memories.

I was walking a day or two after with an English
friend, who was also a delegate to the International
Literary Congress, in the Exhibition, when we approached the side gate, or rear entrance of the Hungarian café. Six or seven dark and strange-looking
men stood about, dressed in the uniform of a military
band. I caught their glances, and saw that they were
Romany.

"Now you shall see something queer," I said to
my friend.

So advancing to the first dark man I greeted him
in gypsy.

"I do not understand you," he promptly replied —
or lied.

I turned to a second.

"You have more sense, and you do understand.
Adro miro tem penena mande o baro rai." (In my
country the gypsies call me the great gentleman.)

This phrase may be translated to mean either the
"tall gentleman" or the "great lord." It was apparently taken in the latter sense, for at once all the

party bowed very low, raising their hands to their foreheads, in Oriental fashion.

"Hallo!" exclaimed my English friend, who had not understood what I had said. "What game is this you are playing on these fellows?"

Up to the front came a superior, the leader of the band.

"Great God!" he exclaimed, "what is this I hear? This is wonderful. To think that there should be anybody here to talk with! I can only talk Magyar and Romanes."

"And what do you talk?" I inquired of the first violin.

"*Ich spreche nur Deutsch!*" he exclaimed, with a strong Vienna accent and a roar of laughter. "I only talk German."

This worthy man, I found, was as much delighted with my German as the leader with my gypsy; and in all my experience I never met two beings so charmed at being able to converse. That I should have met with them was of itself wonderful. Only there was this difference: that the Viennese burst into a laugh every time he spoke, while the gypsy grew more sternly solemn and awfully impressive. There are people to whom mere talking is a pleasure, — never mind the ideas, — and here I had struck two at once. I once knew a gentleman named Stewart. He was the mayor, first physician, and postmaster of St. Paul, Minnesota. While camping out, *en route*, and in a tent with him, it chanced that among the other gentlemen who had tented with us there were two terrible snorers. Now Mr. Stewart had heard that you may stop a man's snoring by whistling. And here was a wonderful opportunity.

"So I waited," he said, "until one man was coming down with his snore, *diminuendo*, while the other was rising, *crescendo*, and at the exact point of intersection, *moderato*, I blew my car-whistle, and so got both birds at one shot. I stopped them both." Even as Mayor Stewart had winged his two birds with one ball had I hit my two peregrines.

"We are now going to perform," said the gypsy captain. "Will you not take seats on the platform, and hear us play?"

I did not know it at the time, but I heard afterwards that this was a great compliment, and one rarely bestowed. The platform was small, and we were very near our new friends. Scarcely had the performance begun ere I perceived that, just as the gypsies in Russia had sung their best in my honor, these artists were exerting themselves to the utmost, and, all unheeding the audience, playing directly at me and into me. When any *tour* was deftly made the dark master nodded to me with gleaming eyes, as if saying, "What do you think of *that*, now?" The Viennese laughed for joy every time his glance met mine, and as I looked at the various Lajoshes and Joshkas of the band, they blew, beat, or scraped with redoubled fury, or sank into thrilling tenderness. Hurrah! here was somebody to play to who knew gypsy and all the games thereof; for a very little, even a word, reveals a great deal, and I must be a virtuoso, at least by Rommany, if not by art. It was with all the joy of success that the first piece ended amid thunders of applause.

"That was not the *racoczy*," I said. "Yet it sounded like it."

"No," said the captain. "But *now* you shall hear

the *racoczy* and the *czardas* as you never heard them
before. For we can play that better than any orchestra in Vienna. Truly, you will never forget us
after hearing it."

And then they played the *racoczy*, the national
Hungarian favorite, of gypsy composition, with heart
and soul. As these men played for me, inspired with
their own music, feeling and enjoying it far more than
the audience, and all because they had got a gypsy
gentleman to play to, I appreciated what a *life* that
was to them, and what it should be ; not cold-blooded
skill, aiming only at excellence or preëxcellence and
at setting up the artist, but a fire and a joy, a self-
forgetfulness which whirls the soul away as the soul
of the Mœnad went with the stream adown the
mountains, — *Evoë Bacchus !* This feeling is deep in
the heart of the Hungarian gypsy ; he plays it, he
feels it in every air, he knows the rush of the stream
as it bounds onwards, — knows that it expresses his
deepest desire ; and so he has given it words in a
song which, to him who has the key, is one of the
most touching ever written : —

> " Dyal o pañi repedishis,
> M'ro pirano hegedishis ;
>
> " Dyal o pañi tale vatra,
> M'ro pirano klauetaha.
>
> " Dyal o pañi pe kishai
> M'ro pirano tsino rai."

> " The stream runs on with rushing din
> As I hear my true love's violin ;

> " And the river rolls o'er rock and stone
> As he plays the flute so sweet alone.

> " Runs o'er the sand as it began,
> Then my true love lives a gentleman."

Yes, music whirling the soul away as on a rushing
river, the violin notes falling like ripples, the flute
tones all aflow among the rocks ; and when it sweeps
adagio on the sandy bed, then the gypsy player is
at heart equal to a lord, then he feels a gentleman.
The only true republic is art. There all earthly dis-
tinctions pass away ; there he is best who lives and
feels best, and makes others feel, not that he is cleverer than they, but that he can awaken sympathy
and joy.

The intense reality of musical art as a comforter
to these gypsies of Eastern Europe is wonderful.
Among certain inedited songs of the Transylvanian
gypsies, in the Kolosvárer dialect, I find the following : —

> " Na janav ko dad m'ro as,
>   Niko mälleu mange as,
>   Miro gule dai merdyas
>   Pirani me pregelyas.
>   Uva tu o hegedive
>   Tu sal mindik pash mange."

> " I 've known no father since my birth,
>   I have no friend alive on earth ;
>   My mother 's dead this many day,
>   The girl I loved has gone her way ;
>   Thou violin with music free
>   Alone art ever true to me."

It is very wonderful that the charm of the Russian
gypsy girls' singing was destroyed by the atmosphere
or applause of a Paris concert-room, while the Hungarian Romanys conquered it as it were by sheer
force, and by conquering gave their music the charm
of intensity. I do not deny that in this music, be it
of voice or instruments, there is much which is perhaps imagined, which depends on association, which
is plain to John but not to Jack ; but you have only

to advance or retreat a few steps to find the same in the highest art. This, at least, we know: that no performer at any concert in London can awake the feeling of intense enjoyment which these wild minstrels excite in themselves and in others by sympathy. Now it is a question in many forms as to whether art for enjoyment is to die, and art for the sake of art alone survive. Is joyous and healthy nature to vanish step by step from the heart of man, and morbid, egoistic pessimism to take its place? Are over-culture, excessive sentiment, constant self-criticism, and all the brood of nervous curses to monopolize and inspire art? A fine alliance this they are making, the ascetic monk and the atheistic pessimist, to kill Nature! They will never effect it. It may die in many forms. It may lose its charm, as the singing of Sarsha and of Liubasha was lost among the rustling and noise of thousands of Parisian *badauds* in the Orangerie. But there will be stronger forms of art, which will make themselves heard, as the Hungarian Romanys heeded no din, and bore all away with their music.

" *Latcho dívvus miri pralia! — miduvel atch pa tumende!* " (Good-day, my brothers. God rest on you) I said, and they rose and bowed, and I went forth into the Exhibition. It was a brave show, that of all the fine things from all parts of the world which man can make, but to me the most interesting of all were the men themselves. Will not the managers of the next world show give us a living ethnological department?

Of these Hungarian gypsies who played in Paris during the Exhibition much was said in the newspapers, and from the following, which appeared in an

American journal, written by some one to me unknown, the reader may learn that there were many others to whom their music was deeply thrilling or wildly exciting : —

"The Hungarian Tziganes (Zigeuner) are the rage just now at Paris. The story is that Liszt picked out the individuals composing the band one by one from among the gypsy performers in Hungary and Bohemia. Half-civilized in appearance, dressed in an unbecoming half-military costume, they are nothing while playing Strauss' waltzes or their own ; but when they play the Radetsky Defile, the Racoksky March, or their marvelous czardas, one sees and hears the battle, and it is easy to understand the influence of their music in fomenting Hungarian revolutions ; why for so long it was made treasonable to play or listen to these czardas ; and why, as they heard them, men rose to their feet, gathered together, and with tears rolling down their faces, and throats swelling with emotion, departed to do or die."

And when I remember that they played for me as they said they had played for no other man in Paris, "into the ear," — and when I think of the gleam in their eyes, I verily believe they told the truth, — I feel glad that I chanced that morning on those dark men and spoke to them in Romany.

Since the above was written I have met in an entertaining work called "Unknown Hungary," by Victor Tissot, with certain remarks on the Hungarian gypsy musicians which are so appropriate that I cite them in full : —

"The gypsy artists in Hungary play by inspiration, with inimitable *verve* and spirit, without even knowing their notes, and nothing whatever of the rhymes and rules of the masters. Liszt, who has closely studied them, says, The art of music being for them a sublime language, a song, mystic in itself, though dear to the initiated, they use it according to the wants of the moment which they wish to express. They have invented their music for their own use, to sing about themselves to themselves, to express themselves in the most heartfelt and touching monologues.

" Their music is as free as their lives ; no intermediate modulation, no chords, no transition, it goes from one key to another. From ethereal heights they precipitate you into the howling depths of hell ; from the plaint, barely heard, they pass brusquely to the warrior's song, which bursts loudly forth, passionate and tender, at once burning and calm. Their melodies plunge you into a melancholy reverie, or carry you away into a stormy whirlwind ; they are a faithful expression of the Hungarian character, sometimes quick, brilliant, and lively, sometimes sad and apathetic.

" The gypsies, when they arrived in Hungary, had no music of their own ; they appropriated the Magyar music, and made from it an original art which now belongs to them."

I here break in upon Messieurs Tissot and Liszt to remark that, while it is very probable that the Roms reformed Hungarian music, it is rather boldly assumed that they had no music of their own. It was, among other callings, as dancers and musicians that they left India and entered Europe, and among them were doubtless many descendants of the ten thousand Indo-Persian Luris or Nuris. But to resume quotation :—

" They made from it an art full of life, passion,

laughter, and tears. The instrument which.the gypsies prefer is the violin, which they call *bas' alja*, 'the
king of instruments.' They also play the viola, the
cymbal, and the clarionet.

" There was a pause. The gypsies, who had perceived at a table a comfortable-looking man, evidently wealthy, and on a pleasure excursion in the
town, came down from their platform, and ranged
themselves round him to give him a serenade all to
himself, as is their custom. They call this ' playing
into the ear.'

" They first asked the gentleman his favorite air,
and then played it with such spirit and enthusiasm
and overflowing richness of variation and ornament,
and with so much emotion, that it drew forth the
applause of the whole company. After this they
executed a czardas, one of the wildest, most feverish,
harshest, and, one may say, tormenting, as if to pour
intoxication into the soul of their listener. They
watched his countenance to note the impression produced by the passionate rhythm of their instruments ;
then, breaking off suddenly, they played a hushed,
soft, caressing measure ; and again, almost breaking
the trembling cords of their bows, they produced
such an intensity of effect that the listener was almost beside himself with delight and astonishment.
He sat as if bewitched ; he shut his eyes, hung his
head in melancholy, or raised it with a start, as the
music varied ; then jumped up and struck the back
of his head with his hands. He positively laughed
and cried at once ; then, drawing a roll of bank-notes
from his pocket-book, he threw it to the gypsies, and
fell back in his chair, as if exhausted with so much
enjoyment. And in *this* lies the triumph of the

gypsy music; it is like that of Orpheus, which moved
the rocks and trees. The soul of the Hungarian
plunges, with a refinement of sensation that we can
understand, but cannot follow, into this music, which,
like the unrestrained indulgence of the imagination in
fantasy and caprice, gives to the initiated all the in-
toxicating sensations experienced by opium smokers."

The Austrian gypsies have many songs which perfectly reflect their character. Most of them are only
single verses of a few lines, such as are sung everywhere in Spain; others, which are longer, seem to
have grown from the connection of these verses. The
following translation from the Roumanian Romany
(Vassile Alexandri) gives an idea of their style and
spirit : –

GYPSY SONG.

The wind whistles over the heath,
The moonlight flits over the flood;
And the gypsy lights up his fire,
In the darkness of the wood.
    Hurrah!
In the darkness of the wood.

Free is the bird in the air,
And the fish where the river flows;
Free is the deer in the forest,
And the gypsy wherever he goes.
    Hurrah!
And the gypsy wherever he goes.

A GORGIO GENTLEMAN SPEAKS.

Girl, wilt thou live in my home?
I will give thee a sable gown,
And golden coins for a necklace,
If thou wilt be my own.

GYPSY GIRL.

No wild horse will leave the prairie
For a harness with silver stars;

6

Nor an eagle the crags of the mountain,
For a cage with golden bars;

Nor the gypsy girl the forest,
Or the meadow, though gray and cold,
For garments made of sable,
Or necklaces of gold.

THE GORGIO.

Girl, wilt thou live in my dwelling,
For pearls and diamonds true ?[1]
I will give thee a bed of scarlet,
And a royal palace, too.

GYPSY GIRL.

My white teeth are my pearlins,
My diamonds my own black eyes;
My bed is the soft green meadow,
My palace the world as it lies.

Free is the bird in the air,
And the fish where the river flows;
Free is the deer in the forest,
And the gypsy wherever he goes.
          Hurrah!
And the gypsy wherever he goes.

There is a deep, strange element in the gypsy character, which finds no sympathy or knowledge in the
German, and very little in other Europeans, but
which is so much in accord with the Slavonian and
Hungarian that he who truly feels it with love is often
disposed to mingle them together. It is a dreamy
mysticism; an indefinite semi-supernaturalism, often
passing into gloom; a feeling as of Buddhism which
has glided into Northern snows, and taken a new and
darker life in winter-lands. It is strong in the Czech
or Bohemian, whose nature is the worst understood
in the civilized world. That he should hate the Ger-

---

[1] Diamonds true. *O latcho bar* (in England, *tatcho bar*), " the true
or real stone," is the gypsy for a diamond.

man with all his heart and soul is in the order of things. We talk about the mystical Germans, but German self-conscious mysticism is like a problem of Euclid beside the natural, unexpressed dreaminess of the Czech. The German mystic goes to work at once to expound his "system" in categories, dressing it up in a technology which in the end proves to be the only mystery in it. The Bohemian and gypsy, each in their degrees of culture, form no system and make no technology, but they feel all the more. Now the difference between true and imitative mysticism is that the former takes no form; it is even narrowed by religious creeds, and wing-clipt by pious " illumination." Nature, and nature alone, is its real life. It was from the Southern Slavonian lands that all real mysticism, and all that higher illumination which means freedom, came into Germany and Europe; and after all, Germany's first and best mystic, Jacob Böhme, was Bohemian by name, as he was by nature. When the world shall have discovered who the as yet unknown Slavonian German was who wrote all the best part of " Consuelo," and who helped himself in so doing from " Der letzte Taborit," by Herlossohn, we shall find one of the few men who understood the Bohemian.

Once in a while, as in Fanny Janauschek, the Czech bursts out into art, and achieves a great triumph. I have seen Rachel and Ristori many a time, but their best acting was shallow compared to Janauschek's, as I have seen it in by-gone years, when she played Iphigenia and Medea in German. No one save a Bohemian could ever so *intuit* the gloomy profundity and unearthly fire of the Colchian sorceress. These are the things required to perfect every artist, — above all, the tragic artist, — that the tree of his or her genius shall not only soar to heaven among the angels, but also have roots in the depths of darkness and fire ; and that he or she shall play not only to the audience, and in sympathy with them, but also unto one's self and down to one's deepest dreams.

No one will accuse me of wide discussion or padding who understands my drift in this chapter. I am speaking of the gypsy, and I cannot explain him more clearly than by showing his affinities with the Slavonian and Magyar, and how, through music and probably in many other ways, he has influenced them. As the Spaniard perfectly understands the objective vagabond side of the Gitano, so the Southeastern European understands the musical and wild-forest yearnings of the Tsigane. Both to gypsy and Slavonian there is that which makes them dream so that even debauchery has for them at times an unearthly inspiration ; and as smoking was inexpressibly sacred to the red Indians of old, so that when the Guatemalan Christ harried hell, the demons offered him cigars ; in like manner tipiness is often to the gypsy and Servian, or Czech, or Croat, something so serious and impressive that it is a thing not to be lightly thought of, but to be undertaken with intense deliberation and under due appreciation of its benefits.

Many years ago, when I had begun to feel this strange element I gave it expression in a poem which I called " The Bohemian," as expressive of both gypsy and Slavonian nature : —

THE BOHEMIAN.

Chces li tajnou vec aneb pravdu vyzvédéti
Blazen, dité opily člověk o tom umeji povodeti.

Wouldst thou know a truth or mystery,
A drunkard, fool, or child may tell it thee
BOHEMIAN PROVERB

And now I'll wrap my blanket o'er me,
 And on the tavern floor I'll lie,
A double spirit-flask before me,
 And watch my pipe clouds, melting, die.

They melt and die, but ever darken
 As night comes on and hides the day,
Till all is black ; then, brothers, hearken, '
 And if ye can write down my lay.

In yon long loaf my knife is gleaming,
 Like one black sail above the boat ;
As once at Pesth I saw it beaming,
 Half through a dark Croatian throat.

Now faster, faster, whirls the ceiling,
 And wilder, wilder, turns my brain ;
And still I'll drink, till, past all feeling,
 My soul leaps forth to light again.

Whence come these white girls wreathing round me ?
 Barushka ! — long I thought thee dead ;
Katchenka ! — when these arms last bound thee
 Thou laid'st by Rajrad, cold as lead.

And faster, faster, whirls the ceiling,
 And wilder, wilder, turns my brain ;
And from afar a star comes stealing
 Straight at me o'er the death-black plain.

Alas ! I sink. My spirits miss me.
 I swim, I shoot from shore to shore !
Klara ! thou golden sister — kiss me !
 I rise — I'm safe — I'm strong once more.

And faster, faster, whirls the ceiling,
 And wilder, wilder, whirls my brain ;.

The star ! — it strikes my soul, revealing
All life and light to me again.

———

Against the waves fresh waves are dashing,
Above the breeze fresh breezes blow;
Through seas of light new light is flashing,
And with them all I float and flow.

Yet round me rings of fire are gleaming, —
Pale rings of fire, wild eyes of death !
Why haunt me thus, awake or dreaming?
Methought I left ye with my breath!

Ay, glare and stare, with life increasing,
And leech-like eyebrows, arching in ;
Be, if ye must, my fate unceasing,
But never hope a fear to win.

He who knows all may haunt the haunter,
He who fears naught hath conquered fate ;
Who bears in silence quells the daunter,
And makes his spoiler desolate.

O wondrous eyes, of star-like lustre,
How have ye changed to guardian love !
Alas ! where stars in myriads cluster,
Ye vanish in the heaven above.

———

I hear two bells so softly ringing ;
How sweet their silver voices roll !
The one on distant hills is ringing,
The other peals within my soul.

I hear two maidens gently talking,
Bohemian maids, and fair to see:
The one on distant hills is walking,
The other maiden, — where is she ?

Where is she ?   When the moonlight glistens
O'er silent lake or murmuring stream,
I hear her call my soul, which listens,
"Oh, wake no more !   Come, love, and dream!"

She came to earth, earth's loveliest creature;
 She died, and then was born once more;
Changed was her race, and changed each feature,
 , But yet I loved her as before.

We live, but still, when night has bound me
 In golden dreams too sweet to last,
A wondrous light-blue world around me,
 She comes, — the loved one of the past.

I know not which I love the dearest,
 For both the loves are still the same:
The living to my life is nearest,
 The dead one feeds the living flame.

And when the sun, its rose-wine quaffing,
 Which flows across the Eastern deep,
Awakes us, Klara chides me, laughing,
 And says we love too well in sleep.

And though no more a Voivode's daughter,
 As when she lived on earth before,
The love is still the same which sought her,
 And I am true, and ask no more.

Bright moonbeams on the sea are playing,
 And starlight shines upon the hill,
And I should wake, but still delaying
 In our old life I linger still.

For as the wind clouds flit above me,
 And as the stars above them shine,
My higher life 's in those who love me,
 And higher still, our life 's divine.

And thus I raise my soul by drinking,
 As on the tavern floor I lie;
It heeds not whence begins our thinking
 If to the end its flight is high.

E'en outcasts may have heart and feeling,
 The blackest wild Tsigan be true,
And love, like light in dungeons stealing,
 Though bars be there, will still burst through.

It is the reëcho of more than one song of those
strange lands, of more than one voice, and of many a
melody; and those who have heard them, though not
more distinctly than François Villon when he spoke of
flinging the question back by silent lake and streamlet
lone, will understand me, and say it is true to nature.

In a late work on Magyarland, by a lady Fellow
of the Carpathian Society, I find more on Hungarian
gypsy music, which is so well written that I quote
fully from it, being of the opinion that one ought,
when setting forth any subject, to give quite as good
an opportunity to others who are in our business as
to ourselves. And truly this lady has felt the charm
of the Tsigan music and describes it so well that one
wishes she were a Romany in language and by adop-
tion, like unto a dozen dames and damsels whom I
know.

" The Magyars have a perfect passion for this
gypsy music, and there is nothing that appeals so
powerfully to their emotions, whether of joy or sorrow. These singular musicians are, as a rule, well
taught, and can play almost any music, greatly pre-
ferring, however, their own compositions. Their music, consequently, is highly characteristic. It is the
language of their lives and strange surroundings, a
wild, weird banshee music : now all joy and sparkle,
like sunshine on the plains ; now sullen, sad, and pathetic by turns, like the wail of a crushed and op-
pressed people, — an echo, it is said, of the minstrelsy
of the *hegedösök* or Hungarian bards, but sounding
to our ears like the more distant echo of that exceeding bitter cry, uttered long centuries ago by their
forefathers under Egyptian bondage, and borne over
the time-waves of thousands of years, breaking forth
in their music of to-day."

Here I interrupt the lady — with all due courtesy — to remark that I cannot agree with her, nor with her probable authority, Walter Simson, in believing that the gypsies are the descendants of the mixed races who followed Moses out of Egypt. The Rom in Egypt is a Hindoo stranger now, as he ever was. But that the echo of centuries of outlawry and wretchedness and wildness rises and falls, like the ineffable discord in a wind-harp, in Romany airs is true enough, whatever its origin may have been. But I beg pardon, madam, — I interrupted you.

" The soul-stirring, madly exciting, and martial strains of the Racoczys — one of the Revolutionary airs — has just died upon the ear. A brief interval of rest has passed. Now listen with bated breath to that recitative in the minor key, — that passionate wail, that touching story, the gypsies' own music, which rises and falls on the air. Knives and forks are set down, hands and arms hang listless, all the seeming necessities of the moment being either suspended or forgotten, — merged in the memories which those vibrations, so akin to human language, reawaken in each heart. Eyes involuntarily fill with tears, as those pathetic strains echo back and make present some sorrow of long ago, or rouse from slumber that of recent time. . . .

" And now, the recitative being ended, and the last chord struck, the melody begins, of which the former was the prelude. Watch the movements of the supple figure of the first violin, standing in the centre of the other musicians, who accompany him softly. How every nerve is *en rapport* with his instrument, and how his very soul is speaking through it ! See how gently he draws the bow across the trembling strings,

and how lovingly he lays his cheek upon it, as if listening to some responsive echo of his heart's inmost
feeling, for it is his mystic language! How the instrument lives and answers to his every touch, sending forth in turn utterances tender, sad, wild, and
joyous! The audience once more hold their breath
to catch the dying tones, as the melody, so rich, so
beautiful, so full of pathos, is drawing to a close. The
tension is absolutely painful as the gypsy dwells on
the last lingering note, and it is a relief when, with a
loud and general burst of sound, every performer
starts into life and motion. *Then* what crude and
wild dissonances are made to resolve themselves into
delicious harmony! What rapturous and fervid
phrases, and what energy and impetuosity, are there
in every motion of the gypsies' figures, as their dark
eyes glisten and emit flashes in unison with the
tones!"

The writer is gifted in giving words to gypsy music. One cannot say, as the inexhaustible Cad writes
of Niagara ten times on a page in the Visitors' Book,
that it is indescribable. I think that if language
means anything this music has been very well described by the writers whom I have cited. When I
am told that the gypsies' impetuous and passionate
natures make them enter into musical action with
heart and soul, I feel not only the strains played long
ago, but also hear therein the horns of Elfland blow-
ing, — which he who has not heard, of summer days,
in the drone of the bee, by reedy rustling stream,
will never know on earth in any wise. But once
heard it comes ever, as I, though in the city, heard
it last night in the winter wind, with Romany words
mingled in wild refrain : —

" Kamava tute, miri chelladi !"

II.

AUSTRIAN GYPSIES IN PHILADELPHIA.

It was a sunny Sunday afternoon, and I was walking down Chestnut Street, Philadelphia, when I met with three very dark men.

Dark men are not rarities in my native city. There is, for instance, Eugene, who has the invaluable faculty of being able to turn his hand to an infinite helpfulness in the small arts. These men were darker than Eugene, but they differed from him in this, that while he is a man of color, they were not. For in America the man of Aryan blood, however dark he may be, is always "off" color, while the lightest-hued quadroon is always on it. Which is not the only paradox connected with the descendants of Africans of which I have heard.

I saw at a glance that these dark men were much nearer to the old Aryan stock than are even my purely white readers. For they were more recently from India, and they could speak a language abounding in Hindi, in pure old Sanskrit, and in Persian. Yet they would make no display of it; on the contrary, I knew that they would be very likely at first to deny all knowledge thereof, as well as their race and blood. For · they were gypsies; it was very apparent in their eyes, which had the Gitano gleam as one seldom sees it in England. I confess that I experienced a thrill as I exchanged glances with

them. It was a long time since I had seen a Romany, and, as usual, I knew that I was going to astonish them. They were singularly attired, having
very good clothes of a quite theatrical foreign fashion, bearing silver buttons as large as and of the
shape of hen's eggs. Their hair hung in black ring-
lets down their shoulders, and I saw that they had
come from the Austrian Slavonian land.

I addressed the eldest in Italian. He answered
fluently and politely. I changed to Ilirski or Illyrian and to Serb, of which I have a few phrases in
stock. They spoke all these languages fluently, for
one was a born Illyrian and one a Serb. They also
spoke Nemetz, or German; in fact, everything except English.

"Have you got through all your languages?" I at
last inquired.

"Tutte, signore, — all of them."

"Is n't there *one* left behind, which you have forgotten? Think a minute."

"No, signore. None."

"What, not *one!* You know so many that perhaps a language more or less makes no difference to
you."

"By the Lord, signore, you have seen every egg
in the basket."

I looked him fixedly in the eyes, and said, in a low
tone, —

"*Ne rakesa tu Romanes miro prala?*"

There was a startled glance from one to the other,
and a silence. I had asked him if he could not talk
Romany. And I added, —

"*Won't* you talk a word with a gypsy brother?"

That moved them. They all shook my hands with

great feeling, expressing intense joy and amazement at meeting with one who knew them.

"*Mishto hom me dikava tute.*" (I am glad to see you.) So they told me how they were getting on, and where they were camped, and how they sold horses, and so on, and we might have got on much farther had it not been for a very annoying interruption. As I was talking to the gypsies, a great number of men, attracted by the sound of a foreign language, stopped, and fairly pushed themselves up to us, endeavoring to make it all out. When there were at least fifty, they crowded in between me and the foreigners, so that I could hardly talk to them. The crowd did not consist of ordinary people, or snobs. They were well dressed, — young clerks, at least, — who would have fiercely resented being told that they were impertinent.

" Eye-talians, ain't they ? " inquired one man, who was evidently zealous in pursuit of knowledge.

" Why don't you tell us what they are sayin' ? "

" What kind of fellers air they, any way ? "

I was desirous of going with the Hungarian Roms. But to walk along Chestnut Street with an augmenting procession of fifty curious Sunday promenaders was not on my card. In fact, I had some difficulty in tearing myself from the inquisitive, questioning, well-dressed people. The gypsies bore the pressure with the serene equanimity of cosmopolite superiority, smiling at provincial rawness. Even so in China and Africa the traveler is mobbed by the many, who, there as here, think that " I want to know " is full excuse for all intrusiveness. *C'est tout comme chez nous.* I confess that I was vexed, and, considering that it was in my native city, mortified.

A few days after I went out to the *tan* where
these Roms had camped. But the birds had flown,
and a little pile of ashes and the usual débris of a
gypsy camp were all that remained. The police told
me that they had some very fine horses, and had gone
to the Northwest; and that is all I ever saw of them.

I have heard of a philanthropist who was turned
into a misanthrope by attempting to sketch in public
and in galleries. Respectable strangers, even clergymen, would stop and coolly look over his shoulder,
and ask questions, and give him advice, until he could
work no longer. Why is it that people who would
not speak to you for life without an introduction
should think that their small curiosity to see your
sketches authorizes them to act as aquaintances?
Or why is the pursuit of knowledge assumed among
the half-bred to be an excuse for so much intrusion?
"I want to know." Well, and what if you do? The
man who thinks that his desire for knowledge is an
excuse for impertinence — and there are too many who
act on this in all sincerity — is of the kind who knocks
the fingers off statues, because " he wants them "
for his collection; who chips away tombstones, and
hews down historic trees, and not infrequently steals
outright, and thinks that his pretense of culture is
full excuse for all his mean deeds. Of this tribe is
the man who cuts his name on all walls and smears
it on the pyramids, to proclaim himself a fool to the
world; the difference being that, instead of wanting
to know anything, he wants everybody to know that
His Littleness was once in a great place.

I knew a distinguished artist, who, while in the
East, only secured his best sketch of a landscape by
employing fifty men to keep off the multitude. I

have seen a strange fellow take a lady's sketch out
of her hand, excusing himself with the remark that
he was so fond of pictures. Of course my readers
do not act thus. When they are passing through the
Louvre or British Museum they never pause and
overlook artists, despite the notices requesting them
not to do so. Of course not. Yet I once knew a
charming young American lady, who scouted the idea
as nonsense that she should not watch artists at
work. " Why, we used to make up parties for the
purpose of looking at them ! " she said. " It was half
the fun of going there. I 'm sure the artists were
delighted to get a chance to talk to us." Doubtless.
And yet there are really very few artists who do
not work more at their ease when not watched, and
I have known some to whom such watching was misery. They are not, O intruder, painting for *your*
amusement !

This is not such a far cry from my Romanys as
it may seem. When I think of what I have lost in
this life by impertinence coming between me and
gypsies, I feel that it could not be avoided. The
proportion of men, even of gentlemen, or of those
who dress decently, who cannot see another well-
dressed man talking with a very poor one in public,
without at once surmising a mystery, and endeavoring to solve it, is amazing. And they do not stop
at a trifle, either.

It is a marked characteristic of all gypsies that
they are quite free from any such mean intrusiveness. Whether it is because they themselves are
continually treated as curiosities, or because great
knowledge of life in a small way has made them
philosophers, I will not say, but it is a fact that in

this respect they are invariably the politest people in the world. Perhaps their calm contempt of the *galerly*, or green Gorgios, is founded on a consciousness of their superiority in this matter.

The Hungarian gypsy differs from all his brethren of Europe in being more intensely gypsy. He has deeper, wilder, and more original feeling in music, and he is more inspired with a love of travel. Numbers of Hungarian Romany chals — in which I include all Austrian gypsies — travel annually all over Europe, but return as regularly to their own country. I have met with them exhibiting bears in Baden-Baden. These Ričinari, or bear-leaders, form, however, a set within a set, and are in fact more nearly allied to the gypsy bear-leaders of Turkey and Syria than to any other of their own people. They are wild and rude to a proverb, and generally speak a peculiar dialect of Romany, which is called the Bear-leaders' by philologists. I have also seen Syrian-gypsy Ričinari in Cairo. Many of the better caste make a great deal of money, and some are rich. Like all really pure-blooded gypsies, they have deep feelings, which are easily awakened by kindness, but especially by sympathy and interest.

ENGLISH GYPSIES.

I.

OATLANDS PARK.

OATLANDS PARK (between Weybridge and Walton-upon-Thames) was once the property of the Duke of York, but now the lordly manor-house is a hotel. The grounds about it are well preserved and very picturesque. They should look well, for they cover a vast and wasted fortune. There is, for instance, a grotto which cost forty thousand pounds. It is one of those wretched and tasteless masses of silly rock-rococo work which were so much admired at the beginning of the present century, when sham ruins and sham caverns were preferred to real. There is, also, close by the grotto, a dogs' burial-ground, in which more than a hundred animals, the favorites of the late duchess, lie buried. Over each is a tomb-stone, inscribed with a rhyming epitaph, written by the titled lady herself, and which is in sober sadness in every instance doggerel, as befits the subject. In order to degrade the associations of religion and church rites as effectually as possible, there is attached to these graves the semblance of a ruined chapel, the stained-glass window of which was taken from a church.[1] I confess that I could never see either

---

[1] Within a mile, Maginn lies buried, without a monument.

grotto or grave-yard without sincerely wishing, out of regard to the memory of both duke and duchess, that these ridiculous relics of vulgar taste and affected sentimentalism could be completely obliterated. But, apart from them, the scenes around are very beautiful; for there are grassy slopes and pleasant lawns, ancient trees and broad gravel walks, over which, as the dry leaves fall on the crisp sunny morning, the feet are tempted to walk on and on, all through the merry golden autumn day.

The neighborhood abounds in memories of olden time. Near Oatlands is a modernized house, in which Henry the Eighth lived in his youth. It belonged then to Cardinal Wolsey; now it is owned by Mr. Lindsay, — a sufficient cause for wits calling it Lindsay-Wolsey, that being also a " fabric." Within an hour's walk is the palace built by Cardinal Wolsey, while over the river, and visible from the portico, is the little old Gothic church of Shepperton, and in the same view, to the right, is the old Walton Bridge, by Cowie Stakes, supposed to cover the exact spot where Cæsar crossed. This has been denied by many, but I know that the field adjacent to it abounds in ancient British jars filled with burned bones, the relics of an ancient battle, — probably that which legend states was fought on the neighboring Battle Island. Stout-hearted Queen Bessy has also left her mark on this neighborhood, for within a mile is the old Saxon-towered church of Walton, in which the royal dame was asked for her opinion of the sacrament when it was given to her, to which she replied : —

> " Christ was the Word who spake it,
> He took the bread and brake it ;
> And what that Word did make it,
> That I believe, and take it."

In memory of this the lines were inscribed on the massy Norman pillar by which she stood. From the style and cutting it is evident that the inscription dates from the reign of Elizabeth. And very near Oatlands, in fact on the grounds, there are two ancient yew-trees, several hundred yards apart. The story runs that Queen Elizabeth once drew a long bow and shot an arrow so far that, to commemorate the deed, one of these trees was planted where she stood, and the other where the shaft fell. All England is a museum of touching or quaint relics; to me one of its most interesting cabinets is this of the neighborhood of Weybridge and Walton-upon-Thames.

I once lived for eight months at Oatlands Park, and learned to know the neighborhood well. I had many friends among the families in the vicinity, and, guided by their advice, wandered to every old church and manor-house, ruin and haunted rock, fairy-oak, tower, palace, or shrine within a day's ramble. But there was one afternoon walk of four miles, round by the river, which I seldom missed. It led by a spot on the bank, and an old willow-tree near the bridge, which spot was greatly haunted by the Romany, so that, excepting during the hopping-season of autumn, when they were away in Kent, I seldom failed to see from afar a light rising smoke, and near it a tent and a van, as the evening shadows blended with the mist from the river in phantom union.

It is a common part of gypsy life that the father shall be away all day, lounging about the next village, possibly in the *kitchema* or ale-house, or trying to trade a horse, while the wife trudges over the country, from one farm-house or cottage to another,

loaded with baskets, household utensils, toys, or cheap
ornaments, which she endeavors, like a true Autolyca,
with wily arts and wheedling tones, to sell to the rus-
tics. When it can be managed, this hawking is often
an introduction to fortune-telling, and if these fail the
gypsy has recourse to begging. But it is a weary life,
and the poor *dye* is always glad enough to get home.
During the day the children have been left to look
out for themselves or to the care of the eldest, and
have tumbled about the van, rolled around with the
dog, and fought or frolicked as they chose. But
though their parents often have a stock of cheap toys,
especially of penny dolls and the like, which they
put up as prizes for games at races and fairs, I have
never seen these children with playthings. The little girls have no dolls; the boys, indeed, affect whips,
as becomes incipient jockeys, but on the whole they
never seemed to me to have the same ideas as to play
as ordinary house-children. The author of "My Indian Garden" has made the same observation of Hindoo little ones, whose ways are not as our ways were
when we were young. Roman and Egyptian children
had their dolls; and there is something sadly sweet
to me in the sight of these barbarous and naïve fac-
similes of miniature humanity, which come up like
little spectres out of the dust of ancient days. They
are so rude and queer, these Roman puppets; and yet
they were loved once, and had pet names, and their
owl-like faces were as tenderly kissed as their little
mistresses had been by their mothers. So the Romany
girl, unlike the Roman, is generally doll-less and toy-
less. But the affection between mother and child is
as warm among these wanderers as with any other
people; and it is a touching sight to see the gypsy who

has been absent all the weary day returning home. And when she is seen from afar off there is a race among all the little dark-brown things to run to mother and get kissed, and cluster and scramble around her, and perhaps receive some little gift which mother's thoughtful love has provided. Knowing these customs, I was wont to fill my pockets with chestnuts or oranges, and, distributing them among the little ones, talk with them, and await the sunset return of their parents. The confidence or love of all children is delightful ; but that of gypsy children resembles the friendship of young foxes, and the study of their artless-artful ways is indeed attractive.

I can remember that one afternoon six small Romany boys implored me to give them each a penny. I replied, —

" If I had sixpence, how would you divide it ? "

" That would be a penny apiece," said the eldest boy.

" And if threepence ? "

" A ha'penny apiece."

" And three ha'pence ? "

" A farden all round. And then it could n't go no furder, unless we bought tobacco an' diwided it."

" Well, I have some tobacco. But can any of you smoke ? "

They were from four to ten years of age, and at the word every one pulled out the stump of a blackened pipe, — such depraved-looking fragments I never saw, — and holding them all up, and crowding closely around, like hungry poultry with uplifted bills, they began to clamor for *tūvalo*, or tobacco. They were connoisseurs, too, and the elder boy, as he secured his share, smelled it with intense satisfaction, and said, " That 's *rye's tŭvalo;* " that is, " gentleman's tobacco," or best quality.

One evening, as the shadows were darkening the day, I met a little gypsy boy, dragging along, with incredible labor, a sack full of wood, which one needed not go far afield to surmise was neither purchased nor begged. The alarmed and guilty or despairing look which he cast at me was very touching. Perhaps he thought I was the gentleman upon whose property he had " found " the wood ; or else a magistrate. How he stared when I spoke to him in Romany, and offered to help him carry it! As we bore it along I suggested that we had better be careful and avoid the police, which remark established perfect confidence between us. But as we came to the tent, what was the amazement of the boy's mother to see him returning with a gentleman helping him to carry his load ! And to hear me say in Romany, and in a cheerful tone, " Mother, here is some wood we 've been stealing for you."

Gypsies have strong nerves and much cheek, but this was beyond her endowment ; she was appalled at the unearthly strangeness of the whole proceeding, and when she spoke there was a skeleton rattle in her words and a quaver of startled ghastliness in her laugh. She had been alarmed for her boy, and when I appeared she thought I was a swell bringing him in under arrest; but when I announced myself in Romany as an accomplice, emotion stifled thought. And I lingered not, and spoke no more, but walked away into the woods and the darkness. However, the legend went forth on the roads, even unto Kingston, and was told among the rollicking Romanys of 'Appy Ampton ; for there are always a merry, loafing lot of them about that festive spot, looking out for excursionists through the months when the gorse blooms, and kissing is in season — which is always. And he who seeks them on Sunday may find them camped in Green Lane.

When I wished for a long ramble on the hedge-lined roads — the sweet roads of old England — and by the green fields, I was wont to take a day's walk to Netley Abbey. Then I could pause, as I went, before many a quiet, sheltered spot, adorned with arbors and green alleys, and protected by trees and hawthorn hedges, and again surrender my soul, while walking, to tender and vague reveries, in which all definite thoughts swim overpowered, yet happy, in a sea of voluptuous emotions inspired by clouds lost in the blue sea of heaven and valleys visioned away into the purple sky. What opium is to one, what hasheesh may be to another, what *kheyf* or mere repose concentrated into actuality is to the Arab, that is Nature to him who has followed her for long years through poets and mystics and in works of art, until at last he pierces through dreams and pictures to reality.

The ruins of Netley Abbey, nine or ten miles from Oatlands Park, are picturesque and lonely, and well fitted for the dream-artist in shadows among sunshine. The priory was called Newstead or De Novo Loco in Norman times, when it was founded by Ruald de Calva, in the day of Richard Cœur de Lion. The ruins rise gray, white, and undressed with ivy, that they may contrast the more vividly with the deep emerald of the meadows around. "The surrounding scenery is composed of rivers and rivulets," — for seven streams run by it, according to Aubrey, — " of foot-bridge and fords, plashy pools and fringed, tangled hollows, trees in groups or alone, and cattle dotted over the pastures : " an English Cuyp from many points of view, beautiful and English-home-like from all. Very near it is the quaint, out-of-the-way, darling little old church of Pirford, up a hill, nestling among trees, a half-Norman, decorated beauty, out of the age, but altogether in the heart. As I came near, of a summer afternoon, the waving of leaves and the buzzing of bees without, and the hum of the voices of children at school within the adjoining building, the cool shade and the beautiful view of the ruined Abbey beyond, made an impression which I can never forget. Among such scenes one learns why the English love so heartily their rural life, and why every object peculiar to it has brought forth a picture or a poem. I can imagine how many a man, who has never known what poetry was at home, has wept with yearning inexpressible, when sitting among burning sands and under the palms of the East, for such scenes as these.

But Netley Abbey is close by the river Wey, and the sight of that river and the thought of the story of the monks of the olden time who dwelt in the Abbey drive away sentiment as suddenly as a north wind scatters sea-fogs. For the legend is a merry one, and the reader may have heard it ; but if he has not I will give it in one of the merriest ballads ever written. By whom I know not, — doubtless many know. I sing, while walking, songs of olden time.

THE MONKS OF THE WEY.

A TRUE AND IMPORTANT RELATION OF THE WONDERFUL TUN-
NELL OF NEWARKE ABBEY AND OF THE UNTIMELY ENDE OF
SEVERALL OF YE GHOSTLY BRETH'REN.

The monks of the Wey seldom sung any psalms,
And little they thought of religion or qualms;
Such rollicking, frolicking, ranting, and gay,
And jolly old boys were the monks of the Wey.

To the sweet nuns of Ockham devoting their cares,
They had little time for their beads and their prayers;
For the love of these maidens they sighed night and day,
And neglected devotion, these monks of the Wey.

And happy i' faith might these brothers have been
If the river had never been rolling between
The abbey so grand and the convent so gray,
That stood on the opposite side of the Wey.

For daily they sighed, and then nightly they pined,
But little to anchorite precepts inclined,
So smitten with beauty's enchantments were they,
These rollicking, frolicking monks of the Wey.

But scandal was rife in the country near,
They dared not row over the river for fear;
And no more could they swim it, so fat were they,
These oily and amorous monks of the Wey.

Loudly they groaned for their fate so hard,
From the love of these beautiful maidens debarred,
Till a brother just hit on a plan which would stay
The woe of these heart-broken monks of the Wey.

"Nothing," quoth he, "should true love sunder;
Since we cannot go over, then let us go under!
Boats and bridges shall yield to clay,
We'll dig a long tunnel clean under the Wey."

So to it they went with right good will,
With spade and shovel and pike and bill;

And from evening's close till the dawn of day
They worked like miners all under the Wey.

And at vesper hour, as their work begun,
Each sung of the charms of his favorite nun ;
"How surprised they will be, and how happy ! " said they,
"When we pop in upon them from under the Wey!"

And for months they kept grubbing and making no sound
Like other black moles, darkly under the ground ;
And no one suspected such going astray,
So sly were these mischievous monks of the Wey.

At last their fine work was brought near to a close
And early one morn from their pallets they rose,
And met in their tunnel with lights to survey
If they 'd scooped a free passage right under the Wey.

But alas for their fate ! As they smirked and they smiled.
To think how completely the world was beguiled,
The river broke in, and it grieves me to say
It drowned all the frolicksome monks of the Wey.

O churchmen beware of the lures of the flesh,
The net of the devil has many a mesh !
And remember whenever you 're tempted to stray,
The fate that befell the poor monks of the Wey.

It was all long ago, and now there are neither
monks nor nuns ; the convent has been converted,
little by little, age by age, into cottages, even as the
friars and nuns themselves may have been organically
changed possibly into violets, but more probably into
the festive sparrows which flit and hop and flirt about
the ruins with abrupt startles, like pheasants sudden
bursting on the wing. There is a pretty little Latin
epigram, written by a gay monk, of a pretty little
lady, who, being very amorous, and observing that
sparrows were like her as to love, hoped that she
might be turned into one after death ; and it is not

difficult for a dreamer in an old abbey, of a golden
day to fancy that these merry, saucy birdies, who
dart and dip in and out of the sunshine or shadow,
chirping their shameless ditties *pro et con*, were once
the human dwellers in the spot, who sang their gau-
drioles to pleasant strains.

I became familiar with many such scenes for many
miles about Oatlands, not merely during solitary
walks, but by availing myself of the kind invitations
of many friends, and by hunting afoot with the bea-
gles. In this fashion one has hare and hound, but
no horse. It is not needed, for while going over crisp
stubble and velvet turf, climbing fences and jump-
ing ditches, a man has a keen sense of being his own
horse, and when he accomplishes a good leap of being
intrinsically well worth £200. And indeed, so long
as anybody can walk day in and out a greater distance than would tire a horse, he may well believe
he is really worth one. It may be a good thing for
us to reflect on the fact that if slavery prevailed at
the present day as it did among the polished Greeks
the average price of young gentlemen, and even of
young ladies, would not be more than what is paid
for a good hunter. Divested of diamonds and of
Worth's dresses, what would a girl of average charms
be worth to a stranger? Let us reflect!

It was an October morning, and, pausing after a
run, I let the pack and the "course-men" sweep
away, while I sat in a pleasant spot to enjoy the air
and scenery. The solemn grandeur of groves and
the quiet dignity of woodland glades, barred with
rays of solid-seeming sunshine, such as the saint of
old hung his cloak on, the brook into which the over-
hanging chestnuts drop, as if in sport, their creamy

golden little boats of leaves, never seem so beautiful
or impressive as immediately after a rush and cry of
many men, succeeded by solitude and silence. Little
by little the bay of the hounds, the shouts of the
hunters, and the occasional sound of the horn grew
fainter; the birds once more appeared, and sent forth
short calls to their timid friends. I began again
to notice who my neighbors were, as to daisies and
heather which resided around the stone on which I
sat, and the exclusive circle of a fairy-ring at a little
distance, which, like many exclusive circles, consisted
entirely of mushrooms.

As the beagle-sound died away, and while the hounds
were " working around " to the road, I heard footsteps
approaching, and looking up saw before me a gypsy
woman and a boy. She was a very gypsy woman,
an ideal witch, nut-brown, tangle-haired, aquiline of
nose, and fierce-eyed; and fiercely did she beg! As
amid broken Gothic ruins, overhung with unkempt
ivy, one can trace a vanished and strange beauty, so
in this worn face of the Romany, mantled by neglected
tresses, I could see the remains of what must have
been once a wonderful though wild loveliness. As I
looked into those serpent eyes, trained for a long life
to fascinate in fortune-telling simple dove-girls, I
could readily understand the implicit faith with which
many writers in the olden time spoke of the "fascination" peculiar to female glances. " The multipli-
cation of women," said the rabbis, " is the increase
of witches," for the belles in Israel were killing girls,
with arrows, the bows whereof are formed by pairs of
jet-black eyebrows joined in one. And thus it was
that these black-eyed beauties, by *mashing* [1] men for

---

[1] *Mashing,* a word of gypsy origin (*mashāva*), meaning fascination
by the eye, or taking in.

many generations, with shafts shot sideways and most wantonly, at last sealed their souls into the corner of their eyes, as you have heard before. Cotton Mather tells us that these witches with peaked eye-corners could never weep but three tears out of their long-tailed eyes. And I have observed that such tears, as they sweep down the cheeks of the brunette witches, are also long-tailed, and recall by their shape and glitter the eyes from which they fell, even as the daughter recalls the mother. For all love's witchcraft lurks in flashing eyes, — *lontan del occhio lontan dal' cuor.*

It is a great pity that the pigeon-eye-peaks, so pretty in young witches, become in the old ones crow's-feet and crafty. When I greeted the woman, she answered in Romany, and said she was a Stanley from the North. She lied bravely, and I told her so. It made no difference in any way, nor was she hurt. The brown boy, who seemed like a goblin, umber-colored fungus, growing by a snaky black wild vine, sat by her and stared at me. I was pleased, when he said *tober*, that she corrected him, exclaiming earnestly, " Never say *tober* for road; that is *canting*. Always say *drom;* that is good Romanes." There is always a way of bringing up a child in the way he should go, — though it be a gypsy one, — and *drom* comes from the Greek *dromos*, which is elegant and classical. Then she began to beg again, to pass the time, and I lectured her severely on the sin and meanness of her conduct, and said, with bitterness, " Do dogs eat dogs, or are all the Gorgios dead in the land, that you cry for money to me? Oh, you are a fine Stanley ! a nice Beshaley you, to sing mumpin and mongerin, when a half-blood Matthews has too much decency to trouble the rye! And how much will you take? Whatever the gentleman pleases, and thank you, my kind sir, and the blessings of the poor gypsy woman on you. Yes, I know that, *givelli*, you mother of all the liars. You expect a sixpence, and here it is, and may you get drunk on the money, and be well thrashed by your man for it. And now see what I had in my hand all the time to give you. A lucky half crown, my deary; but that's not for you now. I only give a sixpence to a beggar, but I stand a *pash-korauna* to any Romany who's a pal and amāl."

This pleasing discourse made us very good friends, and, as I kept my eyes sharply fixed on her viper orbs with an air of intense suspicion, everything like ill-feeling or distrust naturally vanished from her mind; for it is of the nature of the Romanys and all their kind to like those whom they respect, and respect those whom they cannot deceive, and to measure mankind exactly by their capacity of being taken in, especially by themselves. As is also the case, in good society, with many ladies and some gentlemen, — and much good may it do them!

There was a brief silence, during which the boy still looked wistfully into my face, as if wondering what kind of gentleman I might be, until his mother said, —

" How do you do with them *ryas* [swells] ? What do you tell 'em — about — what do they think — you know ?"

This was not explicit, but I understood it perfectly. There is a great deal of such loose, disjointed conversation among gypsies and other half-thinkers. An educated man requires, or pretends to himself to require, a most accurately-detailed and form-polished statement of anything to understand it. The gypsy is less exacting. I have observed among rural Americans much of this lottery style of conversation, in which one man invests in a dubious question, not knowing exactly what sort of a prize or blank answer he may draw. What the gypsy meant effectively was, " How do you account to the Gorgios for knowing so much about us, and talking with us? Our life is as different from yours as possible, and you never acquired such a knowledge of all our tricky ways as you have just shown without much experience of us and a double life. You are related to us in some way, and you deceive the Gorgios about it. What is your little game of life, on general principles? "

For the gypsy is so little accustomed to having any congenial interest taken in him that he can clearly explain it only by consanguinity. And as I was questioned, so I answered, —

" Well, I tell them I like to learn languages, and am trying to learn yours; and then I 'm a foreigner in the country, anyhow, and they don't know my *droms* [ways], and they don't care much what I do, — don't you see? "

This was perfectly satisfactory, and as the hounds came sweeping round the corner of the wood she rose and went her way, and I saw her growing less and less along the winding road and up the hill, till she disappeared, with her boy, in a small ale-house. " Bang went the sixpence."

When the last red light was in the west I went down to the river, and as I paused, and looked alternately at the stars reflected and flickering in the water and at the lights in the little gypsy camp,

I thought that as the dancing, restless, and broken sparkles were to their serene types above, such were the wandering and wild Romany to the men of culture in their settled homes. It is from the house-dweller that the men of the roads and commons draw the elements of their life, but in that life they are as shaken and confused as the starlight in the rippling river. But if we look through our own life we find that it is not the gypsy alone who is merely a reflection and an imitation of the stars above him, and a creature of second-hand fashion.

I found in the camp an old acquaintance, named Brown, and also perceived at the first greeting that the woman Stanley had told Mrs. Brown that I would not be *mongerdo,* or begged from, and that the latter, proud of her power in extortion, and as yet invincible in mendicancy, had boasted that she would succeed, let others weakly fail. And to lose no time she went at me with an abruptness and dramatic earnestness which promptly betrayed the secret. And on the spot I made a vow that nothing should get a farthing from me, though I should be drawn by wild horses. And a horse was, indeed, brought into requisition to draw me, or my money, but without success ; for Mr. Brown, as I very well knew, — it being just then the current topic in the best society on the road, — had very recently been involved in a tangled trouble with a stolen horse. This horse had been figuratively laid at his door, even as a " love-babe " is sometimes placed on the front steps of a virtuous and grave citizen, — at least, this is what White George averred, — and his very innocence and purity had, like a shining mark, attracted the shafts of the wicked. He had come out unscathed, with a package of papers from a lawyer, which established his character above par; but all this had cost money, beautiful golden money, and brought him to the very brink of ruin! Mrs. Brown's attack was a desperate and determined effort, and there was more at stake on its success than the reader may surmise. Among gypsy women skill in begging implies the possession of every talent which they most esteem, such as artfulness, cool effrontery, and the power of moving pity or provoking generosity by pique or humor. A quaint and racy book might be written, should it only set forth the manner in which the experienced matrons give straight-tips or suggestions to the maidens as to the manner and lore of begging; and it is something worth hearing when several sit together and devise dodges, and tell anecdotes illustrating the noble art of mendicity, and how it should be properly practiced.

Mrs. Brown knew that to extort alms from me would place her on the pinnacle as an artist. Among all the Cooper clan, to which she was allied, there was not one who ever begged from me, they having all found that the ripest nuts are those which fall from the tree of their own accord, or are blown earthward by the soft breezes of benevolence, and not those which are violently beaten down. She began by pitiful appeals; she was moving, but I did not budge. She grew pathetic; she touched on the stolen horse; she paused, and gushed almost to tears, as much as to say, If it must be, you *shall* know all. Ruin stared them in the face; poverty was crushing them. It was well acted, — rather in the Bernhardt style, which, if M. Ondit speaks the truth, is also employed rather extensively for acquiring " de mon-ish." I looked at the van, of which the Browns are proud, and inquired if it were true that it had been insured for a hundred pounds, as George had recently boasted. Persuasion having failed, Mrs. Brown tried bold defiance, saying that they needed no company who were no good to them, and plainly said to me I might be gone. It was her last card, thinking that a threat to dissolve our acquaintance would drive me to capitulate, and it failed. I laughed, went into the van, sat down, took out my brandy flask, and then accepted some bread and ale, and, to please them, read aloud all the papers acquitting George from all guilt as concerned the stolen horse, — papers which, he declared, had cost him full five pounds. This was a sad come-down from the story first told. Then I seriously rated his wife for begging from me. " You know well enough," I said, " that I give all I can spare to your family and your people when they are sick or poor. And here you are, the richest Romanys on the road between Windsor and the Boro Gav, begging a friend, who knows all about you, for money! Now, here is a shilling. Take it. Have half a crown? Two of 'em! No! Oh, you don't want it here in your own house. Well, you have some decency left, and to save your credit I won't make you take it. And you scandalize me, a gentleman and a friend, just to show this tramp of a Stanley *juva*, who has n't even got a drag [wagon], that you can beat her *a mongerin mandy* [begging me]."

Mrs. Brown assented volubly to everything, and all the time I saw in her smiling eyes, ever agreeing to all, and heard from her voluble lips nothing but the *lie*, — that lie which is the mental action and

inmost grain of the Romany, and especially of the
diddikai, or half-breed. Anything and everything
— trickery, wheedling or bullying, fawning or threat-
ening, smiles, or rage, or tears — for a sixpence. All
day long flattering and tricking to tell fortunes or
sell trifles, and all life one greasy lie, with ready
frowns or smiles : as it was in India in the beginning, as it is in Europe, and as it will be in America,
so long as there shall be a rambler on the roads,
amen !

Sweet peace again established, Mrs. Brown became
herself once more, and acted the hospitable hostess,
exactly in the spirit and manner of any woman who
has " a home of her own," and a spark of decent feeling in her heart. Like many actors, she was a bad
lot on the boards, but a very nice person off them.
Here in her rolling home she was neither a beggar
nor poor, and she issued her orders grandly. " Boil
some tea for the *rye* — cook some coffee for the *rye*
— wait a few minutes, my darling gentleman, and I 'll
brile you a steak — or here 's a fish, if you 'd like it ? "
But I declined everything except the corner of a loaf
and some ale ; and all the time a little brown boy, with
great black eyes, a perfect Murillo model, sat con-
densed in wondrous narrow space by the fire, baking
small apples between the bars of the grate, and rolling up his orbs at me as if wondering what could have
brought me into such a circle, — even as he had done
that morning in the greenwood.

Now if the reader would know what the interior of
a gypsy van, or " drag," or *wardo*, is like, he may see
it in the following diagram.

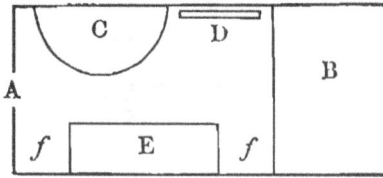

A is the door; *B* is the bed, or rather two beds, each six feet long, like berths, with a vacant space below; *C* is a grate cooking-stove; *D* is a table, which hangs by hinges from the wall; *E* is a chest of drawers; *f* and *f* are two chairs. The general appearance of a well-kept van is that of a state-room. Brown's is a very good van, and quite clean. They are admirably well adapted for slow traveling, and it was in such vans, purchased from gypsies, that Sir Samuel Baker and his wife explored the whole of Cyprus.

Mrs. Brown was proud of her van and of her little treasures. From the great recess under the bed she raked out as a rare curiosity an old Dolly Varden or damasked skirt, not at all worn, quite pretty, and evidently of considerable value to a collector. This had belonged to Mrs. Brown's grandmother, an old gypsy queen. And it may be observed, by the way, that the claims of every Irishman of every degree to be descended from one of the ancient kings of Ireland fade into nothing before those of the gypsy women, all of whom, with rare exception, are the own daughters of royal personages, granddaughterhood being hardly a claim to true nobility. Then the bed itself was exhibited with pride, and the princess sang its praises, till she affirmed that the *rye* himself did not sleep on a better one, for which George reprimanded her. But she vigorously defended its excellence, and, to please her, I felt it,

and declared it was indeed much softer than the one
I slept on, which was really true, — thank Heaven!
—and was received as a great compliment, and afterwards proclaimed on the roads even unto the ends of
Surrey.

" Yes," said Brown, as I observed some osiers in
the cupboard, " when I feels like it I sometimes
makes a pound a day a-making baskets."

" I should think," I said, " that it would be cheaper
to buy French baskets of Bulrose [Bulureaux] in
Houndsditch, ready made."

" So one would think ; but the *ranyor* [osiers]
costs nothin', and so it's all profit, any way."

Then I urged the greater profit of living in America, but both assured me that so long as they could
make a good living and be very comfortable, as they
considered themselves, in England, it would be nonsense to go to America.

For all things are relative, and many a gypsy whom
the begged-from pity sincerely, is as proud and happy
in a van as any lord in the land. A very nice, neat
young gypsy woman, camped long before just where
the Browns were, once said to me, " It is n't having
everything fine and stylish that makes you happy.
Now we 've got a van, and have everything so elegant
and comfortable, and sleep warm as anybody ; and
yet I often say to my husband that we used to be
happier when we used to sleep under a hedge, with,
may be, only a thin blanket, and wake up covered
with snow." Now this woman had only a wretched
wagon, and was always tramping in the rain, or cow-
ering in a smoky, ragged tent and sitting on the
ground, but she had food, fire, and fun, with warm
clothes, and believed herself happy. Truly, she had

better reason to think so than any old maid with a
heart run to waste on church gossip, or the latest
engagements and marriages; for it is better to be a
street-boy in a corner with a crust than one who,
without it, discusses, in starvation, with his friend,
the sausages and turtle-soup in a cook-shop window,
between which and themselves there is a great pane
of glass fixed, never to be penetrated.

II.

WALKING AND VISITING.

I NEVER shall forget the sparkling splendor of that frosty morning in December when I went with a younger friend from Oatlands Park for a day's walk. I may have seen at other times, but I do not remember, such winter lace-work as then adorned the hedges. The gossamer spider has within her an inward monitor which tells if the weather will be fine; but it says nothing about sudden changes to keen cold, and the artistic result was that the hedges were hung with thousands of Honiton lamp-mats, instead of the thread fly-catchers which their little artists had intended. And on twigs and dead leaves, grass and rock and wall, were such expenditures of Brussels and Spanish point, such a luxury of real old Venetian run mad, and such deliria of Russian lace as made it evident that Mrs. Jack Frost is a very extravagant fairy, but one gifted with exquisite taste. When I reflect how I have in my time spoken of the taste for lace and diamonds in women as entirely without foundation in nature, I feel that I sinned deeply. For Nature, in this lace-work, displays at times a sympathy with humanity, — especially womanity, — and coquets and flirts with it, as becomes the subject, in a manner which is merrily awful. There was once in Philadelphia a shop the windows of which were always filled with different kinds of the richest

and rarest lace, and one cold morning I found that
the fairies had covered the panes with literal frost
fac-similes of the exquisite wares which hung behind.
This was no fancy ; the copies were as accurate as
photographs. Can it be that in the invisible world
there are Female Fairy Schools of Design, whose
scholars combine in this graceful style Etching on
Glass and Art Needlework ?

We were going to the village of Hersham to make
a call. It was not at any stylish villa or lordly manor-
house, — though I knew of more than one in the vicinity where we would have been welcome, — but at a
rather disreputable-looking edifice, which bore on its
front the sign of " Lodgings for Travellers." Now
" traveller " means, below a certain circle of English
life, not the occasional, but the habitual wanderer, or
one who dwells upon the roads, and gains his living
thereon. I have in my possession several cards of
such a house. I found them wrapped in a piece of
paper, by a deserted gypsy camp, where they had
been lost : —

A NEW HOUSE.

*Good Lodging for Travellers. With a Large
Private Kitchen.*

THE CROSS KEYS,

WEST STREET . . . . . . MAIDENHEAD.

BY J. HARRIS.

The " private kitchen " indicates that the guests
will have facilities for doing their own cooking, as
all of them bring their own victuals in perpetual
picnic. In the inclosure of the house in Hersham,
the tops of two or three gypsy vans could always be
seen above the high fence, and there was that gen-

eral air of mystery about the entire establishment
which is characteristic of all places haunted by people whose ways are not as our ways, and whose little
games are not as our little games. I had become
acquainted with it and its proprietor, Mr. Hamilton,
in that irregular and only way which is usual with
such acquaintances. I was walking by the house
one summer day, and stopped to ask my way. A
handsome dark-brown girl was busy at the wash-tub,
two or three older women were clustered at the gate,
and in all their faces was the manner of the *diddikai*
or *chureni*, or half-blood gypsy. As I spoke I dropped
my voice, and said, inquiringly, —

" Romanes ? "

" Yes," was the confidential answer.

They were all astonished, and kept quiet till I had
gone a few rods on my way, when the whole party,
recovering from their amazement, raised a gentle
cheer, expressive of approbation and sympathy. A
few days after, walking with a lady in Weybridge,
she said to me, —

" Who is that man who looked at you so closely ? "

" I do not know."

" That's very strange. I am quite sure I heard
him utter two words in a strange language, as you
passed, as if he only meant them for you. They
sounded like *sarshaun baw.*" Which means, " How
are you, sir ? " or friend. As we came up the street,
I saw the man talking with a well-dressed, sporting-
looking man, not quite a gentleman, who sat cheekily
in his own jaunty little wagon. As I passed, the one
of the wagon said to the other, speaking of me, and
in pure Romany, evidently thinking I did not understand, —

" *Dikk'adovo Gorgio, adoi!* " (Look at that Gorgio, there !)

Being a Romany rye, and not accustomed to be spoken of as a Gorgio, I looked up at him, angrily, when he, seeing that I understood him, smiled, and bowed politely in apology. I laughed and passed on. But I thought it a little strange, for neither of the men had the slightest indication of gypsiness. I met the one who had said *sarishān bā* again, soon after. I found that he and the one of the wagon were not of gypsy blood, but of a class not uncommon in England, who, be they rich or poor, are affected towards gypsies. The wealthy one lived with a gypsy mistress; the poorer one had a gypsy wife, and was very fond of the language. There is a very large class of these mysterious men everywhere about the country. They haunt fairs; they pop up unexpectedly as Jack-in-boxes in unsuspected guise; they look out from under fatherly umbrellas; their name is Legion; their mother is Mystery, and their uncle is Old Tom, — not of Virginia, but of Gin. Once, in the old town of Canterbury, I stood in the street, under the Old Woman with the Clock, one of the quaintest pieces of drollery ever imagined during the Middle Ages. And by me was a tinker, and as his wheel went *siz-'z-'z-'z, uz-uz-uz-z-z!* I talked with him, and there joined us a fat, little, elderly, spectacled, shabby-genteel, but well-to-do-looking sort of a punchy, small tradesman. And, as we spoke, there went by a great, stout, roaring Romany woman, — a scarlet-runner of Babylon run to seed, — with a boy and a hand-cart to carry the seed in. And to her I cried, " *Hav akai te mandy'll del tute a shāori!* " (Come here, and I'll stand a sixpence !) But she did not

believe in my offer, but went her way, like a Burning
Shame, through the crowd, and was lost evermore. I
looked at the little old gentleman to see what effect
my outcry in a strange language had upon him. But
he only remarked, soberly, " Well, now, I *should* 'a'
thought a sixpence would 'a' brought her to! " And
the wheel said, " Suz-zuz-zuz-z-z I should 'a' suz-suz 'a'
thought a suz-z-zixpence would 'a' suz-zuz 'a' brought
her, too-z-z-z ! " And I looked at the Old Woman
with the Clock, and she ticked, " A — six — pence
— would — have — brought — *me* — two — three —
four " — and I began to dream that all Canterbury
was Romany.

We came to the house, the landlord was up-stairs,
ill in bed, but would be glad to see us; and he welcomed us warmly, and went deeply into Romany
family matters with my friend, the Oxford scholar.
Meanwhile, his daughter, a nice brunette, received
and read a letter ; and he tried to explain to me the
mystery of the many men who are not gypsies, yet
speak Romany, but could not do it, though he was
one of them. It appeared from his account that
they were "a kind of mixed, you see, and dusted in,
you know, and on it, out of the family, it peppers
up; but not exactly, you understand, and that 's the
way it is. And I remember a case in point, and that
was one day, and I had sold a horse, and was with my
boy in a *moramengro's buddika* [barber's shop], and
my boy says to me, in Romanes, ' Father, I 'd like
to have my hair cut.' ' It 's too dear here, my son,'
said I, Romaneskes ; ' for the bill says threepence.'
And then the barber, he ups and says, in Romany,
' Since you 're Romanys, I 'll cut it for *two*pence,
though it 's clear out of all my rules.' And he did

it; but why that man *rakkered Romanes* I don't know, nor how it comes about; for he had n't no more call to it than a pig has to be a preacher. But I 've known men in Sussex to take to diggin' truffles on the same principles, and one Gorgio in Hastings that adopted sellin' fried fish for his livin', about the town, because he thought it was kind of romantic. That 's it."

Over the chimney-piece hung a large engraving of Milton and his daughters. It was out of place, and our host knew it, and was proud. He said he had bought it at an auction, and that it was a picture of Middleton, — a poet, he believed; " anyhow, he was a writing man." But, on second thought, he remembered that the name was not Middleton, but Millerton. And on further reflection, he was still more convinced that Millerton *was* a poet.

I once asked old Matthew Cooper the Romany word for a poet. And he promptly replied that he had generally heard such a man called a *givellengero* or *gilliengro*, which means a song-master, but that he himself regarded *shereskero-mush*, or head-man, as more elegant and deeper; for poets make songs out of their heads, and are also ahead of all other men in head-work. There is a touching and unconscious tribute to the art of arts in this definition which is worth recording. It has been said that, as people grow polite, they cease to be poetical; it is certain that in the first circles they do not speak of their poets with such respect as this.

Out again into the fresh air and the frost on the crisp, crackling road and in the sunshine. At such a time, when cold inspires life, one can understand why the old poets and mystics believed that there was fire in ice. Therefore, Saint Sebaldus, coming into the hut of a poor and pious man who was dying of cold, went out, and, bringing in an armful of icicles, laid them on the andirons and made a good fire. Now this fire was the inner glowing glory of God, and worked both ways, — of course you see the connection, — as was shown in Adelheid von Sigolsheim, the Holy Nun of Unterlinden, who was so full of it that she passed the night in a freezing stream, and then stood all the morning, ice-clad, in the choir, and never caught cold. And the pious Peroneta, to avoid a sinful suitor, lived all winter, up to her neck, in ice-water, on the highest Alp in Savoy.[1] These were saints. But there was a gypsy, named Dighton, encamped near Brighton, who told me nearly the same story of another gypsy, who was no saint, and which I repeat merely to show how extremes meet. It was that this gypsy, who was inspired with anything but the inner glowing glory of God, but who was, on the contrary, cram full of pure cussedness, being warmed by the same, — and the devil, — when chased by the constable, took refuge in a river full of freezing slush and broken ice, where he stood up to his neck and defied capture; for he verily cared no more for it than did Saint Peter of Alcantara, who was both ice and fire proof. "Come out of that, my good man," said the gentleman, whose hen he had stolen, "and I'll let you go." "No, I won't come out," said the gypsy. "My blood be on your head!" So the gentleman offered him five pounds, and then a suit of clothes, to come ashore. The gypsy reflected, and at last said, "Well, if you'll add a drink of spirits, I'll come; but it's only to oblige you that I budge."

[1] Goerres, *Christliche Mystik*, i. 296. 1. 23.

Then we walked in the sober evening, with its gray gathering shadows, as the last western rose light rippled in the river, yet fading in the sky, — like a good man who, in dying, speaks cheerfully of earthly things, while his soul is vanishing serenely into heaven. The swans, looking like snowballs, unconscious of cold, were taking their last swim towards the reedy, brake-tangled islets where they nested, gossiping as they went. The deepening darkness, at such a time, becomes more impressive from the twinkling stars, just as the subduing silence is noted only by the far-borne sounds from the hamlet or farm-house, or the occasional whispers of the night-breeze. So we went on in the twilight, along the Thames, till we saw the night-fire of the Romanys and its gleam on the *tan.* A *tan* is, strictly speaking, a tent, but a tent is a dwelling, or stopping-place; and so from earliest Aryan time, the word *tan* is like Alabama, or " here we rest," and may be found in *tun*, the ancestor of town, and in *stan*, as in Hindostan, — and if I blunder, so much the better for the philological gentlemen, who, of all others, most delight in setting erring brothers right, and never miss a chance to show, through others' shame, how much they know.

There was a bark of a dog, and a voice said, " The Romany rye ! " They had not seen us, but the dog knew, and they knew his language.

" *Sarishan ryor !* "

" *O boro duvel atch' pa leste !* " (The great Lord be on you !) This is not a common Romany greeting. It is of ancient days and archaic. Sixty or seventy years ago it was current. Old Gentilla Cooper, the famous fortune-teller of the Devil's Dike, near Brighton, knew it, and when she heard it from me she was moved, — just as a very old negro in London was, when I said to him, "*Sady*, uncle." I said it because I had recognized by the dog's bark that it was Sam Smith's tan. Sam likes to be considered as *deep* Romany. He tries to learn old gypsy words, and he affects old gypsy ways. He is pleased to be called Petulengro, which means Smith. Therefore, my greeting was a compliment.

In a few minutes we were in camp and at home. We talked of many things, and among others of witches. It is remarkable that while the current English idea of a witch is that of an old woman who has sold herself to Satan, and is a distinctly marked character, just like Satan himself, that of the witch among gypsies is general and Oriental. There is no Satan in India. Mrs. Smith — since dead — held that witches were to be found everywhere. "You may know a natural witch," she said, "by certain signs. One of these is straight hair which curls at the ends. Such women have it in them."

It was only recently, as I write, that I was at a very elegant art reception, which was fully reported in the newspapers. And I was very much astonished when a lady called my attention to another young and very pretty lady, and expressed intense disgust at the way the latter wore her hair. It was simply parted in the middle, and fell down on either side, smooth as a water-fall, and then broke into curls at the ends, just as water, after falling, breaks into waves and rapids. But as she spoke, I felt it all, and saw that Mrs. Petulengro was in the right. The girl with the end-curled hair was uncanny. Her hair curled at the ends, — so did her eyes; she *was* a witch.

"But there's a many witches as knows clever things," said Mrs. Petulengro. "And I learned from one of them how to cure the rheumatiz. Suppose you 've got the rheumatiz. Well, just you carry a potato in your pocket. As the potato dries up, your rheumatiz will go away."

Sam Smith was always known on the roads as Fighting Sam. Years have passed, and when I have asked after him I have always heard that he was either in prison or had just been let out. Once it happened that, during a fight with a Gorgio, the Gorgio's watch disappeared, and Sam was arrested under suspicion of having got up the fight in order that the watch might disappear. All of his friends declared his innocence. The next trouble was for *chorin a gry*, or stealing a horse, and so was the next, and so on. As horse-stealing is not a crime, but only "rough gambling," on the roads, nobody defended him on these counts. He was, so far as this went, only a sporting character. When his wife died he married Athalía, the widow of Joshua Cooper, a gypsy, of whom I shall speak anon. I always liked Sam. Among the travelers, he was always spoken of as genteel, owing to the fact, that whatever the state of his wardrobe might be, he always wore about his neck an immaculate white woolen scarf, and on *jours de fête*, such as horse-races, sported a *boro stardī*, or chimney-pot hat. O my friend, Colonel Dash, of the —— club! Change but the name, this fable is of thee!

"There's to be a *walgoro, kaliko i sala* — a fair, to-morrow morning, at Cobham," said Sam, as he departed.

"All right. We 'll be there."

As I went forth by the river into the night, and the stars looked down like loving eyes, there shot a meteor across the sky, one long trail of light, out of darkness into darkness, one instant bright, then dead forever. And I remembered how I once was told that stars, like mortals, often fall in love. O love, forever in thy glory go! And that they send their starry angels forth, and that the meteors are their messengers. O love, forever in thy glory go! For love and light in heaven, as on earth, were ever one, and planets speak with light. Light is their language; as they love they speak. O love, forever in thy glory go!

9

III.

COBHAM FAIR.

THE walk from Oatlands Park Hotel to Cobham is beautiful with memorials of Older England. Even on the grounds there is a quaint brick gateway, which is the only relic of a palace which preceded the present pile. The grandfather was indeed a stately edifice, built by Henry VIII., improved and magnified, according to his lights, by Inigo Jones, and then destroyed during the civil war. The river is here very beautiful, and the view was once painted by Turner. It abounds in " short windings and reaches." Here it is, indeed, the Olerifera Thamesis, as it was called by Guillaume le Breton in his " Phillipeis," in the days of Richard the Lion Heart. Here the eyots and banks still recall Norman days, for they are " wild and were;" and there is even yet a wary otter or two, known to the gypsies and fishermen, which may be seen of moonlight nights plunging or swimming silently in the haunted water.

Now we pass Walton Church, and look in, that my friend may see the massy Norman pillars and arches, the fine painted glass, and the brasses. One of these represents John Selwyn, who was keeper of the royal park of Oatlands in 1587. Tradition, still current in the village, says that Selwyn was a man of wondrous strength and of rare skill in horse-

manship. Once, when Queen Elizabeth was present
at a stag hunt, he leaped from his horse upon the
back of the stag, while both were running at full
speed, kept his seat gracefully, guided the animal
towards the queen, and stabbed him so deftly that
he fell dead at her majesty's feet. It was daintily
done, and doubtless Queen Bess, who loved a proper
man, was well pleased. The brass plate represents
Selwyn as riding on the stag, and there is in the village a shop where the neat old dame who presides,
or her daughter, will sell you for a penny a picture
of the plate, and tell you the story into the bargain.
In it the valiant ranger sits on the stag, which he is
stabbing through the neck with his *couteau de chasse*,
looking meanwhile as solemn as if he were sitting in
a pew and listening to *De profundis*. He who is
great in one respect seldom fails in some other, and
there is in the church another and a larger brass,
from which it appears that Selwyn not only had a
wife, but also eleven children, who are depicted in
successive grandeur or gradation. There are monuments by Roubiliac and Chantrey in the church, and
on the left side of the altar lies buried William Lilly,
the great astrologer, the Sidrophel of Butler's " Hu-
dibras." And look into the chancel. There is a
tablet to his memory, which was put up by Elias
Ashmole, the antiquary, who has left it in print that
this " fair black marble stone " cost him £6 4s. 6d.
When I was a youth, and used to pore in the old
Franklin Library of Philadelphia over Lilly, I never
thought that his grave would be so near my home.
But a far greater literary favorite of mine lies buried
in the church-yard without. This is Dr. Maginn, the
author of " Father Tom and the Pope," and many

another racy, subtle jest. A fellow of infinite humor, — the truest disciple of Rabelais, — and here he lies without a monument!

Summon the sexton, and let us ask him to show us the scold's, or gossip's, bridle. This is a rare curiosity, which is kept in the vestry. It would seem, from all that can be learned, that two hundred years ago there were in England viragoes so virulent, women so gifted with gab and so loaded and primed with the devil's own gunpowder, that all moral suasion was wasted on them, and simply showed, as old Reisersberg wrote, that *fatue agit qui ignem conatur extinguere sulphure* ('t is all nonsense to try to quench fire with brimstone). For such diavolas they had made — what the sexton is just going to show you — a muzzle of thin iron bars, which pass around the head and are padlocked behind. In front a flat piece of iron enters the mouth and keeps down the tongue. On it is the date 1633, and certain lines, no longer legible : —

> " Chester presents Walton with a bridle,
> To curb women's tongues that talk too idle."

A sad story, if we only knew it all! What tradition tells is that long ago there was a Master Chester, who lost a fine estate through the idle, malicious clack of a gossiping, lying woman. " What is good for a bootless bene?" What he did was to endow the church with this admirable piece of head-gear. And when any woman in the parish was unanimously adjudged to be deserving of the honor, the bridle was put on her head and tongue, and she was led about town by the beadle as an example to all the scolding sisterhood. Truly, if it could only be applied to the women and men who repeat gossip, rumors, reports, *on dits*, small slanders, proved or unproved; to all gobe-mouches, club-gabblers, tea-talkers and tattlers, chatterers, church-twaddlers, wonderers if-it-be-true-what-they-say; in fine, to the entire sister and brother hood of tongue-waggers, I for one would subscribe my mite to have one kept in every church in the world, to be zealously applied to their vile jaws. For verily the mere Social Evil is an angel of light on this earth as regards doing evil, compared to the Sociable Evil, — and thus endeth the first lesson.

We leave the church, so full of friendly memories. In this one building alone there are twenty things known to me from a boy. For from boyhood I have held in my memory those lines by Queen Elizabeth which she uttered here, and have read Lilly and Ashmole and Maginn; and this is only one corner in merrie England! Am I a stranger here? There is a father-land of the soul, which has no limits to him who, far sweeping on the wings of song and history, goes forth over many lands.

We have but a little farther to go on our way before we come to the quaint old manor-house which was of old the home of President Bradshaw, the grim old Puritan. There is an old sailor in the village, who owns a tavern, and he says, and the policeman agrees with him, that it was in this house that the death-warrant of King Charles the First was signed. Also, that there is a subterranean passage which leads from it to the Thames, which was in some way connected with battle, murder, plots, Puritans, sudden death, and politics; though how this was is more than legend can clearly explain. Whether his sacred majesty was led to execution through this

cavity, or whether Charles the Second had it for one
of his numerous hiding-places, or returned through
it with Nell Gwynn from his exile, are other obscure
points debated among the villagers.   The truth is
that the whole country about Walton is subterrened
with strange and winding ways, leading no one knows
whither, dug in the days of the monks or knights,
from one long-vanished monastery or castle to the
other.   There is the opening to one of these hard
by the hotel, but there was never any gold found in
it that ever I heard of.   And all the land is full of
legend, and ghosts glide o' nights along the alleys,
and there is an infallible fairy well at hand, named
the Nun, and within a short walk stands the tremendous Crouch oak, which was known of Saxon
days.   Whoever gives but a little of its bark to a
lady will win her love.   It takes its name from *croix*
(a cross), according to Mr. Kemble,[1] and it is twenty-
four feet in girth.   Its first branch, which is forty-
eight feet long, shoots out horizontally, and is almost
as large as the trunk.   Under this tree Wickliffe
preached, and Queen Elizabeth dined.

It has been well said by Irving that the English,
from the great prevalence of rural habits throughout
every class of society, have been extremely fond of
those festivals and holidays which agreeably interrupt the stillness of country life.   True, the days
have gone when burlesque pageant and splendid procession made even villages magnificent.   Harp and
tabor and viol are no longer heard in every inn when
people would be merry, and men have forgotten how
to give themselves up to headlong roaring revelry.
The last of this tremendous frolicking in Europe

[1] *The Saxons in England,* i. 3.

died out with the last yearly *kermess* in Amsterdam, and it was indeed wonderful to see with what utter *abandon* the usually stolid Dutch flung themselves into a rushing tide of frantic gayety. Here and there in England a spark of the old fire, lit in mediæval times, still flickers, or perhaps flames, as at Dorking in the annual foot-ball play, which is carried on with such vigor that two or three thousand people run wild in it, while all the windows and street lamps are carefully screened for protection. But notwithstanding the gradually advancing republicanism of the age, which is dressing all men alike, bodily and mentally, the rollicking democracy of these old-fashioned festivals, in which the peasant bonneted the peer without ceremony, and rustic maids ran races *en chemise* for a pound of tea, is entirely too leveling for culture. There are still, however, numbers of village fairs, quietly conducted, in which there is much that is pleasant and picturesque, and this at Cobham was as pretty a bit of its kind as I ever saw. These are old-fashioned and gay in their little retired nooks, and there the plain people show themselves as they really are. The better class of the neighborhood, having no sympathy with such sports or scenes, do not visit village fairs. It is, indeed, a most exceptional thing to see any man who is a " gentleman," according to the society standard, in any fair except Mayfair in London.

Cobham is well built for dramatic display. Its White Lion Inn is of the old coaching days, and the lion on its front is a very impressive monster, one of the few relics of the days when signs were signs in spirit and in truth. In this respect the tavern keeper of to-day is a poor snob, that he thinks a sign painted

or carven is degenerate and low, and therefore an-
nounces, in a line of letters, that his establishment is
the Pig and Whistle, just as his remote predecessor
thought it was low, or slow, or old-fashioned to dedicate his ale-shop to Pigen Wassail or Hail to the
Virgin, and so changed it to a more genteel and sec-
ular form. In the public place were rows of booths
arranged in streets forming *imperium in imperio*, a
town within a town. There was of course the tradi-
tional gilt gingerbread, and the cheering but not ine-
briating ginger-beer, dear to the youthful palate, and
not less loved by the tired pedestrian, when, mixed
half and half with ale, it foams before him as *shandy
gaff*. There, too, were the stands, presided over by
jaunty, saucy girls, who would load a rifle for you
and give you a prize or a certain number of shots for
a shilling. You may be a good shot, but the better
you shoot the less likely will you be to hit the bull's-
eye with the rifle which that black-eyed Egyptian
minx gives you; for it is artfully curved and false-
sighted, and the rifle was made only to rifle your
pocket, and the damsel to sell you with her smiles,
and the doll is stuffed with sawdust, and life is not
worth living for, and Miching Mallocko says it, —
albeit I believe he lives at times as if there might be
moments when it was forgot.

And we had not been long on the ground before
we were addressed furtively and gravely by a man
whom it required a second glance to recognize as
Samuel Petulengro, so artfully was he disguised as a
simple-seeming agriculturalist of the better lower-
class. But that there remained in Sam's black eyes
that glint of the Romany which nothing could disguise, one would have longed to buy a horse of him.

And in the same quiet way there came, one by one, out of the crowd, six others, all speaking in subdued voices, like conspirators, and in Romany, as if it were a sin. And all were dressed rustically, and the same with intent to deceive, and all had the solemn air of very small farmers, who must sell that horse at any sacrifice. But when I saw Sam's horses I marked that his disguise of himself was nothing to the wondrous skill with which he had converted his five-pound screws into something comparatively elegant. They had been curried, clipped, singed, and beautified to the last resource, and the manner in which the finest straw had been braided into mane and tail was a miracle of art. This was a *jour de fête* for Sam and his *diddikai*, or half-blood pals; his foot was on his native heath in the horse-fair, where all inside the ring knew the gypsy, and it was with pride that he invited us to drink ale, and once in the bar-room, where all assembled were jockeys and sharps, conversed loudly in Romany, in order to exhibit himself and us to admiring friends. A Romany rye, on such occasions, is to a Sam Petulengro what a scion of royalty is to minor aristocracy when it can lure him into its nets. To watch one of these small horse-dealers at a fair, and to observe the manner in which he conducts his bargains, is very curious. He lounges about all day, apparently doing nothing; he is the only idler around. Once in a while somebody approaches him and mutters something, to which he gives a brief reply. Then he goes to a tap-room or stable-yard, and is merged in a mob of his mates. But all the while he is doing sharp clicks of business. There is somebody talking to another party about *that horse;* somebody telling a farmer that he knows a young man as has got a likely 'oss at 'arf price, the larst of a lot which he wants to clear out, and it may be 'ad, but if the young man sees 'im [the farmer] he may put it on 'eavy.

Then the agent calls in one of the disguised Romanys to testify to the good qualities of the horse. They look at it, but the third *deguisé*, who has it in charge, avers that it has just been sold to a gentleman. But they have another. By this time the farmer wishes he had bought the horse. When any coin slips from between our fingers, and rolls down through a grating into the sewer, we are always sure that it was a sovereign, and not a half-penny. Yes, and the fish which drops back from the line into the river is always the biggest take — or mistake — of the day. And this horse was a bargain, and the three in disguise say so, and wish they had a hundred like it. But there comes a Voice from the depths, a casual remark, offering to bet that 'ere gent won't close on that hoss. " Bet yer ten bob he will." " Done." " How do yer know he don't take the hoss?" " He carn't; he's too heavy loaded with Bill's mare. Says he'll sell it for a pound better." The farmer begins to see his way. He is shrewd; it may be that he sees through all this myth of "the gentleman." But his attention has been attracted to the horse. Perhaps he pays a little more, or " the pound better;" in greater probability he gets Sam's horse for the original price. There are many ways among gypsies of making such bargains, but the motive power of them all is *táderin*, or drawing the eye of the purchaser, a game not unknown to Gorgios. I have heard of a German *yahūd* in Philadelphia, whose little boy Moses would shoot from the door with a pop-gun or squirt at passers-by, or abuse them vilely, and then run into the shop for shelter. They of course pursued him and complained to the parent, who immediately whipped his son, to the great solace of the afflicted ones. And then the afflicted seldom failed to buy something in that shop, and the corrected son received ten per cent. of the profit. The attention of the public had been drawn.

As we went about looking at people and pastimes, a Romany, I think one of the Ayres, said to me, —

"See the two policemen? They're following you two gentlemen. They saw you pallin' with Bowers. That Bowers is the biggest blackguard on the roads between London and Windsor. I don't want to hurt his charáckter, but it's no bad talkin' nor *dusherin* of him to say that no decent Romanys care to go with him. Good at a mill? Yes, he's that. A reg'lar *wastimengro*, I call him. And that's why it is."

Now there was in the fair a vast institution which proclaimed by a monstrous sign and by an excessive eruption of advertisement that it was THE SENSA-TION OF THE AGE. This was a giant hand-organ in connection with a forty-bicycle merry-go-round, all propelled by steam. And as we walked about the fair, the two rural policemen, who had nothing better to do, shadowed or followed us, their bucolic features expressing the intensest suspicion allied to the extremest stupidity; when suddenly the Sensation of the Age struck up the Gendarme's chorus, "We'll run 'em in," from Genevieve de Brabant, and the arrangement was complete. Of all airs ever com posed this was the most appropriate to the occasion, and therefore it played itself. The whole formed quite a little opera-bouffe, gypsies not being wanting.

And as we came round, in our promenade, the pretty girl, with her rifle in hand, implored us to take a shot, and the walk wound up by her finally letting fly herself and ringing the bell.

That pretty girl might or might not have a touch of Romany blood in her veins, but it is worth noting that among all these show-men and show-women, acrobats, exhibitors of giants, purse-droppers, gingerbread-wheel gamblers, shilling knife-throwers, pitch-in-his-mouths, Punches, Cheap-Jacks, thimble-rigs, and patterers of every kind there is always a leaven and a suspicion of gypsiness. If there be not descent, there is affinity by marriage, familiarity, knowledge of words and ways, sweethearting and trafficking, so that they know the children of the Rom as the house-world does not know them, and they in some sort belong together. It is a muddle, perhaps, and a puzzle; I doubt if anybody quite understands it. No novelist, no writer whatever, has as yet *clearly* explained the curious fact that our entire nomadic population, excepting tramps, is not, as we thought in our childhood, composed of English people like ourselves. It is leavened with direct Indian blood; it has, more or less modified, a peculiar *morale*. It was old before the Saxon heptarchy.

I was very much impressed at this fair with the extensive and unsuspected amount of Romany existent in our rural population. We had to be satisfied, as we came late into the tavern for lunch, with cold boiled beef and carrots, of which I did not complain, as cold carrots are much. nicer than warm, a fact too little understood in cookery. There were many men in the common room, mostly well dressed, and decent even if doubtful looking. I ob-

served that several used Romany words in casual conversation. I came to the conclusion at last that all
who were present knew something of it. The greatly
reprobated Bowers was not himself a gypsy, but he
had a gypsy wife. He lived in a cottage not far
from Walton, and made baskets, while his wife roamed
far and near, selling them ; and I have more than once
stopped and sent for a pot of ale, and shared it with
Bill, listening meantime to his memories of the road
as he caned chairs or "basketed." I think his reputation came rather from a certain Bohemian disre-
gard of *convenances* and of appearances than from any
deeply-seated sinfulness. For there are Bohemians
even among gypsies ; everything in this life being
relative and socially-contractive. When I came to
know the disreputable William well, I found in him
the principles of Panurge, deeply identified with the
morale of Falstaff ; a wondrous fund of unbundled
humor, which expressed itself more by tones than
words ; a wisdom based on the practices of the prize-
ring ; and a perfectly sympathetic admiration of my
researches into Romany. One day, at Kingston Fair,
as I wished to depart, I asked Bill the way to the
station. "I will go with you and show you," he
said. But knowing that he had business in the fair
I declined his escort. He looked at me as if hurt.

"*Does tute pen mandy'd chore tute ?*" (Do you
think I would rob *you* or pick your pockets ?) For
he believed I was afraid of it. I knew Bill better. I
knew that he was perfectly aware that I was about
the only man in England who had a good opinion
of him in any way, or knew what good there was
in him. When a *femme incomprise*, a woman not as
yet found out, discovers at last the man who is so

much a master of the art of flattery as to satisfy
somewhat her inordinate vanity, she is generally
grateful enough to him who has thus gratified her
desires to refrain from speaking ill of him, and abuse
those who do, especially the latter. In like manner,
Bill Bowers, who was every whit as interesting as
any *femme incomprise* in Belgravia, or even Russell
Square, believing that I had a little better opinion
of him than anybody else, would not only have re-
frained from robbing me, but have proceeded to lam
with his fists anybody else who would have done so,
— the latter proceeding being, from his point of view,
only a light, cheerful, healthy, and invigorating exercise, so that, as he said, and as I believe truthfully,
"I'd rather be walloped than not fight." Even as
my friend H. had rather lose than not play "farrer."

This was a very pretty little country fair at Cobham ; pleasant and purely English. It was very
picturesque, with its flags, banners, gayly bedecked
booths, and mammoth placards, there being, as usual,
no lack of color or objects. I wonder that Mr. Frith,
who has given with such idiomatic genius the humors
of the Derby, has never painted an old-fashioned rural fair like this. In a few years the last of them
will have been closed, and the last gypsy will be there
to look on.

There was a pleasant sight in the afternoon, when
all at once, as it seemed to me, there came hundreds
of pretty, rosy-cheeked children into the fair. There
were twice as many of them as of grown people. I
think that, the schools being over for the day, they
had been sent a-fairing for a treat. They swarmed
in like small bee-angels, just escaped from some upset
celestial hive ; they crowded around the booths, buy-

ing little toys, chattering, bargaining, and laughing, when my eye caught theirs, as though to be noticed was the very best joke in the whole world. They soon found out the Sensation of the Age, and the mammoth steam bicycle was forthwith crowded with the happy little creatures, raptured in all the glory of a ride. The cars looked like baskets full of roses. It was delightful to see them: at first like grave and stolid little Anglo-Saxons, occupied seriously with the new Sensation; then here and there beaming with thawing jollity; then smiling like sudden sun-gleams; and then laughing, until all were in one grand chorus, as the speed became greater, and the organ roared out its notes as rapidly as a runaway musical locomotive, and the steam-engine puffed in time, until a high-pressure scream told that the penn'orth of fun was up.

As we went home in the twilight, and looked back at the trees and roofs of the village, in dark silhouette against the gold-bronze sky, and heard from afar and fitfully the music of the Great Sensation mingled with the beat of a drum and the shouts of the crowd, rising and falling with the wind, I felt a little sad, that the age, in its advancing refinement, is setting itself against these old-fashioned merry-makings, and shrinking like a weakling from all out-of-doors festivals, on the plea of their being disorderly, but in reality because they are believed to be vulgar. They come down to us from rough old days; but they are relics of a time when life, if rough, was at least kind and hearty. We admire that life on the stage, we ape it in novels, we affect admiration and appreciation of its rich picturesqueness and vigorous originality, and we lie in so doing; for there is not an æsthetic prig in London who could have lived an hour in it.   Truly, I should like to know what François Villon and Chaucer would have thought of some of their modern adorers, or what the lioness Fair-sinners of the olden time would have had to say to the nervous weaklings who try to play the genial blackguard in their praise!   It is to me the best joke of the age that those who now set themselves up for priests of the old faith are the men, of all others, whom the old gods would have kicked, *cum magna injuria*, out of the temple.   When I sit by Bill Bowers, as he baskets, and hear the bees buzz about his marigolds, or in Plato Buckland's van, or with a few hearty and true men of London town of whom I wot, *then* I know that the old spirit liveth in its ashes; but there is little of it, I trow, among its penny prig-trumpeters.

IV.

THE MIXED FORTUNES.

" Thus spoke the king to the great Master: ' Thou didst bless and
ban the people ; thou didst give benison and curse, luck and sorrow, to
the evil or the good.'

" And the Master said, ' It may be so.'

" And the king continued, ' There came two men, and one was good
and the other bad. And one thou didst bless, thinking he was good ;
but he was wicked. And the other thou didst curse, and thought him
bad ; but he was good.'

" The Master said, ' And what came of it ? '

" The king answered, ' All evil came upon the good man, and all
happiness to the bad.'

" And the Master said, ' I write letters, but I am not the messenger ;
I hunt the deer, but I am not the cook ; I plant the vine, but I do not
pour the wine to the guests ; I ordain war, yet do not fight ; I send
ships forth on the sea, but do not sail them. There is many a slip
between cup and lip, as the chief of the rebel spirits said when he
was thrown out of heaven, and I am not greater nor wiser than he
was before he fell. Hast thou any more questions, O son ? "

" And the king went his way."

ONE afternoon I was walking with three ladies.
One was married, one was a young widow, and one,
no longer very young, had not as yet husbanded her
resources. And as we went by the Thames, conversation turned upon many things, and among them the
mystery of the future and mediums ; and the widow
at last said she would like to have her fortune told.

" You need not go far to have it done," I said.
" There is a gypsy camp not a mile away, and in it
one of the cleverest fortune-tellers in England."

" I am almost afraid to go," said the maiden lady.

10

" It seems to me to be really wrong to try to look into the awful secrets of futurity. One can never be certain as to what a gypsy may not know. It 's all very well, I dare say, to declare it 's all rubbish, but then you know you never can tell what may be in a rubbish-heap, and they may be predicting true things all the time while they think they 're humbugging you. And they do often foretell the most wonderful things ; I know they do. My aunt was told that she would marry a man who would cause her trouble, and, sure enough, she did ; and it was such a shame, she was such a sweet-tempered, timid woman, and he spent half her immense fortune. Now was n't that wonderful ? "

It would be a curious matter for those who like studying statistics and chance to find out what proportion in England of sweet-tempered, timid women of the medium-middle class, in newly-sprouted families, with immense fortunes, do *not* marry men who only want their money. Such heiresses are the natural food of the noble shark and the swell sucker, and even a gypsy knows it, and can read them at a glance. I explained this to the lady ; but she knew what she knew, and would not know otherwise.

So we came along the rippling river, watching the darting swallows and light water-gnats, as the sun sank afar into the tawny, golden west, and Night, in ever-nearing circles, wove her shades around us. We saw the little tents, like bee-hives, — one, indeed, not larger than the hive in which Tyll Eulenspiegel slept his famous nap, and in which he was carried away by the thieves who mistook him for honey and found him vinegar. And the outposts, or advanced pickets of small, brown, black-eyed elves, were tumbling about

as usual, and shouted their glad greeting ; for it was
only the day before that I had come down with two
dozen oranges, which by chance proved to be just
one apiece for all to eat except for little Synfie Cooper,
who saved hers up for her father when he should return.

I had just an instant in which to give the gypsy
sorceress a "straight tip," and this I did, saying in
Romany that one of the ladies was married and one
a widow. I was indeed quite sure that she must
know the married lady as such, since she had lived
near at hand, within a mile, for months. And so,
with all due solemnity, the sorceress went to her
work.

"You will come first, my lady, if you please," she
said to the married dame, and led her into a hedge-
corner, so as to be remote from public view, while we
waited by the camp.

The hand was inspected, and properly crossed with
a shilling, and the seeress began her prediction.

"It's a beautiful hand, my lady, and there's luck
in it. The line o' life runs lovely and clear, just like
a smooth river from sea to sea, and that means you'll
never be in danger before you die, nor troubled with
much ill. And it's written that you'll have another
husband very soon."

"But I don't want another," said the lady.

"Ah, my dear lady, so you'll say till you get him,
but when he comes you'll be glad enough; so do you
just get the first one out of your head as soon as
you can, for the next will be the better one. And
you'll cross the sea and travel in a foreign land, and
remember what I told you to the end of your life
days."

Then the widow had her turn.

"This is a lucky hand, and little need you had to have your fortune told. You 've been well married once, and once is enough when it 's all you need. There 's others as is never satisfied and wants everything, but you 've had the best, and more you need n't want, though there 'll be many a man who 'll be in love with you. Ay, indeed, there 's fair and dark as will feel the favor of your beautiful eyes, but little good will it do them, and barons and lords as would kiss the ground you tread on ; and no wonder, either, for you have the charm which nobody can tell what it is. But it will do 'em no good, nevermore."

"Then I 'm never to have another husband," said the widow.

"No, my lady. He that you married was the best of all, and, after him, you 'll never need another ; and that was written in your hand when you were born, and it will be your fate, forever and ever : and that is the gypsy's production over the future, and what she has producted will come true. All the stars in the fermentation of heaven can't change it. But if you ar'n't satisfied, I can set a planet for you, and try the cards, which comes more expensive, for I never do that under ten shillings."

There was a comparing of notes among the ladies and much laughter, when it appeared that the priestess of the hidden spell, in her working, had mixed up the oracles. Jacob had manifestly got Esau's blessing. It was agreed that the *bonnes fortunes* should be exchanged, that the shillings might not be regarded as lost, and all this was explained to the unmarried lady. She said nothing, but in due time was also *dukkered*, or fortune-told. With the same mystery she was con-

ducted to the secluded corner of the hedge, and a very
long, low-murmuring colloquy ensued. What it was
we never knew, but the lady had evidently been
greatly impressed and awed. All that she would
tell was that she had heard things that were "very
remarkable, which she was sure no person living
could have known," and in fact that she believed
in the gypsy, and even the blunder as to the married lady and the widow, and all my assurances that
chiromancy as popularly practiced was all humbug,
made no impression. There was once "a disciple
in Yabneh" who gave a hundred and fifty reasons
to prove that a reptile was no more unclean than
any other animal. But in those days people had not
been converted to the law of turtle soup and the gospel of Saint Terrapin, so the people said it was a vain
thing. And had I given a hundred and fifty reasons
to this lady, they would have all been vain to her, for
she wished to believe; and when our own wishes are
served up unto us on nice brown pieces of the well-
buttered toast of flattery, it is not hard to induce us
to devour them.

It is written that when Ashmedai, or Asmodeus,
the chief of all the devils of mischief, was being led
a captive to Solomon, he did several mysterious things
while on the way, among others bursting into extravagant laughter, when he saw a magician conjur-
ing and predicting. On being questioned by Benaiah,
the son of Jehoiada, why he had seemed so much
amused, Ashmedai answered that it was because the
seer was at the very time sitting on a princely treasure, and he did not, with all his magic and promising
fortune to others, know this. Yet, if this had been
told to all the world, the conjurer's business would

not have suffered. Not a bit of it. *Entre Jean, passe Jeannot:* one comes and goes, another takes his place, and the poor will disappear from this world before the too credulous shall have departed.

It was on the afternoon of the following day that I, by chance, met the gypsy with a female friend, each with a basket, by the roadside, in a lonely, furzy place, beyond Walton.

"You are a nice fortune-teller, are n't you now?" I said to her. "After getting a tip, which made it all as clear as day, you walk straight into the dark. And here you promise a lady two husbands, and she married already; but you never promised me two wives, that I might make merry withal. And then to tell a widow that she would never be married again! You 're a *bori chovihani* [a great witch], — indeed, you are n't."

"*Rye,*" said the gypsy, with a droll smile and a shrug, — I think I can see it now, — "the *dukkerin* [prediction] was all right, but I pet the right *dukkerins* on the wrong ladies."

And the Master said, "I write letters, but I am not the messenger." His orders, like the gypsy's, had been all right, but they had gone to the wrong shop. Thus, in all ages, those who affect superior wisdom and foreknowledge absolute have found that a great practical part of the real business consisted in the plausible explanation of failures. The great Canadian weather prophet is said to keep two clerks busy, one in recording his predictions, the other in explaining their failures; which is much the case with the rain-doctors in Africa, who are as ingenious and fortunate in explaining a miss as a hit, as, indeed, they need be, since they must, in case of error, submit to be devoured alive by ants, — insects which in Africa correspond in several respects to editors and critics, particularly the stinging kind. "*Und ist man bei der Prophezeiung angestellt,*" as Heine says; "when a man has a situation in a prophecy-office," a great part of his business is to explain to the customers why it is that so many of them draw blanks, or why the trains of fate are never on time.

V.

HAMPTON RACES.

On a summer day, when waking dreams softly wave before the fancy, it is pleasant to walk in the noon-stillness along the Thames, for then we pass a series of pictures forming a gallery which I would not exchange for that of the Louvre, could I impress them as indelibly upon the eye-memory as its works are fixed on canvas. There exists in all of us a spiritual photographic apparatus, by means of which we might retain accurately all we have ever seen, and bring out, at will, the pictures from the pigeon-holes of the memory, or make new ones as vivid as aught we see in dreams, but the faculty must be developed in childhood. So surely as I am now writing this will become, at some future day, a branch of education, to be developed into results of which the wildest imagination can form no conception, and I put the prediction on record. As it is, I am sorry that I was never trained to this half-thinking, half-painting art, since, if I had been, I should have left for distant days to come some charming views of Surrey as it appears in this decade.

The reedy eyots and the rising hills; the level meadows and the little villes, with their antique perpendicular Gothic churches, which form the points around which they have clustered for centuries, even as groups of boats in the river are tied around their mooring-posts; the bridges and trim cottages or elegant mansions with their flower-bordered grounds sweeping down to the water's edge, looking like rich carpets with new baize over the centre, make the pictures of which I speak, varying with every turn of the Thames; while the river itself is, at this season, like a continual regatta, with many kinds of boats, propelled by stalwart young Englishmen or healthy, handsome damsels, of every rank, the better class by far predominating. There is a disposition among the English to don quaint holiday attire, to put on the picturesque, and go to the very limits which custom permits, which would astonish an American. Of late years this is becoming the case, too, in Trans-Atlantis, but it has always been usual in England, to mark the fête day with a festive dress, to wear gay ribbons, and to indulge the very harmless instinct of youth to be gallant and gay.

I had started one morning on a walk by the Thames, when I met a friend, who asked, —

" Are n't you going to-day to the Hampton races ? "

" How far is it ? "

" Just six miles. On Molesy Hurst."

Six miles, and I had only six shillings in my pocket. I had some curiosity to see this race, which is run on the Molesy Hurst, famous as the great place for prize-fighting in the olden time, and which has never been able to raise itself to respectability, inasmuch as the local chronicler says that "the course attracts considerable and not very reputable gatherings." In fact, it is generally spoken of as the Costermonger's race, at which a mere welsher is a comparatively respectable character, and every man in a good coat a swell. I was nicely attired, by chance, for the oc-

casion, for I had come out, thinking of a ride, in a
white hat, new corduroy pantaloons and waistcoat,
and a velveteen coat, which dress is so greatly admired by the gypsies that it may almost be regarded
as their "national costume."

There was certainly, to say the least, a rather *bour-
geois* tone at the race, and gentility was conspicuous by
its absence ; but I did not find it so outrageously low
as I had been led to expect.   I confess that I was not
encouraged to attempt to increase my little hoard of
silver by betting, and the certainty that if I lost I
could not lunch made me timid.   But the good are
never alone in this world, and I found friends whom
I dreamed not of.   Leaving the crowd, I sought the
gypsy vans, and by one of these was old Liz Buckland.

"*Sarishan rye!*   And glad I am to see you.   Why
did n't you come down into Kent to see the hoppin'?
Many a time the Romanys says they expected to see
their *rye* there.   Just the other night, your Coopers
was a-lyin' round their fire, every one of 'em in a new
red blanket, lookin' so beautiful as the light shone on
'em, and I says, 'If our *rye* was to see you, he'd
just have that book of his out, and take all your pictures.' "

After much gossip over absent friends, I said, —

" Well, *dye*, I stand a shilling for beer, and that's
all I can do to-day, for I've come out with only *shove
trin-grushi.*"

Liz took the shilling, looked at it and at me with
an earnest air, and shook her head.

" It 'll never do, *rye*, — never.   A gentleman wants
more than six shillin's to see a race through, and a
reg'lar Romany rye like you ought to slap down his

lovvo with the best of 'em for the credit of his people.
And if you want a *bar* [a pound] or two, I 'll lend
you the money, and never fear about your payment."

It was kind of the old *dye*, but I thought that I
would pull through on my five shillings, before I would
draw on the Romany bank. To be considered with
sincere sympathy, as an object of deserving charity, on
the lowest race-ground in England, and to be offered
eleemosynary relief by a gypsy, was, indeed, touching
the hard pan of humiliation. I went my way, idly
strolling about, mingling affably with all orders, for
my watch was at home. *Vacuus viator cantabit.* As I
stood by a fence, I heard a gentlemanly-looking young
man, who was evidently a superior pickpocket, or "a
regular fly gonoff," say to a friend, —

"She 's on the ground, — a great woman among
the gypsies. What do they call her?"

"Mrs. Lee."

"Yes. A swell Romany she is."

Whenever one hears an Englishman, not a scholar,
speak of gypsies as "Romany," he may be sure that
man is rather more on the loose than becomes a
steady citizen, and that he walks in ways which, if
not of darkness, are at least in a shady *demi-jour*,
with a gentle down grade. I do not think there was
anybody on the race-ground who was not familiar
with the older word.

It began to rain, and before long my new velveteen
coat was very wet. I looked among the booths for
one where I might dry myself and get something to
eat, and, entering the largest, was struck by the appearance of the landlady. She was a young and
decidedly pretty woman, nicely dressed, and was un-

mistakably gypsy. I had never seen her before, but I knew who she was by a description I had heard. So I went up to the bar and spoke : —

"How are you, Agnes ?"

"Bloomin'. What will you have, sir ?"

"*Dui curro levinor, yeck for tute, yeck for mandy.*" (Two glasses for ale, — one for you, one for me.)

She looked up with a quick glance and a wondering smile, and then said, —

"You must be the Romany rye of the Coopers. I'm glad to see you. Bless me, how wet you are. Go to the fire and dry yourself. Here, Bill, I say ! Attend to this gentleman."

There was a tremendous roaring fire at the farther end of the booth, at which were pieces of meat, so enormous as to suggest a giant's roast or a political barbecue rather than a kitchen. I glanced with some interest at Bill, who came to aid me. In all my life I never saw a man who looked so thoroughly the regular English bull-dog bruiser of the lowest type, but battered and worn out. His nose, by oft-repeated pummeling, had gradually subsided almost to a level with his other features, just as an ancient British grave subsides, under the pelting storms of centuries, into equality with the plain. His eyes looked out from under their bristly eaves like sleepy wild-cats from a pig-pen, and his physique was tremendous. He noticed my look of curiosity.

"Old Bruisin' Bill, your honor. I was well knowed in the prize-ring once. Been in the newspapers. Now, you mus'n't dry your coat that way ! New welwe-teen ought always to be wiped afore you dry it. I was a gamekeeper myself for six years, an' wore it all that time nice and proper, I did, and know how

May be you 've got a thrip'ny bit for old Bill.
Thanky."

I will do Mrs. Agnes Wynn the credit to say that
in her booth the best and most abundant meal that
I ever saw for the price in England was given for
eighteen pence. Fed and dried, I was talking with
her, when there came up a pretty boy of ten, so
neat and well dressed and altogether so nice that he
might have passed current for a gentleman's son anywhere.

"Well, Agnes. You 're Wynn by name and winsome by nature, and all the best you have has gone
into that boy. They say you gypsies used to steal
children. I think it 's time to turn the tables, and
when I take the game up I 'll begin by stealing your
chavo."

Mrs. Wynn looked pleased. " He is a good boy,
as good as he looks, and he goes to school, and don't
keep low company."

Here two or three octoroon, duodecaroon, or vigin-
tiroon Romany female friends of the landlady came
up to be introduced to me, and of course to take
something at my expense for the good of the house.
This they did in the manner specially favored by
gypsies; that is to say, a quart of ale, being ordered,
was offered first to me, in honor of my social position, and then passed about from hand to hand. This
rite accomplished, I went forth to view the race.
The sun had begun to shine again, the damp flags
and streamers had dried themselves in its cheering
rays, even as I had renewed myself at Dame Wynn's
fire, and I crossed the race-course. The scene was
lively, picturesque, and thoroughly English. There
are certain pleasures and pursuits which, however

they may be perfected in other countries, always seem to belong especially to England, and chief among these is the turf. As a fresh start was made, as the spectators rushed to the ropes, roaring with excitement, and the horses swept by amid hurrahs, I could realize the sympathetic feeling which had been developed in all present by ancient familiarity and many associations with such scenes. Whatever the moral value of these may be, it is certain that anything so racy with local color and so distinctly fixed in popular affection as the *race* will always appeal to the artist and the student of national scenes.

I found Old Liz lounging with Old Dick, her husband, on the other side. There was a canvas screen, eight feet high, stretched as a background to stop the sticks hurled by the players at " coker-nuts," while the nuts themselves, each resting on a stick five feet high, looked like disconsolate and starved spectres, waiting to be cruelly treated. In company with the old couple was a commanding-looking, eagle-eyed Romany woman, in whom I at once recognized the remarkable gypsy spoken of by the pickpocket.

" My name is Lee," she said, in answer to my greeting. " What is yours ? "

" Leland."

" Yes, you have added land to the lee. You are luckier than I am. I'm a Lee without land."

As she spoke she looked like an ideal Meg Merrilies, and I wished I had her picture. It was very strange that I made the wish at that instant, for just then she was within an ace of having it taken, and therefore arose and went away to avoid it. An itinerant photographer, seeing me talking with the gypsies, was attempting, though I knew it not, to take the group. But the keen eye of the Romany saw it all, and she went her way, because she was of the real old kind, who believe it is unlucky to have their portraits taken. I used to think that this aversion was of the same kind as that which many good men evince in a marked manner when requested by the police to sit for their photographs for the rogues' gallery. But here I did the gypsies great injustice; for they will allow their likenesses to be taken if you will give them a shoe-string. That this old superstition relative to the binding and loosing of ill-luck by the shoe-string should exist in this connection is of itself curious. In the earliest times the shoe-latchet brought luck, just as the shoe itself did, especially when filled with corn or rice, and thrown after the bride. It is a great pity that the ignorant Gentiles, who are so careful to do this at every wedding, do not know that it is all in vain unless they cry aloud in Hebrew, " *Peru urphu!* "[1] with all their might when the shoe is cast, and that the shoe should be filled with rice.

She went away, and in a few minutes the photographer came in great glee to show a picture which he had taken.

" 'Ere you are, sir. An elegant photograph, surroundin' sentimental scenery and horiental cokernuts thrown in, — all for a diminitive little shillin'."

"Now that time you missed it," I said; " for on my honor as a gentleman, I have only ninepence in all my pockets."

" A gent like you with only ninepence!" said the artist.

---

[1] *Peru urphu!* "Increase and multiply!" *Vide* Bodenschatz, *Kirchliche Verfassung der Juden*, part IV. ch. 4, sect. 2.

"If he has n't got money in his pocket now," said Old Liz, speaking up in my defense, "he has plenty at home. He has given pounds and pounds to us gypsies."

"*Dovo's a huckaben*," I said to her in Romany. "*Mandy kekker delled tute kūmi'n a trin-grushi.*" (That is untrue. I never gave you more than a shilling.)

"Anyhow," said Liz, "ninepence is enough for it." And the man, assenting, gave it to me. It was a very good picture, and I have since had several copies taken of it.

"Yes, *rya,*" said Old Liz, when I regretted the absence of my Lady Lee, and talked with her about shoe-strings and old shoes, and how necessary it was to cry out "*Peru urphu!*" when you throw them, — "yes. That's the way the Gorgis always half does things. You see 'em get a horse-shoe off the roads, and what do they do with it! Goes like *dinneli* idiots and nails it up with the p'ints down, which, as is well beknown, brings all the bad luck there is flyin' in the air into the house, and *taders chovihanees* [draws witches] like anise-seed does rats. Now common sense ought to teach that the shoe ought to be put like horns, with the p'ints up. For if it 's lucky to put real horns up, of course the horse-shoe goes the same *drom* [road]. And it 's lucky to pick up a red string in the morning, — yes, or at any time; but it 's sure love from a girl if you do, — specially silk. And if so be she gives you a red string or cord, or a strip of red stuff, *that* means she 'll be bound to you and loves you."

VI.

STREET SKETCHES.

LONDON, during hot weather, after the close of
the wise season, suggests to the upper ten thousand,
and to the lower twenty thousand who reflect their
ways, and to the lowest millions who minister to them
all, a scene of doleful dullness. I call the time which
has passed wise, because that which succeeds is universally known as the silly season. Then the editors
in town have recourse to the American newspapers for
amusing murders, while their rural brethren invent
great gooseberries. Then the sea-serpent again lifts
his awful head. I am always glad when this sterling inheritance of the Northern races reappears; for
while we have *him* I know that the capacity for swal-
lowing a big bouncer, or for inventing one, is not lost.
He is characteristic of a fine, bold race. Long may
he wave! It is true that we cannot lie as gloriously
as our ancestors did about him. When the great
news-dealer of Norse times had no home-news he took
his lyre, and either spun a yarn about Vinland such
as would smash the "Telegraph," or else sung about
"that sea-snake tremendous curled, whose girth en-
circles half the world." It is wonderful, it is awful,
to consider how true we remain to the traditions of
the older time. The French boast that they invented
the *canard*. Let them boast. They also invented
the shirt-collar; but hoary legends say that an Eng-

11

lishman invented the shirt for it, as well as the art of washing it. What the shirt is to the collar, that is the glorious, tough old Northern *saga*, or maritime-spun yarn, to the *canard*, or duck. The yarn will wash ; it passes into myth and history ; it fits exactly, because it was made to order ; its age and glory illustrate the survival of the fittest.

I have, during three or four summers, remained a month in London after the family had taken flight to the sea-side. I stayed to finish books promised for the autumn. It is true that nearly four million of people remain in London during the later summer ; but it is wonderful what an influence the absence of a few exerts on them and on the town. Then you realize by the long lines of idle vehicles in the ranks how few people in this world can afford a cab ; then you find out how scanty is the number of those who buy goods at the really excellent shops ; and then you may finally find out by satisfactory experience, if you are inclined to grumble at your lot in life or your fortune, how much better off you are than ninety-nine in a hundred of your fellow-murmurers at fate.

It was my wont to walk out in the cool of the evening, to smoke my cigar in Regent's Park, seated on a bench, watching the children as they played about the clock-and-bull fountain, — for it embraces these objects among its adornments, — presented by Cowasie Jehanguire, who added to these magnificent Persian names the prosaic English postscript of Ready Money. In this his name sets forth the history of his Parsee people, who, from being heroic Ghebers, have come down to being bankers, who can " do " any Jew, and who might possibly tackle a Yankee so long as they kept out of New Jersey. One evening I walked outside of the Park, passing by the Gloucester Bridge to a little walk or boulevard, where there are a few benches. I was in deep moon-shadow, formed by the trees; only the ends of my boots shone like eyes in the moonlight as I put them out. After a while I saw a nice-looking young girl, of the humble-decent class, seated by me, and with her I entered into casual conversation. On the bench behind us were two young Italians, conversing in strongly marked Florentine dialect. They evidently thought that no one could understand them; as they became more interested they spoke more distinctly, letting out secrets which I by no means wished to hear.

At that instant I recalled the famous story of Prince Bismarck and the Esthonian young ladies and the watch-key. I whispered to the girl, —

" When I say something to you in a language which you do not understand, answer ' *Si* ' as distinctly as you can."

The damsel was quick to understand. An instant after I said, —

" *Ha veduto il mio 'havallo la sera?* "

" *Si.* "

There was a dead silence, and then a rise and a rush. My young friend rolled her eyes up at me, but said nothing. The Italians had departed with their awful mysteries. Then there came by a man who looked much worse. He was a truculent, untamable rough, evidently inspired with gin. At a glance I saw by the manner in which he carried his coat that he was a traveler, or one who lived on the roads. Seeing me he stopped, and said, grimly, —

" Do you love your Jesus? "

This is certainly a pious question; but it was ut-

uttered in a tone which intimated that if I did not answer it affirmatively I might expect anything but Christian treatment. I knew why the man uttered it. He had just come by an open-air preaching in the Park, and the phrase had, moreover, been recently chalked and stenciled by numerous zealous and busy nonconformists all over northwestern London. I smiled, and said, quietly, —

"*Pal, mor rakker sā drován. Jā pukenus on the drum.*" (Don't talk so loud, brother. Go away quietly.")

The man's whole manner changed. As if quite sober, he said, —

"*Mang your shūnaben, rye. But tute jins chomany. Kushti ratti!*" (Beg your pardon, sir. But you *do* know a thing or two. Good-night!)

"I was awfully frightened," said the young girl, as the traveler departed. "I'm sure he meant to pitch into us. But what a wonderful way you have, sir, of sending people away! I was n't so much astonished when you got rid of the Italians. I suppose ladies and gentlemen know Italian, or else they would n't go to the opera. But this man was a common, bad English tramp; yet I'm sure he spoke to you in some kind of strange language, and you said something to him that changed him into as peaceable as could be. What was it?"

"It was gypsy, young lady, — what the gypsies talk among themselves."

"Do you know, sir, I think you're the most mysterious gentleman I ever met."

"Very likely. Good-night."

"Good night, sir."

I was walking with my friend the Palmer, one afternoon in June, in one of the several squares which lie to the west of the British Museum. As we went I saw a singular-looking. slightly-built man, lounging at a corner. He was wretchedly clad, and appeared to be selling some rudely-made, but curious contrivances of notched sticks, intended to contain flowerpots. He also had flower-holders made of twisted copper wire. But the greatest curiosity was the man himself. He had such a wild, wasted, wistful expression, a face marked with a life of almost unconscious misery. And most palpable in it was the unrest, which spoke of an endless struggle with life, and had ended by goading him into incessant wandering. I cannot imagine what people can be made of who can look at such men without emotion.

"That is a gypsy," I said to the Palmer. "*Sarishan, pal!*"

The wanderer seemed to be greatly pleased to hear Romany. He declared that he was in the habit of talking it so much to himself when alone that his ordinary name was Romany Dick.

"But if you come down to the Potteries, and want to find me, you mus'n't ask for Romany Dick, but Divius Dick." "That means Wild Dick." "Yes." "And why?" Because I wander about so, and can never stay more than a night in any one place. I can't help it. I must keep going." He said this with that wistful, sad expression, a yearning as for something which he had never comprehended. Was it *rest?*

"And so I *rakker* Romany [talk gypsy to myself], when I'm alone of a night, when the wind blows. It's better company than talkin' Gorginess. More sociable. *He* says — no — *I* say more sensible things

Romaneskas than in English. You understand me?" he exclaimed suddenly, with the same wistful stare.

" Perfectly. It's quite reasonable. It must be like having two heads instead of one, and being twice as knowing as anybody else."

" Yes, that's it. But everybody don't know it."

" What do you ask for one of those flower-stands, Dick?"

" A shillin', sir."

" Well, here is my name and where I live, on an envelope. And here are two shillings. But if you *chore mandy* [cheat me] and don't leave it at the house, I'll look you up in the Potteries, and *koor tute* [whip you].

He looked at me very seriously. " Ah, yes. You could *koor me kennā* [whip me now]. But you could n't have *koored* my *dadas* [whipped my father]. Leastways not afore he got his leg broken fightin' Lancaster Sam. You must have heard of my father, — Single-stick Dick. But if your 're comin' down to the Potteries, don't come next Sunday. Come Sunday three weeks. My brother is *stardo kennā* for *chorin* a *gry* [in prison for horse-stealing]. In three weeks he'll be let out, and we 're goin' to have a great family party to welcome him, and we'll be glad to see you. Do come."

The flower-stand was faithfully delivered, but another engagement prevented an acceptance of the invitation, and I have never seen Dick since.

I was walking along Marylebone Road, which always seems to be a worn and wind-beaten street, very pretty once, and now repenting it; when just beyond Baker Street station I saw a gypsy van, hung all round with baskets and wooden - ware. Smoke issued from its pipe, and it went along smoking like any careless pedestrian. It always seems strange to think of a family being thus conveyed with its dinner cooking, the children playing about the stove, over rural roads, past common and gorse and hedge. in and out of villages, and through Great Babylon itself, as if the family had a *pied à terre*, and were as secluded all the time as though they lived in Little Pedlington or Tinnecum. For they have just the same narrow range of gossip, and just the same set of friends, though the set are always on the move. Traveling does not make a cosmopolite.

By the van strolled the lord and master, with his wife. I accosted him.

" *Sarishan?* "

" *Sarishan rye !* "

" Did you ever see me before ? Do you know me ? "

" No, sir."

" I 'm sorry for that. I have a nice velveteen coat which I have been keeping for your father. How 's your brother Frank ? Traveling about Kingston, I suppose. As usual. But I don't care about trusting the coat to anybody who don't know me."

" I 'll take it to him, safe enough, sir."

" Yes, I dare say. On your back. And wear it yourself six months before you see him."

Up spoke his wife: " That he shan't. I 'll take good care that the *pooro mush* [the old man] gets it all right, in a week."

" Well, *dye*, I can trust you. You remember me. And, Anselo, here is my address. Come to the house in half an hour."

In half an hour the housekeeper, said with a quiet smile, —

"If you please, sir, there's a gentleman — a *gypsy* gentleman — wishes to see you."

It is an English theory that the master can have no "visitors" who are not gentlemen. I must admit that Anselo's dress was not what could be called gentlemanly. From his hat to his stout shoes he looked the impenitent gypsy and sinful poacher, unaffected and natural. There was a cutaway, sporting look about his coat which indicated that he had grown to it from boyhood "in woodis grene." He held a heavy-handled whip, a regular Romany *tchupni* or *chŭckni,* which Mr. Borrow thinks gave rise to the word "jockey." I thought the same once, but have changed my mind, for there were "jockeys" in England before gypsies. Altogether, Anselo (which comes from Wenceslas) was a determined and vigorous specimen of an old-fashioned English gypsy, a type which, with all its faults, is not wanting in sundry manly virtues.

I knew that Anselo rarely entered any houses save ale-houses, and that he had probably never before been in a study full of books, arms, and bric-a-brac. And he knew that I was aware of it. Now, if he had been more of a fool, like a red Indian or an old-fashioned fop, he would have affected a stoical indifference, for fear of showing his ignorance. As it was, he sat down in an arm-chair, glanced about him, and said just the right thing.

"It must be a pleasant thing, at the end of the day, after one has been running about, to come home to such a room as this, so full of fine things, and sit down in such a comfortable chair." "Will I have a glass of old ale ? Yes, I thank you." "That is *kushto levinor* [good ale]. I never tasted better." "Would I rather have wine or spirits ? No, I thank you ; such ale as this is fit for a king."

Here Anselo's keen eye suddenly rested on something which he understood.

" What a beautiful little rifle ! That's what I call a *rinkno yāg-engree* [pretty gun]."

" Has it been a *wafedo wen* [hard winter], Anselo ? "

" It has been a dreadful winter, sir. We have been hard put to it sometimes for food. It's dreadful to think of. I've acti'lly seen the time when I was almost desperated, and if I'd had such a gun as that I'm afraid, if I'd been tempted, I could a-found it in my heart to knock over a pheasant."

I looked sympathetically at Anselo. The idea of his having been brought to the very brink of such a terrible temptation and awful crime was touching. He met the glance with the expression of a good man, who had done no more than his duty, closed his eyes, and softly shook his head. Then he took another glass of ale, as if the memory of the pheasants or something connected with the subject had been too much for him, and spoke : —

" I came here on my horse. But he's an ugly old white punch. So as not to discredit you, I left him standing before a gentleman's house, two doors off."

Here Anselo paused. I acknowledged this touching act of thoughtful delicacy by raising my glass. He drank again, then resumed : —

" But I feel uneasy about leaving a horse by himself in the streets of London. He'll stand like a driven nail wherever you put him — but there's always plenty of claw-hammers to draw such nails."

"Don't be afraid, Anselo. The park-keeper will not let anybody take him through the gates. I'll pay for him if he goes."

But visions of a stolen horse seemed to haunt Anselo. One would have thought that something of the kind had been familiar to him. So I sent for the velveteen coat, and, folding it on his arm, he mounted the old white horse, while waving an adieu with the heavy-handled whip, rode away in the mist, and was seen no more.

Farewell, farewell, thou old brown velveteen! I had thee first in by-gone years, afar, hunting ferocious fox and horrid hare, near Brighton, on the Downs, and wore thee well on many a sketching tour to churches old and castles dark or gray, when winter went with all his raines wete. Farewell, my coat, and benedicite! I bore thee over France unto Marseilles, and on the steamer where we took aboard two hundred Paynim pilgrims of Mahound. Farewell, my coat, and benedicite! Thou wert in Naples by great Virgil's tomb, and borest dust from Posilippo's grot, and hast been wetted by the dainty spray from bays and shoals of old Etrurian name. Farewell, my coat, and benedicite! And thou wert in the old Egyptian realm : I had thee on that morning 'neath the palms when long I lingered where of yore had stood the rose-red city, half as old as time. Farewell, my coat, and benedicite! It was a lady called thee into life. She said, Methinks ye need a velvet coat. It is a seemly guise to ride to hounds. Another gave me whip and silvered spurs. Now all have vanished in the darkening past. Ladies and all are gone into the gloom. Farewell, my coat, and benedicite! Thou'st had a venturous and traveled life, for thou wert once in Moscow in the snow. A true Bohemian thou hast ever been, and as a right Bohemian thou wilt die, the garment of a roving Romany. Fain would I see and hear what thou 'rt to know of reckless riding and the gypsy *tan*, of camps in dark green lanes, afar from towns. Farewell, mine coat, and benedicite!

VII.

OF CERTAIN GENTLEMEN AND GYPSIES.

ONE morning I was walking with Mr. Thomas Carlyle and Mr. Froude. We went across Hyde Park, and paused to rest on the bridge. This is a remarkable place, since there, in the very heart of London, one sees a view which is perfectly rural. The old oaks rise above each other like green waves, the houses in the distance are country-like, while over the trees, and far away, a village-looking spire completes the picture. I think that it was Mr. Froude who called my attention to the beauty of the view, and I remarked that it needed only a gypsy tent and the curling smoke to make it in all respects perfectly English.

" You have paid some attention to gypsies," said Mr. Carlyle. " They 're not altogether so bad a people as many think. In Scotland, we used to see many of them. I 'll not say that they were not rovers and reivers, but they could be honest at times. The country folk feared them, but those who made friends wi' them had no cause to complain of their conduct. Once there was a man who was persuaded to lend a gypsy a large sum of money. My father knew the man. It was to be repaid at a certain time. The day came; the gypsy did not. And months passed, and still the creditor had nothing of money but the memory of it; and ye remember

'*nessun maggior dolore*,' — that there 's na greater
grief than to remember the siller ye once had. Weel,
one day the man was surprised to hear that his frien'
the gypsy wanted to see him — interview, ye call it
in America. And the gypsy explained that, having
been arrested, and unfortunately detained, by some
little accident, in preeson, he had na been able to
keep his engagement. 'If ye 'll just gang wi' me,'
said the gypsy, 'aw 'll mak' it all right.' 'Mon, aw
wull,' said the creditor, — they were Scotch, ye know,
and spoke in deealect. So the gypsy led the way to
the house which he had inhabited, a cottage which
belonged to the man himself to whom he owed the
money. And there he lifted up the hearthstone ; the
hard-stane they call it in Scotland, and it is called so
in the prophecy of Thomas of Ercildowne. And under the hard-stane there was an iron pot. It was full
of gold, and out of that gold the gypsy carle paid his
creditor. Ye wonder how 't was come by? Well,
ye 'll have heard it 's best to let sleeping dogs lie."

"Yes. And what was said of the Poles who had,
during the Middle Ages, a reputation almost as good
as that of gypsies? *Ad secretas Poli, curas extendere
noli.*" (Never concern your soul as to the secrets of a
Pole.)

Mr. Carlyle's story reminds me that Walter Simp-
son, in his history of them, says that the Scottish
gypsies have ever been distinguished for their gratitude to those who treated them with civility and
kindness, anent which he tells a capital story, while
other instances sparkle here and there with many
brilliant touches in his five hundred-and-fifty-page
volume.

I have more than once met with Romanys, when

I was in the company of men who, like Carlyle and
Bilderdijk, " were also in the world of letters known,"
or who might say, " We have deserved to be."   One
of the many memories of golden days, all in the
merrie tyme of summer song in England, is of the
Thames, and of a pleasure party in a little steam-
launch.   It was a weenie affair, — just room for six
forward outside the cubby, which was called the
cabin ; and of these six, one was Mr. Roebuck, —
" the last Englishman," as some one has called him,
but as the late Lord Lytton applies the same term to
one of his characters about the time of the Conquest,
its accuracy may be doubted.   Say the last type of a
certain phase of the Englishman ; say that Roebuck
was the last of the old iron and oak men, the *triplex
æs et robur* chiefs of the Cobbet kind, and the phrase
may pass.   But it will only pass over into a new variety of true manhood.   However frequently the last
Englishman may die, I hope it will be ever said of
him, *Le roi est mort*, — *vive le roi !* I have had talks
with Lord Lytton on gypsics.   He, too, was once a
Romany rye in a small way, and in the gay May
heyday of his young manhood once went off with a
band of Romanys, and passed weeks in their tents, —
no bad thing, either, for anybody.   I was more than
once tempted to tell him the strange fact that, though
he had been among the black people and thought
he had learned their language, what they had imposed upon him for that was not Romany, but cant,
or English thieves' slang.   For what is given, in good
faith, as the gypsy tongue in " Paul Clifford " and the
" Disowned," is only the same old mumping *kennick*
which was palmed off on Bampfylde Moore Carew ;
or which he palmed on his readers, as the secret of

the Roms. But what is the use or humanity of désil-lusioning an author by correcting an error forty years old. If one could have corrected it in the proof, *à la bonne heure!* Besides, it was of no particular conse-quence to anybody whether the characters in " Paul Clifford " called a clergyman a *patter-cove* or a *rashai.* It is a supreme moment of triumph for a man when he discovers that his specialty — whatever it be — is not of such value as to be worth troubling anybody with it. As for Everybody, *he* is fair game.

The boat went up the Thames, and I remember that the river was, that morning, unusually beautiful. It is graceful, as in an outline, even when leaden with November mists, or iron-gray in the drizzle of December, but under the golden sunlight of June it is lovely. It becomes every year, with gay boating parties in semi-fancy dresses, more of a carnival, in which the carnivalers and their carnivalentines as-sume a more decided character. It is very strange to see this tendency of the age to unfold itself in new festival forms, when those who believe that there can never be any poetry or picturing in life but in the past are wailing over the vanishing of May-poles and old English sports. There may be, from time to time, a pause between the acts; the curtain may be down a little longer than usual; but in the long run the world-old play of the Peoples' Holiday will go on, as it has been going ever since Satan suggested that little apple-stealing excursion to Eve, which, as ex-plained by the Talmudists, was manifestly the direct cause of all the flirtations and other dreadful doings in all little outings down to the present day, in the drawing-room or " on the leads," world without end.

And as the boat went along by Weybridge we

passed a bank by which was a small gypsy camp; tents and wagons, donkeys and all, reflected in the silent stream, as much as were the swans in the fore-water. And in the camp was a tall, handsome, wild beauty, named Britannia, who knew me well; a dam-sel fond of larking, with as much genuine devil's gun-powder in her as would have made an entire pack or a Chinese hundred of sixty-four of the small crack-ers known as fast girls, in or around society. She was a splendid creature, long and lithe and lissom, but well rounded, of a figure suggestive of leaping hedges; and as the sun shone on her white teeth and burning black eyes, there was a hint of biting, too, about her. She lay coiled and basking, in feline fash-ion, in the sun; but at sight of me on the boat, up she bounded, and ran along the bank, easily keeping up with the steamer, and crying out to me in Rom-anes.

Now it just so happened that I by no means felt certain that *all* of the company present were such genial Bohemians as to appreciate anything like the joyous intimacy which Britannia was manifesting, as she, Atalanta-like, coursed along. Consequently, I was not delighted with her attentions.

"What a fine girl!" said Mr. Roebuck. "How well she would look on the stage! She seems to know you."

"Certainly," said one of the ladies, "or she would not be speaking her language. Why don't you an-swer her? Let us hear a conversation."

Thus adjured, I answered, —

"*Miri pen, miri kushti pen, beng lel tute, mā rak-ker sā drován! Or ma rakker Romaneskas. Mān dikesa te rānia shan akai. Miri kameli — mān kair*

mandy ladye!" (My sister, my nice, sweet sister!
— devil take you! don't hallo at me like that! Or
else don't talk Romany. Don't you see there are
ladies here? My dear, don't put me to shame!)

"*Pen the rani ta wusser mandy a trin-grushi —
who—op, hallo!*" (Tell the lady to shy me a shilling — whoop!) cried the fast damsel.

"*Pa miri duvels kām, pen — o bero se ta duro.
Mandy 'll dé tute a pash-korauna keratti if tu tevel
jā. Gorgie shan i foki kavakoi!*" (For the Lord's
sake, sister! — the boat is too far from shore. I'll
give you half a crown this evening if you'll clear out.
These be Gentiles, these here.)

"It seems to be a melodious language," said Mr.
Roebuck, greatly amused. "What are you saying?"

"I am telling her to hold her tongue, and go."

"But how on earth does it happen that you speak
such a language?" inquired a lady. "I always
thought that the gypsies only talked a kind of English slang, and this sounds like a foreign tongue."

All this time Britannia, like the Cork Leg, never
tired, but kept on the chase, neck and neck, till we
reached a lock, when, with a merry laugh like a child,
she turned on her track and left us.

"Mr. L.'s proficiency in Romany," said Mr. Roebuck, "is well known to me. I have heard him
spoken of as the successor to George Borrow."

"That," I replied, "I do not deserve. There are
other gentlemen in England who are by far my superiors in knowledge of the people."

And I spoke very sincerely. Apropos of Mr.
George Borrow, I knew him, and a grand old fellow
he was, — a fresh and hearty giant, holding his six
feet two or three inches as uprightly at eighty as he

12

ever had at eighteen. I believe that was his age, but
may be wrong. Borrow was like one of the old
Norse heroes, whom he so much admired, or an old-
fashioned gypsy bruiser, full of craft and merry tricks.
One of these he played on me, and I bear him no mal-
ice for it. The manner of the joke was this: I had
written a book on the English gypsies and their language; but before I announced it, I wrote a letter to
Father George, telling him that I proposed to print
it, and asking his permission to dedicate it to him.
He did not answer the letter, but " worked the tip "
promptly enough, for he immediately announced in
the newspapers on the following Monday his " Word-
Book of the Romany Language," " with many pieces
in gypsy, illustrative of the way of speaking and
thinking of the English gypsies, with specimens of
their poetry, and an account of various things relat-
ing to gypsy life in England." This was exactly
what I had told him that my book would contain ; for
I intended originally to publish a vocabulary. Father
George covered the track by not answering my letter;
but I subsequently ascertained that it had been faithfully delivered to him by a gentleman from whom I
obtained the information.

It was like the contest between Hildebrand the
elder and his son : —

> " A ready trick tried Hildebrand,
>   That old, gray-bearded man ;
> For when the younger raised to strike,
>   Beneath his sword he ran."

And, like the son, I had no ill feeling about it.
My obligations to him for " Lavengro " and the " Romany Rye " and his other works are such as I owe to
few men. I have enjoyed gypsying more than any

sport in the world, and I owe my love of it all to
George Borrow. I have since heard that a part of
Mr. Borrow's "Romano Lavo-Lil" had been in manuscript for thirty years, and that it might never
have been published but for my own work. I hope
that this is true; for I am sincerely proud to think
that I may have been in any way, directly or indi-
rectly, the cause of his giving it to the world. I
would gladly enough have burnt my own book, as I
said, with a hearty laugh, when I saw the announce-
ment of the "Lavo-Lil," if it would have pleased
the old Romany rye, and I never spoke a truer
word. He would not have believed it; but it would
have been true, all the same.

I well remember the first time I met George Borrow. It was in the British Museum, and I was introduced to him by Mrs. Estelle Lewis, — now dead,
— the well known-friend of Edgar A. Poe. He was
seated at a table, and had a large old German folio
open before him. We talked about gypsies, and I
told him that I had unquestionably found the word
for "green," *shelno*, in use among the English Romany. He assented, and said that he knew it. I
mention this as a proof of the manner in which the
"Romano Lavo-Lil" must have been hurried, because he declares in it that there is no English gypsy
word for "green." In this work he asserts that the
English gypsy speech does not probably amount to
fourteen hundred words. It is a weakness with the
Romany rye fraternity to believe that there are no
words in gypsy which they do not know. I am sure
that my own collection contains nearly four thousand Anglo-Romany terms, many of which I feared
were doubtful, but which I am constantly verifying

America is a far better place in which to study the language than England. As an old Scotch gypsy said to me lately, the deepest and cleverest old gypsies all come over here to America, where they have grown rich, and built the old language up again.

I knew a gentleman in London who was a man of extraordinary energy. Having been utterly ruined, at seventy years of age, by a relative, he left England, was absent two or three years in a foreign country, during which time he made in business some fifty thousand pounds, and, returning, settled down in England. He had been in youth for a long time the most intimate friend of George Borrow, who was, he said, a very wild and eccentric youth. One night, when skylarking about London, Borrow was pursued by the police, as he wished to be, even as Panurge so planned as to be chased by the night-watch. He was very tall and strong in those days, a trained shoulder-hitter, and could run like a deer. He was hunted to the Thames, "and there they thought they had him." But the Romany rye made for the edge, and, leaping into the wan water, like the Squyre in the old ballad, swam to the other side, and escaped.

I have conversed with Mr. Borrow on many subjects, — horses, gypsies, and Old Irish. Anent which latter subject I have heard him declare that he doubted whether there was any man living who could really read an old Irish manuscript. I have seen the same statement made by another writer. My personal impressions of Mr. Borrow were very agreeable, and I was pleased to learn afterwards from Mrs. Lewis that he had expressed himself warmly as regarded myself. As he was not invariably disposed to like those whom he met, it is a source of great pleasure to me to reflect that I have nothing but pleasant memories of the good old Romany rye, the Nestor of gypsy gentlemen. It is commonly reported among gypsies that Mr. Borrow was one by blood, and that his real name was Boro, or great. This is not true. He was of pure English extraction.

When I first met "George Eliot" and G. H. Lewes, at their house in North Bank, the lady turned the conversation almost at once to gypsies. They spoke of having visited the Zincali in Spain, and of several very curious meetings with the *Chabos.* Mr. Lewes, in fact, seldom met me — and we met very often about town, and at many places, especially at the Trübners' — without conversing on the Romanys. The subject evidently had for him a special fascination. I believe that I have elsewhere mentioned that after I returned from Russia, and had given him, by particular request, an account of my visits to the gypsies of St. Petersburg and Moscow, he was much struck by the fact that I had chiromanced to the Romany clan of the latter city. To tell the fortunes of gypsy girls was, he thought, the refinement of presumption. " There was in this world nothing so impudent as a gypsy when determined to tell a fortune ; and the idea of not one, but many gypsy girls believing earnestly in my palmistry was like a righteous retribution."

The late Tom Taylor had, while a student at Cambridge, been *aficionado,* or smitten, with gypsies, and made a manuscript vocabulary of Romany words, which he allowed me to use, and from which I obtained several which were new to me. This fact should make all smart gypsy scholars "take tent" and heed as to believing that they know everything.

I have many Anglo-Romany words — purely Hindi as to origin — which I have verified again and again, yet which have never appeared in print. Thus far the Romany vocabulary field has been merely scratched over.

Who that knows London knoweth not Sir Patrick Colquhoun? I made his acquaintance in 1848, when, coming over from student-life in Paris and the Revolution, I was most kindly treated by his family. A glorious, tough, widely experienced man he was even in early youth. For then he already bore the enviable reputation of being the first amateur sculler on the Thames, the first gentleman light-weight boxer in England, a graduate with honors of Cambridge, a Doctor Ph. of Heidelberg, a diplomat, and a linguist who knew Arabic, Persian, and Gaelic, Modern Greek and the Omnium Botherum tongues. They don't make such men nowadays, or, if they do, they leave out the genial element.

Years had passed, and I had returned to London in 1870, and found Sir Patrick living, as of yore, in the Temple, where I once and yet again and again dined with him. It was in the early days of this new spring of English life that we found ourselves by chance at a boat-race on the Thames. It was on the Thames, by his invitation, that I had twenty years before first seen an English regatta, and had a place in the gayly decked, superbly luncheoned barge of his club. It is a curious point in English character that the cleverest people do not realize or understand how festive and genial they really are, or how gayly and picturesquely they conduct their sports. It is a generally accepted doctrine with them that they do this kind of thing better in France; they believe sincerely

that they take their own amusements sadly ; it is the
tone, the style, with the wearily-witty, dreary clowns
of the weekly press, in their watery imitations of
Thackeray's worst, to ridicule all English festivity
and merry-making, as though sunshine had faded out
of life, and God and Nature were dead, and in their
place a great wind-bag Jesuit-Mallock were crying, in
tones tainted with sulphuretted hydrogen, "*Ah bah!*"
Reader mine, I have seen many a fête in my time,
all the way from illuminations of Paris to the Khe-
dive's fifteen-million-dollar spree in 1873 and the last
grand flash of the Roman-candle carnival of 1846,
but for true, hearty enjoyment and quiet beauty give
me a merry party on the Thames. Give me, I say,
its sparkling waters, its green banks, the joyous, beautiful girls, the hearty, handsome men. Give me the
boats, darting like fishes, the gay cries. And oh —
oh! — give me the Alsopp's ale in a quart mug, and
not a remark save of approbation when I empty it.

I had met Sir Patrick in the crowd, and our conversation turned on gypsies. When living before-time
in Roumania, he had Romany servants, and learned
a little of their language. Yes, he was inclined to be
"affected" into the race, and thereupon we went
gypsying. Truly, we had not far to seek, for just
outside the crowd a large and flourishing community
of the black-blood had set itself up in the *pivlioi*
(cocoa-nut) or *kashta* (stick) business, and as it was
late in the afternoon, and the entire business-world
was about as drunk as mere beer could make it, the
scene was not unlively. At that time I was new to
England, and unknown to every gypsy on the ground.
In after-days I learned to know them well, very well,
for they were chiefly Coopers and their congeners,

who came to speak of me as *their* rye and own special property or proprietor, — an allegiance which involved on one side an amount of shillings and beer
which concentrated might have set up a charity, but
which was duly reciprocated on the other by jocular
tenures of cocoa-nuts, baskets, and choice and deep
words in the language of Egypt.

As we approached the cock-shy, where sticks were
cast at cocoa-nuts, a young gypsy *chai*, whom I learned
to know in after-days as Athalia Cooper, asked me to
buy some sticks. A penny a throw, all the cocoa-nuts
I could hit to be my own. I declined; she became
urgent, jolly, riotous, insistive. I endured it well, for
I held the winning cards. *Qui minus propĕrè, minus
prospĕrè.* And then, as her voice rose *crescendo* into
a bawl, so that all the Romanys around laughed aloud
to see the green Gorgio so chaffed and bothered, I
bent me low, and whispered softly in her ear a single
monosyllable.

Why are all those sticks dropped so suddenly?
Why does Athalia in a second become sober, and
stand up staring at me, all her chaff and urgency forgotten. Quite polite and earnest now. But there is
joy behind in her heart. This *is* a game, a jolly
game, and no mistake. And uplifting her voice again,
as the voice of one who findeth an exceeding great
treasure even in the wilderness, she cried aloud, —

"*It 's a Romany rye!*"

The spiciest and saltest and rosiest of Sir Patrick's
own stories, told after dinner over his own old port to
a special conventicle of clergymen about town, was
never received with such a roar of delight as that cry
of Athalia's was by the Romany clan. Up went three
cheers at the find; further afield went the shout pro-

claiming the discovery of an aristocratic stranger of their race, a *rye*, who was to them as wheat, — a gypsy gentleman. Neglecting business, they threw down their sticks, and left their cocoanuts to grin in solitude; the *dyes* turned aside from fortune-telling to see what strange fortune had sent such a visitor. In ten minutes Sir Patrick and I were surrounded by such a circle of sudden admirers and vehement applauders, as it seldom happens to any mortal to acquire — out of Ireland — at such exceedingly short notice and on such easy terms.

They were not particular as to what sort of a gypsy I was, or where I came from, or any nonsense of that sort, you know. It was about *cerevisia vincit omnia*, or the beery time of day with them, and they cared not for anything. I was extremely welcome; in short, there was poetry in me. I had come down on them by a way that was dark and a trick that was vain, in the path of mystery, and dropped on Athalia and picked her up. It was gypsily done and very creditable to me, and even Sir Patrick was regarded as one to be honored as an accomplice. It is a charming novelty in every life to have the better class of one's own kind come into it, and nobody feels so keenly as a jolly Romany that *jucundum nihil est nisi quod rĕfĭcit varietas* — naught pleases us without variety.

Then and there I drew to me the first threads of what became in after-days a strange and varied skein of humanity. There was the Thames upon a holiday. Now I look back to it, I ask, *Ubi sunt?* (Where are they all?) Joshua Cooper, as good and earnest a Rom as ever lived, in his grave, with more than one of those who made my acquaintance by hurrahing for me. Some in America, some wandering wide. Yet there by Weybridge still the Thames runs on.

By that sweet river I made many a song. One of these, to the tune of "Waves in Sunlight Dancing," rises and falls in memory like a fitful fairy coming and going in green shadows, and that it may not perish utterly I here give it a place : —

AVELLA PARL O PĀNI.

Av' kushto parl o pāni,
　Av' kushto mir' akai!
Mi kameli chovihani,
　Avel ke tiro rye !

Shan raklia rinkenidiri,
　Mukkellan rinkeni se ;
Kek rakli 'dré i temia
　Se rinkenidiri mi.

Shan dudnidiri yākka,
　Mukkelan dudeni ;
Kek yākk peshel' sā kushti
　Pā miro kameli zi.

Shan balia longi diri,
　Mukk 'lende bori 'pré,
Kek waveri raklia balia,
　Te lian man opré.

Yoi lela angūstrini,
　I miri tācheni,
Kek waver mūsh jinella,
　Sā dovo covva se.

Adré, adré o doeyav
　Patrinia pellelan,
Kennā yek chumer kérdo
　O wavero well' án.

Te wenna būtidiri,
　Ke jana sig akoi

Sa sig sa yeck si gillo
Shan waveri adoi.

Avella parl o pāni,
Avella sig akai!
Mi kamli tāni-rāni
Avell' ke tiro rye!

———

COME OVER THE RIVER.

O love, come o'er the water,
  O love, where'er you be!
My own sweetheart, my darling,
  Come over the river to me!

If any girls are fairer,
  Then fairer let them be;
No maid in all the country
  Is half so fair to me.

If other eyes are brighter,
  Then brighter let them shine;
I know that none are lighter
  Upon this heart of mine.

If other's locks are longer,
  Then longer let them grow;
Hers are the only fish-lines
  Which ever caught me so.

She wears upon her finger
  A ring we know so well,
And we and that ring only
  Know what the ring can tell.

From trees into the water
  Leaves fall and float away,
So kisses come and leave us,
  A thousand in a day.

Yet though they come by thousands,
  Yet still they show their face;

As soon as one has left us
  Another fills its place.

O love, come o'er the water,
  O love, where'er you be !
My own sweetheart, my darling,
  Come over the river to me !

WELSH GYPSIES.

I.

MAT WOODS THE FIDDLER.

THE gypsies of Wales are to those of England what the Welsh themselves are to the English; more antique and quaint, therefore to a collector of human bric-a-brac more curious. The Welsh Rom is specially grateful for kindness or courtesy; he is deeper as to language, and preserves many of the picturesque traits of his race which are now so rapidly vanishing. But then he has such excellent opportunity for gypsying. In Wales there are yet thousands of acres of wild land, deep ravines, rocky corners, and roadside nooks, where he can boil the kettle and *hatch the tan*, or pitch his tent, undisturbed by the rural policeman. For it is a charming country, where no one need weary in summer, when the days are long, or in early autumn, —

> " When the barley is ripe,
> And the frog doth pipe,
> In golden stripe
> And green all dressed;
> When the red apples
> Roll in the chest."

Then it is pleasant walking in Wales, and there too at times, between hedge-rows, you may meet with the Romany.

I was at Aberystwith by the sea, and one afternoon we went, a party of three gentlemen and three ladies, in a char-a-banc, or wagonette, to drive. It was a pleasant afternoon, and we had many a fine view of distant mountains, on whose sides were mines of lead with silver, and of which there were legends from the time of Queen Elizabeth. The hills looked leaden and blue in the distance, while the glancing sea far beyond recalled silver, — for the alchemy of imagery, at least, is never wanting to supply ideal metals, though the real may show a sad *deficit* in the returns.

As we drove we suddenly overtook a singular party, the first of whom was the leader, who had lagged behind. He was a handsome, slender, very dark young man, carrying a violin. Before him went a little open cart, in which lay an old woman, and by her a harp With it walked a good-looking gypsy girl, and another young man, not a gypsy. He was by far the handsomest young fellow, in form and features, whom I ever met among the agricultural class in England; we called him a peasant Apollo. It became evident that the passional affinity which had drawn this rustic to the gypsy girl, and to the roads, was according to the law of natural selection, for they were wonderfully well matched. The young man had the grace inseparable from a fine figure and a handsome face, while the girl was tall, lithe, and pantherine, with the diavolesque charm which, though often attributed by fast-fashionable novelists to their heroines, is really never found except among the low-born beauties of nature. It is the beauty of the Imp and of the Serpent; it fades with letters; it dies in the drawing-room or on the stage. You are mistaken

when you think you see it coming out of the syna-
gogue, unless it be a very vulgar one. Your Lahova
has it not, despite her black eyes, for she is too clever
and too conscious; the devil-beauty never knows
how to read, she is unstudied and no actress. Rachel
and the Bernhardt have it not, any more than Saint
Agnes or Miss Blanche Lapin. It is not of good or
of evil, or of culture, which is both ; it is all and only
of nature, and it does not know itself.

As the wagonette stopped I greeted the young
man at first in English, then in Romany. When he
heard the gypsy tongue he started, his countenance
expressing the utmost surprise and delight. As if
he could hardly believe in such a phenomenon he inquired, "*Romany?*" and as I nodded assent, he
clasped my hand, the tears coming into his eyes. Such
manifestations are not common among gypsies, but I
can remember how one, the wife of black Ben Lee,
was thus surprised and affected. How well I recall
the time and scene, — by the Thames, in the late
twilight, when every tree and twig was violet black
against the amber sky, where the birds were chirp-
chattering themselves to roost and rest, and the river
rippled and murmured a duet with the evening breeze.
I was walking homeward to Oatlands when I met
the tawny Sinaminta, bearing her little stock of baskets to the tent and van which I had just quitted,
and where Ben and his beautiful little boy were lighting the *al fresco* fire. "I have prayed to see this
day!" exclaimed the gypsy woman. "I have so
wanted to see the Romany rye of the Coopers. And
I laid by a little *delaben*, a small present, for you when
we should meet. It's a photograph of Ben and me
and our child." I might have forgotten the evening

and the amber sky, rippling river and dark-green
hedge-rows, but for this strange meeting and greeting
of an unknown friend, but a few kind words fixed
them all for life. That must be indeed a wonderful
landscape which humanity does not make more impressive.

I spoke but a few words to the gypsy with the
violin, and we drove on to a little wayside inn, where
we alighted and rested. After a while the gypsies
came along.

"And now, if you will, let us have a real frolic," I
said to my friends. A word was enough. A quart
of ale, and the fiddle was set going, and I sang in
Romany, and the rustic landlord and his household
wondered what sort of guests we could be. That they
had never before entertained such a mixed party I
can well believe. Here, on one hand, were indubi-
table swells, above their usual range; there, on the
other, were the dusky vagabonds of the road; and it
could be no common condescending patronage, for I
was speaking neither Welsh nor English, and our
friendly fraternity was evident. Yes, many a time,
in England, have I seen the civil landlady or the
neat-handed Phillis awed with bewilderment, as I
have introduced Plato Buckland, or the most disreputable-looking but oily — yea, glycerine-politeful
— old Windsor Frog, into the parlor, and conversed
with him in mystic words. Such an event is a rare
joy to the gypsy. For he loves to be lifted up among
men; he will tell you with pride of the times when he
was pointed at, and people said, "*He's* the man!" and
how a real gentleman once invited him into his house
and gave him a glass of wine. But to enter the best
room of the familiar tavern, to order, in politest but

imperative tones, " beer " — sixpenny beer — for himself and "the other gentleman," is indeed bliss. Then, in addition to the honor of moving in distinguished society, before the very eyes and in the high places of those who have hitherto always considered him as a lowly cuss, the Romany realizes far more than the common peasant the contrast-contradiction, or the humor of the drama, its bit of mystification, and especially the mystification of the house-folk. This is unto him the high hour of the soul, and it is not forgotten. It passes unto the golden legends of the heart, and you are tenderly enshrined in it.

Once, when I was wandering afoot with old Cooper, we stopped at an inn, and in a room by ourselves ordered luncheon. The gypsy might have had poultry of the best; he preferred cold pork. While the attendant was in the room, he sat with exemplary dignity at the table; but as the girl left, he followed her step sounds with his ears, like a dog, moved his head, glanced at me with a nod, turned sideways from the table, and, putting his plate on his knees, proceeded to eat without a fork.

" For it is n't proper for me to eat at the table with you, or *as* you do."

The Welsh gypsy played well, and his sister touched the harp and sang, the ale circulated, and the villagers, assembling, gazed in a crowd into the hall. Then the girl danced solo, just as I have seen her sisters do in Egypt and in Russia, to her brother's fiddling. Even so of old, Syrian and Egyptian girls haunted gardens and taverns, and danced *pas seul* all over the Roman empire, even unto Spain, behaving so gypsily that wise men have conjectured that they were gypsies in very truth. And who shall say they were not? For it is

13

possible that prehistorically, and beyond all records of Persian Luri and Syrian Ballerine and Egyptian Almeh, there was all over the East an outflowing of these children of art from one common primeval Indian stock. From one fraternity, in Italy, at the present day, those itinerant pests, the hand-organ players, proceed to the ends of the earth and to the gold-diggings thereof, and time will yet show that before all time, or in its early dawn, there were root-born Romany itinerants singing, piping, and dancing unto all the known world ; yea, and into the unknown darkness beyond, *in partibus infidelium.*

A gentleman who was in our party had been long in the East. I had known him in Alexandria during the carnival, and he had lived long time *outre mer*, in India. Hearing me use the gypsy numerals — *yeck, dui, trin, shtor, panj,* — he proceeded to count in Hindustani or Persian, in which the same words from one to ten are almost identical with Romany. All of this was carefully noted by the old gypsy mother, — as, also, that my friend is of dark complexion, with sparkling black eyes. Reduced in dress, or diluted down to worn corduroy and a red tie, he might easily pass muster, among the Sons of the Road, as one of them.

And now the ladies must, of course, have their fortunes told, and this, I could observe, greatly astonished the gypsies in their secret souls, though they put a cool face on it. That we, ourselves, were some kind of a mysterious high-caste Romany they had already concluded, and what faith could we put in *dukkerin?* But as it would indubitably bring forth shillings to their benefit, they wisely raised no questions, but calmly took this windfall, which had fallen,

as it were, from the skies, even as they had accepted
the beer, which had come, like a providential rain,
unto them, in the thirst of a dry journey.

It is customary for all gypsy sorceresses to take
those who are to be fortune-told aside, and, if possible,
into a room by themselves. This is done partly to
enhance the mystery of the proceeding, and partly
to avoid the presence of witnesses to what is really an
illegal act. And as the old sorceress led a lady into
the little parlor, the gypsy man, whose name was
Mat, glanced up at me, with a droll, puzzled expression, and said, " Patchessa *tu* adovo ? " (Do *you*
believe in that ?) With a wink, I answered, " Why
not ? I, too, tell fortunes myself." *Anch io sono
pittore.* It seemed to satisfy him, for he replied,
with a nod-wink, and proceeded to pour forth the
balance of his thoughts, if he had any, into the music
of his violin.

When the ladies had all been instructed as to their
future, my friend, who had been in the East, must
needs have his destiny made known unto him. He
did not believe in this sort of thing, you know, — of
course not. But he had lived a long time among
Orientals, and he just happened to wish to know how
certain speculations would fall out, and he loves,
above all things, a lark, or anything out of the common. So he went in. And when alone with the
sybil, she began to talk to him in Romany.

" Oh, I say, now, old lady, stow that ! " he exclaimed. " I don't understand you."

" You don't understand me ! " exclaimed the fortune-teller. " Perhaps you did n't understand your
own mother when she talked Romany to you. What's
the use of your tryin' to make yourself out a Gorgio

to *me?* Don't I know our people? Did n't your
friend there talk Romanes? Is n't he all Romaneskas? And did n't I hear you with my own ears
count up to ten in Romany? And now, after that,
you would deny your own blood and people! Yes,
you 've dwelt in Gorgines so long that you think
your eyes are blue and your hair is yellow, my son,
and you have been far over the sea; but wherever you
went you knew Romanes, if you don't know your own
color. But you shall hear your fortune. There is
lead in the mines and silver in the lead, and wealth
for him who is to win it, and that will be a dark man
who has been nine times over the sea, and eaten his
bread under the black tents, and been three times
near death, once from a horse, and once from a man,
and once through a woman. And you will know
something you don't know now before a month is
over, and something will be found that is now hidden, and has been hidden since the world was made.
And there 's a good fortune coming to the man it was
made for, before the oldest tree that 's a-growing was
a seed, and that 's a man as knows how to count
Romanes up to ten, and many a more thing beside
that, that he 's learned beyond the great water."

And so we went our ways, the harp and violin
sounds growing fainter as we receded, till they were
like the buzzing of bees in drying clover, and the
twilight grew rosier brown. I never met Mat Woods
again, though I often heard of his fame as a fiddler.
Whether my Anglo-Indian friend found the fortune
so vaguely predicted is to me as yet unknown. But
I believe that the prediction encouraged him. That
there are evils in palmistry, and sin in card-drawing,
and iniquity in coffee-grounding, and vice in all the

planets, is established by statute, and yet withal I incline to believe that the art of prediction cheers up many a despondent soul, and does some little good, even as good ale, despite the wickedness of drinking, makes some hearts merry and others stronger. If there are foolish maids who have had their heads turned by being told of coming noblemen and prospective swells, who loved the ground they trod on, and were waiting to woo and win and wed, and if the same maidens herein described have thereby, in the manner set forth, been led by the aforesaid devices unto their great injury, as written in the above indictment, it may also *per contra* and on the other hand be pleaded that divers girls, to wit, those who believe in prediction, have, by encouragement and hope to them held out of legally marrying sundry young men of good estate, been induced to behave better than they would otherwise have done, and led by this hope have acted more morally than was their wont, and thereby lifted themselves above the lowly state of vulgarity, and even of vice, in which they would otherwise have groveled, hoveled, or cottaged. And there have been men who, cherishing in their hearts a prediction, or, what amounts to the same thing, a conviction, or a set fancy, have persevered in hope until the hope was realized. You, O Christian, who believe in a millennium, you, O Jew, who expect a Messiah, and await the fulfillment of your *dukkerin*, are both in the right, for both will come true when you *make* them do so.

II.

THE PIOUS WASHERWOMAN.

THERE is not much in life pleasanter than a long ramble on the road in leaf-green, sun-gold summer. Then it is Nature's merry-time, when fowls in woods them maken blithe, and the crow preaches from the fence to his friends afield, and the honeysuckle winketh to the wild rose in the hedge when she is wooed by the little buzzy bee. In such times it is good for the heart to wander over the hills and far away, into haunts known of old, where perhaps some semi-Saxon church nestles in a hollow behind a hill, where grass o'ergrows each mouldering tomb, and the brook, as it ripples by in a darksome aldered hollow, speaks in a language which man knows no more, but which is answered in the same forgotten tongue by the thousand-year yew as it rustles in the breeze. And when there are Runic stones in this garden of God, where He raises souls, I often fancy that this old dialect is written in their rhythmic lines. The yew-trees were planted by law, lang-syne, to yield bows to the realm, and now archery is dead and Martini-Henry has taken its place, but the yews still live, and the Runic fine art of the twisted lines on the tombs, after a thousand years' sleep, is beginning to revive. Everything at such a time speaks of joy and resurrection, — tree and tomb and bird and flower and bee.

These are all memories of a walk from the town

of Aberystwith, in Wales, which walk leads by an
ancient church, in the soul garden of which are two
Runic cross tombstones. One day I went farther
afield to a more ancient shrine, on the top of a high
mountain. This was to the summit of Cader Idris,
sixteen miles off. On this summit there is a Druid-
ical circle, of which the stones, themselves to ruin
grown, are strange and death-like old. Legend says
that this is the burial-place of Taliesin, the first of
Welsh bards, the primeval poet of Celtic time. Whoever sleeps on the grave will awake either a madman
or a poet, or is at any rate unsafe to become one or
the other. I went, with two friends, afoot on this
little pilgrimage. Both were professors at one of the
great universities. The elder is a gentleman of great
benevolence, learning, and gentleness; the other, a
younger man, has been well polished and sharpened
by travel in many lands. It is rumored that he has
preached Islam in a mosque unto the Moslem even
unto taking up a collection, which is the final test of
the faith which reaches forth into a bright eternity.
That he can be, as I have elsewhere noted, a Persian
unto Persians, and a Romany among Roms, and a
professional among the hanky-pankorites, is likewise
on the cards, as surely as that he knows the roads and
all the devices and little games of them that dwell
thereon. Though elegant enough in his court dress
and rapier when he kisses the hand of our sovereign
lady the queen, he appears such an abandoned rough
when he goes a-fishing that the innocent and guile-
less gypsies, little suspecting that a *rye* lies *perdu* in
his wrap-rascal, will then confide in him as if he and
in-doors had never been acquainted.

We had taken with us a sparing lunch of thin

sandwiches and a frugal flask of modest, blushing brandy, which we diluted at a stingy little fountain spring which dropped economically through a rift in the rock, as if its nymph were conscious that such a delicious drink should not be wasted. As it was, it refreshed us, and we were resting in a blessed repose under the green leaves, when we heard footsteps, and an old woman came walking by.

She was the ideal of decent and extreme poverty. I never saw anybody who was at once so poor and so clean. In her face and in her thin garments was marked the mute, resolute struggle between need and self-respect, which, to him who understands it, is as brave as any battle between life and death. She walked on as if she would have gone past without a word, but when we greeted her she paused, and spoke respectfully. Without forwardness she told her sad and simple story: how she belonged to the Wesleyan confession, how her daughter was dying in the hospital at Caernarvon; how she had walked sixty miles to see her, and hoped to get there in time to close her eyes. In reply to a question as to her means, she admitted that they were exhausted, but that she could get through without money; she did not beg. And then came naturally enough the rest of the little artless narrative, as it generally happens among the simple annals of the poor: how she had been for forty years a washerwoman, and had a letter from her clergyman.

There was a tear in the eye of the elder professor, and his hand was in his pocket. The younger smoked in silence. I was greatly moved myself, — perhaps bewildered would be the better word, — when, all at once, as the old woman turned in the sunlight, I caught the expression *of the corner of an eye!*

My friend Salaman, who boasts that he is of the last of the Sadducees, — that strange, ancient, and secret sect, who disguise themselves as the *Neu Reformirte*, — declares that the Sephardim may be distinguished from the Ashkenazim as readily as from the confounded Goyim, by the corners of their eyes. This he illustrated by pointing out to me, as they walked by in the cool of the evening, the difference between the eyes of Fräulein Eleonora Kohn and Senorita Linda Abarbanel and divers and sundry other young ladies, — the result being that I received in return thirty-six distinct *œillades*, several of which expressed indignation, and in all of which there was evidently an entire misconception of my object in looking at them. Now the eyes of the Sephardesses are unquestionably fascinating; and here it may be recalled that, in the Middle Ages, witches were also recognized by having exactly the same corners, or peaks, to the eye. This is an ancient mystery of darksome lore, that the enchantress always has the bird-peaked eye, which betokens danger to somebody, be she of the Sephardim, or an ordinary witch or enchantress, or a gypsy.

Now, as the old Wesleyan washerwoman turned around in the sunshine, I saw the witch-pointed eye and the glint of the Romany. And then I glanced at her hands, and saw that they had not been long familiar with wash-tubs; for, though clean, they were brown, and had never been blanched with an age of soap-suds. And I spoke suddenly, and said, —

" *Can tute rakker Romanes, miri dye ?* " (Can you speak Romany, my mother ?) And she answered, as if bewildered, —

"The Lord forbid, sir, that I should talk any of them wicked languages."

The younger professor's eyes expressed dawning delight. I followed my shot with, —

"*Tute need n't be attrash to rakker. Mandy's been apré the drom mi-kokero.*" (You need n't be afraid to speak. I have been upon the road myself.)

And, still more confused, she answered in English, —

"Why, sir, you be upon the road now!"

"It seems to me, old lady," remarked the younger professor, "that you understand Romany very well for one who has been for forty years in the Methodist communion."

It may be observed that he here confounded washing with worshiping.

The face of the true believer was at this point a fine study. All her confidence had deserted her. Whether she thought we were of her kind in disguise, or that, in the unknown higher world of respectability, there might be gypsies of corresponding rank, even as there might be gypsy angels among the celestial hierarchies, I cannot with confidence assert. About a week ago a philologist and purist told me that there is no exact synonym in English for the word *flabbergasted*, as it expresses a peculiar state of bewilderment as yet unnamed by scholars, and it exactly sets forth the condition in which our virtuous poverty appeared. She was, indeed, flabbergasted. *Cornix scorpum rapuit*, — the owl had come down on the rabbits, and lo! they had fangs. I resumed, —

"Now, old lady, here is a penny. You are a very poor person, and I pity you so much that I give you this penny for your poverty. But there is a pocketful where this came from, and you shall have the lot if you 'll *rakker*," — that is, talk gypsy.

And at that touch of the Ithuriel spear the old toad flashed up into the Romany devil, as with gleaming eyes and a witch-like grin she cried in a mixture of gypsy and tinker languages, —

"Gents, I 'll have tute jin when you tharis mandy you rakker a reg'lar fly old bewer." Which means, "Gentlemen, I 'll have you know, when you talk to me, you talk to a reg'lar shrewd old female thief."

The face of the elder professor was a study of astonishment for Lavater. His fingers relaxed their grasp of the shilling, his hand was drawn from his pocket, and his glance, like Bill Nye's, remarked: "*Can* this be?" He tells the story to this day, and always adds, "I *never* was so astonished in my life." But the venerable washerwoman was also changed, and, the mask once thrown aside, she became as festive as a witch on the Brocken. Truly, it is a great comfort to cease playing a part, particularly a pious one, and be at home and at ease among your like; and better still if they be swells. This was the delight of Anderson's ugly duck when it got among the swans, "and, blest sensation, felt genteel." And to show her gratitude, the sorceress, who really seemed to have grown several shades darker, insisted on telling our fortunes. I think it was to give vent to her feelings in defiance of the law that she did this; certain it was that just then, under the circumstances, it was the only way available in which the law could be broken. And as it was, indeed, by heath and hill that the priestess of the hidden spell bade the Palmer from over the sea hold out his palm. And she began in the usual sing-song tone, mocking the style of gypsy fortune-tellers, and satirizing herself. And thus she spoke, —

" You 're born under a lucky star, my good gentleman, and you 're a married man ; but there 's a black-eyed young lady that 's in love with you "

" Oh, mother of all the thieves ! " I cried, " you 've put the *dukkerin* on the wrong man. I 'm the one that the dark girls go after."

" Yes, my good gentleman. She 's in love with you both."

" And now tell my fortune ! " I exclaimed, and with a grim expression, casting up my palm, I said, —

" *Pen mengy if mandy 'll be bitchadé pādel for chorin a gry, or nasherdo for mérin a gav-mush.*" (Tell me if I am to be transported for stealing a horse, or hung for killing a policeman.)

The old woman's face changed. " You 'll never need to steal a horse. The man that knows what you know never need be poor like me. I know who *you* are *now ;* you 're not one of these tourists. You 're the boro Romany rye [the tall gypsy gentleman]. And go your way, and brag about it in your house, — and well you may, — that Old Moll of the Roads could n't take you in, and that you found her out. Never another *rye* but you will ever say that again. Never."

And she went dancing away in the sunshine, capering backwards along the road, merrily shaking the pennies in her hand for music, while she sang something in gypsy, — witch to the last, vanishing as witches only can. And there came over me a feeling as of the very olden time, and some memory of another witch, who had said to another man, " *Thou art no traveler. Great master, I know thee now ;*'

and who, when he called her the mother of the giants,
replied, " Go thy way, and boast at home that no man
will ever waken me again with spells. Never." That
was the parting of Odin and the Vala sorceress, and
it was the story of oldest time ; and so the myth of
ancient days becomes a tattered parody, and thus runs
the world away to Romanys and rags — when the gods
are gone.

When I laughed at the younger professor for con-
founding forty years in the church with as many at
the wash-tub, he replied, —

" Cleanliness is with me so near to godliness that
it is not remarkable that in my hurry I mistook one
for the other."

So we went on and climbed Cader Idris, and found
the ancient grave of rocks in a mystic circle, whose
meaning lies buried with the last Druid, who would
perhaps have told you they were —

> " Seats of stone nevir hewin with mennes hand
> But wrocht by Nature as it ane house had bene
> For Nymphes, goddis of floudes and woodis grene."

And we saw afar the beautiful scene, " where
fluddes rynnys in the foaming sea," as Gawain Doug-
las sings, and where, between the fresh water and salt,
stands a village, even where it stood in earliest Cym-
ric prehistoric dawn, and the spot where ran the weir
in which the prince who was in grief because his weir
yielded no fish, at last fished up a poet, even as Pha-
raoh's daughter fished out a prophet. I shall not soon
forget that summer day, nor the dream-like pano-
rama, nor the ancient grave ; nor how the younger
professor lay down on the seat of stone nevir hewin
with mennes hand, and declared he had a nap, — just
enough to make him a poet. To prove which he

wrote a long poem on the finding of Taliesin in the nets, and sent it to the Aberystwith newspaper; while I, not to be behindhand, wrote another, in imitation of the triplets of Llydwarch Hen, which were so greatly admired as tributes to Welsh poetry that they were forthwith translated faithfully into lines of consonants, touched up with so many *w*'s that they looked like saws ; and they circulated even unto Llandudno, and, for aught I know, may be sung at Eistedfodds, now and ever, to the twanging of small harps, — *in sæcula sæculorum*. Truly, the day which had begun with a witch ended fitly enough at the tomb of a prophet poet.

III.

THE GYPSIES AT ABERYSTWITH.

ABERYSTWITH is a little fishing-village, which has of late years first bloomed as a railway-station, and then fruited into prosperity as a bathing-place. Like many *parvenus*, it makes a great display of its Norman ancestor, the old castle, saying little about the long centuries of plebeian obscurity in which it was once buried. This castle, after being woefully neglected during the days when nobody cared for its early respectability, has been suddenly remembered, now that better times have come, and, though not restored, has been made comely with grass banks, benches, and gravel walks, reminding one of an Irish grandfather in America, taken out on a Sunday with " the childher," and looking " gintale " in the clean shirt and whole coat unknown to him for many a decade in Tipperary. Of course the castle and the wealth, or the hotels and parade, are well to the fore, or boldly displayed, as Englishly as possible, while the little Welsh town shrinks quietly into the hollow behind. And being new to prosperity, Aberystwith is also a little muddled as to propriety. It would regard with horror the idea of allowing ladies and gentlemen to bathe together, even though completely clad ; but it sees nothing out of the way when gentlemen in pre-fig-leaf costume disport themselves, bathing just before the young ladies' boarding-school and the chief

hotel, or running joyous races on the beach. I shall
never forget the amazement and horror with which
an Aberystwithienne learned that in distant lands
ladies and gentlemen went into the water arm in arm,
although dressed. But when it was urged that the
Aberystwith system was somewhat peculiar, she replied, " Oh, *that* is a very different thing ! "

On which words for a text a curious sermon might
be preached to the Philistiny souls who live perfectly
reconciled to absurd paradoxes, simply because they
are accustomed to them. Now, of all human beings,
I think the gypsies are freest from trouble with paradoxes as to things being different or alike, and the
least afflicted with moral problems, burning questions,
social puzzles, or any other kind of mental rubbish.
They are even freer than savages or the heathen in
this respect, since of all human beings the Fijian,
New Zealander, Mpongwe, or Esquimaux is most terribly tortured with the laws of etiquette, religion,
social position, and propriety. Among many of these
heathen unfortunates the meeting with an equal involves fifteen minutes of bowing, re-bowing, surre-
bowing, and rejoinder-bowing, with complementary
complimenting, according to old custom, while the
worship of Mrs. Grundy through a superior requires a
half hour wearisome beyond belief. " In Fiji," says
Miss C. F. Gordon Cumming, " strict etiquette rules
every action of life, and the most trifling mistake in
such matters would cause as great dissatisfaction as a
breach in the order of precedence at a European cer-
emonial." In dividing cold baked missionary at a
dinner, especially if a chief be present, the host com-
mitting the least mistake as to helping the proper
guest to the proper piece in the proper way would

find himself promptly put down in the *menu*. In Fiji, as in all other countries, this punctilio is nothing but the direct result of ceaseless effort on the part of the upper classes to distinguish themselves from the lower. Cannibalism is a joint sprout from the same root; "the devourers of the poor" are the scorners of the humble and lowly, and they are all grains of the same corn, of the devil's planting, all the world over. Perhaps the quaintest error which haunts the world in England and America is that so much of this stuff as is taught by rule or fashion as laws for "the *élite*" is the very nucleus of enlightenment and refinement, instead of its being a remnant of barbarism. And when we reflect on the degree to which this naïve and child-like faith exists in the United States, as shown by the enormous amount of information in certain newspapers as to what is the latest thing necessary to be done, acted, or suffered in order to be socially saved, I surmise that some future historian will record that we, being an envious people, turned out the Chinese, because we could not endure the presence among us of a race so vastly our superiors in all that constituted the true principles of culture and "custom."

Arthur Mitchell, in inquiring What is Civilization?[1] remarks that "all the things which gather round or grow upon a high state of civilization are not necessarily true parts of it. These conventionalities are often regarded as its very essence." And it is true that the greater the fool or snob, the deeper is the conviction that the conventional is the core of "culture." "'It is not genteel,' 'in good form,' or 'the mode,' to do this or do that, or say this or say that."

[1] *The Past in the Present,* part 2, lect. 3.

14

"Such things are spoken of as marks of a high civilization, or by those who do not confound civilization with culture as differentiators between the cultured and the uncultured." Dr. Mitchell "neither praises nor condemns these things;" but it is well for a man, while he is about it, to know his own mind, and I, for myself, condemn them with all my heart and soul, whenever anybody declares that such brass counters in the game of life are real gold, and insists that I shall accept them as such. For small play in a very small way with small people, I would endure them; but many men and nearly all women make their capital of them. And whatever may be said in their favor, it cannot be denied that they constantly lead to lying and heartlessness. Even Dr. Mitchell, while he says he does not condemn them, proceeds immediately to declare that "while we submit to them they constitute a sort of tyranny, under which we fret and secretly pine for escape. Does not the exquisite of Rotten Row weary for his flannel shirt and shooting-jacket? Do not 'well-constituted' men want to fish and shoot or kill something, themselves, by climbing mountains, when they can find nothing else? In short, does it not appear that these conventionalities are irksome, and are disregarded when the chance presents itself? And does it not seem as if there were something in human nature pulling men back to a rude and simple life?" To find that *men* suffer under the conventionalities, "adds, on the whole," says our canny, prudent Scot, "to the respectability of human nature." *Tu ha ragione* (right you are), Dr. Mitchell, there. For the conventional, whether found among Fijians as they were, or in Mayfair as it is, whenever it is vexatious and merely serves as a

cordon to separate "sassiety" from society, detracts
from the respectability of humanity, and is in itself
vulgar. If every man in society were a gentleman
and every woman a lady, there would be no more
conventionalism. *Usus est tyrannus* (custom is a ty-
rant), or, as the Talmud proverb saith, "Custom is the
plague of wise men, but is the idol of fools." And
he was a wise Jew, whoever he was, who declared it.

But let us return to our black sheep, the gypsy.
While happy in not being conventional, and while
rejoicing, or at least unconsciously enjoying freedom
from the bonds of etiquette, he agrees with the Chinese, red Indians, May Fairies, and Fifth Avenoodles
in manifesting under the most trying circumstances
that imperturbability which was once declared by an
eminent Philadelphian to be "the Corinthian ornament of a gentleman." He who said this builded
better than he knew, for the ornament in question, if
purely Corinthian, is simply brass. One morning I
was sauntering with the Palmer in Aberystwith,
when we met with a young and good-looking gypsy
woman, with whom we entered into conversation,
learning that she was a Bosville, and acquiring other
items of news as to Egypt and the roads, and then
left.

We had not gone far before we found a tinker.
He who catches a tinker has got hold of half a gypsy
and a whole cosmopolite, however bad the catch may
be. He did not understand the greeting *Sarishan!*
— he really could not remember to have heard it.
He did not know any gypsies, — "he could not get
along with them." They were a bad lot. He had
seen some gypsies three weeks before on the road.
They were curious dark people, who lived in tents.
He could not talk Romany.

This was really pitiable. It was too much. The Palmer informed him that he was wasting his best opportunities, and that it was a great pity that any man who lived on the roads should be so ignorant. The tinker never winked. In the goodness of our hearts we even offered to give him lessons in the *kalo jib*, or black language. The grinder was as calm as a Belgravian image. And as we turned to depart the professor said, —

"*Mandy'd del tute a shahori to pi moro kammaben, if tute jinned sa mandi pukkers.*" (I'd give you a sixpence to drink our health, if you knew what I am saying.)

With undisturbed gravity the tinker replied, —

"Now I come to think of it, I do remember to have heard somethin' in the parst like that. It's a convivial expression arskin' me if I won't have a tanner for ale. Which I will."

"Now since you take such an interest in gypsies," I answered, "it is a pity that you should know so little about them. I have seen them since you have. I saw a nice young woman, one of the Bosvilles here, not half an hour ago. Shall I introduce you?"

"That young woman," remarked the tinker, with the same immovable countenance, "is my wife. And I've come down here, by app'intment, to meet some Romany pals."

And having politely accepted his sixpence, the griddler went his way, tinkling his bell, along the road. He did not disturb himself that his first speeches did not agree with his last; he was not in the habit of being disturbed about anything, and he knew that no one ever learned Romany without learning with it not to be astonished at any little inconsistencies. Serene

and polished as a piece of tin in the sunshine, he would
not stoop to be put out by trifles. He was a typical
tinker. He knew that the world had made up proverbs expressing the utmost indifference either for a
tinker's blessing or a tinker's curse, and he retali-
ated by not caring a curse whether the world blessed
or banned him. In all ages and in all lands the tinker
has always been the type of this droning indifference,
which goes through life bagpiping its single melody,
or whistling, like the serene Marquis de Crabs, " Tou-
jours Santerre."

> " Es ist und bleibt das alte Lied
> Von dem ver-off'nen Pfannenschmied,
> Und wer's nicht weiter singen kann,
> Der fang's von Vorne wieder an."

> 'T will ever be the same old song
> Of tipsy tinkers all day long,
> And he who cannot sing it more
> May sing it over, as before.

I should have liked to know John Bunyan. As a
half-blood gypsy tinker he must have been self-con-
tained and pleasant. He had his wits about him, too,
in a very Romanly way. When confined in prison
he made a flute or pipe out of the leg of his three
legged-stool, and would play on it to pass time. When
the jailer entered to stop the noise, John replaced the
leg in the stool, and sat on it looking innocent as only
a gypsy tinker could, — calm as a summer morning.
I commend the subject for a picture. Very recently,
that is, in the beginning of 1881, a man of the same
tinkering kind, and possibly of the same blood as
Honest John, confined in the prison of Moyamen-
sing, Philadelphia, did nearly the same thing, only
that instead of making his stool leg into a musical

pipe he converted it into a pipe for tobacco. But
when the watchman, led by the smell, entered his cell,
there was no pipe to be found; only a deeply injured
man complaining that "somebody had been smokin'
outside, and it had blowed into his cell through the
door-winder from the corridore, and p'isoned the atmosphere. And he did n't like it." And thus history
repeats itself. 'T is all very well for the sticklers for
Wesleyan gentility to deny that John Bunyan was a
gypsy, but he who in his life cannot read Romany
between the lines knows not the jib nor the cut
thereof. Tough was J. B., "and de-vil-ish sly," and
altogether a much better man than many suppose
him to have been.

The tinker lived with his wife in a "tramps' lodging-house" in the town. To those Americans who
know such places by the abominable dens which are
occasionally reported by American grand juries, the
term will suggest something much worse than it is.
In England the average tramp's lodging is cleaner,
better regulated, and more orderly than many Western "hotels." The police look closely after it, and
do not allow more than a certain number in a room.
They see that it is frequently cleaned, and that clean
sheets are frequently put on the beds. One or two
hand-organs in the hall, with a tinker's barrow or
wheel, proclaimed the character of the lodgers, and in
the sitting-room there were to be found, of an evening,
gypsies, laborers with their families seeking work,
or itinerant musicians. I can recall a powerful and
tall young man, with a badly expressive face, one-
legged, and well dressed as a sailor. He was a beggar, who measured the good or evil of all mankind
by what they gave him. He was very bitter as to

the bad. Yet this house was in its way upper class.
It was not a den of despair, dirt, and misery, and even
the Italians who came there were obliged to be decent
and clean. It would not have been appropriate to
have written for them on the door, " *Voi che intrate
lasciate ogni speranza.*" (He who enters here leaves
soap behind.) The most painful fact which struck
me, in my many visits, was the intelligence and decency of some of the boarders. There was more than
one who conversed in a manner which indicated an
excellent early education; more than one who read
the newspaper aloud and commented on it to the company, as any gentleman might have done. Indeed,
the painful part of life as shown among these poor
people was the manifest fact that so many of them
had come down from a higher position, or were qualified for it. And this is characteristic of such places.
In his " London Labour and the London Poor," vol.
i. p. 217, Mahew tells of a low lodging-house " in
which there were at one time five university men,
three surgeons, and several sorts of broken-down
clerks." The majority of these cases are the result
of parents having risen from poverty and raised their
families to "gentility." The sons are deprived by
their bringing up of the vulgar pluck and coarse energy by which the father rose, and yet are expected to
make their way in the world, with nothing but a so-
called " education," which is too often less a help
than a hindrance. In the race of life no man is so
heavily handicapped as a young " gentleman." The
humblest and raggedest of all the inmates of this
house were two men who got their living by *shelkin
gallopas* (or selling ferns), as it is called in the Shelta,
or tinker's and tramp's slang. One of these, whom I

have described in another chapter as teaching me this dialect, could conjugate a French verb; we thought he had studied law. The other was a poor old fellow called Krooty, who could give the Latin names for all the plants which he gathered and sold, and who would repeat poetry very appropriately, proving sufficiently that he had read it. Both the fern-sellers spoke better English than divers Lord Mayors and Knights to whom I have listened, for they neither omitted *h* like the lowly, nor *r* like the lofty ones of London.

The tinker's wife was afflicted with a nervous disorder, which caused her great suffering, and made it almost impossible for her to sell goods, or contribute anything to the joint support. Her husband always treated her with the greatest kindness; I have seldom seen an instance in which a man was more indulgent and gentle. He made no display whatever of his feelings; it was only little by little that I found out what a heart this imperturbable rough of the road possessed. Now the Palmer, who was always engaged in some wild act of unconscious benevolence, bought for her some medicine, and gave her an order on the first physician in the town for proper advice; the result being a decided amelioration of her health. And I never knew any human being to be more sincerely grateful than the tinker was for this kindness. Ascertaining that I had tools for wood-carving, he insisted on presenting me with crocus powder, " to put an edge on." He had a remarkably fine whetstone, " the best in England; it was worth half a sovereign," and this he often and vainly begged me to accept. And he had a peculiar little trick of relieving his kindly feelings. Whenever we dropped in of an evening to the lodging-house, he would cunningly borrow my knife, and then disappear. Presently the *whiz-whiz, st'st* of his wheel would be heard without, and then the artful dodger would reappear with a triumphant smile, and with the knife sharpened to a razor edge. Anent which gratitude I shall have more to say anon.

One day I was walking on the Front, when I overtook a gypsy van, loaded with baskets and mats, lumbering along. The proprietor, who was a stranger to me, was also slightly or lightly lumbering in his gait, being cheerfully beery, while his berry brown wife, with a little three-year-old boy, peddled wares from door to door. Both were amazed and pleased at being accosted in Romany. In the course of conversation they showed great anxiety as to their child, who had long suffered from some disorder which caused them great alarm. The man's first name was Anselo, though it was painted Onslow on his vehicle. Mr. Anselo, though himself just come to town, was at once deeply impressed with the duty of hospitality to a Romany rye. I had called him *pal*, and this in gypsydom involves the shaking of hands, and with the better class an extra display of courtesy. He produced half a crown, and declared his willingness to devote it all to beer for my benefit. I declined, but he repeated his offer several times, — not with any annoying display, but with a courteous earnestness, intended to set forth a sweet sincerity. As I bade him good-by, he put the crown-piece into one eye, and as he danced backward, gypsy fashion up the street and vanished in the sunny purple twilight towards the sea I could see him winking with the other, and hear him cry, " Don't say no — now's the last chance — do I hear a bid ? "

We found this family in due time at the lodging-house, where the little boy proved to be indeed seriously ill, and we at once discovered that the parents, in their ignorance, had quite misunderstood his malady and were aggravating it by mal-treatment. To these poor people the good Palmer also gave an order on the old physician, who declared that the boy must have died in a few days, had he not taken charge of him. As it was, the little fellow was speedily cured. There was, it appeared, some kind of consanguinity between the tinker or his wife and the Anselo family. These good people, anxious to do anything, yet able to do little, consulted together as to showing their gratitude, and noting that we were specially desirous of collecting old gypsy words gave us all they could think of, and without informing us of their intention, which indeed we only learned by accident a long time after, sent a messenger many miles to bring to Aberystwith a certain Bosville, who was famed as being deep in Romany lore, and in possession of many ancient words. Which was indeed true, he having been the first to teach us *pisāli*, meaning a saddle, and in which Professor Cowell, of Cambridge, promptly detected the Sanskrit for sit-upon, the same double meaning also existing in *boshto*; or, as old Mrs. Buckland said to me at Oaklands Park, in Philadelphia, "a *pisāli* is the same thing with a *boshto*."

"What will gain thy faith?" said Quentin Durward to Hayradden Maugrabhin. "Kindness," answered the gypsy.

The joint families, solely with intent to please us, although they never said a word about it, next sent for a young Romany, one of the Lees, and his wife, whom they supposed we would like to meet. Walking along the Front, I met the tinker's wife with the handsomest Romany girl I ever beheld. In a London ball-room or on the stage she would have been a really startling beauty. This was young Mrs. Lee. Her husband was a clever violinist, and it was very remarkable that when he gave himself up to playing, with *abandon* or self-forgetfulness, there came into his melodies the same wild gypsy expression, the same chords and tones, which abound in the music of the Austrian Tsigane. It was not my imagination which prompted the recognition; the Palmer also observed it, without thinking it remarkable. From the playing of both Mat Woods and young Lee, I am sure that there has survived among the Welsh gypsies some of the spirit of their old Eastern music, just as in the solo dancing of Mat's sister there was precisely the same kind of step which I had seen in Moscow. Among the hundreds of the race whom I have met in Great Britain, I have never known any young people who were so purely Romany as these. The tinker and Anselo with his wife had judged wisely that we would be pleased with this picturesque couple. They always seemed to me in the house like two wild birds, and tropical ones at that, in a cage. There was a tawny-gold, black and scarlet tone about them and their garb, an Indian Spanish duskiness and glow which I loved to look at.

Every proceeding of the tinker and Anselo was veiled in mystery and hidden in the obscurity so dear to such grown-up children, but as I observed after a few days that Lee did nothing beyond acting as assistant to the tinker at the wheel, I surmised that the visit was solely for our benefit. As the tinker

was devoted to his poor wife, so was Anselo and his
dame devoted to their child. He was, indeed, a brave
little fellow, and frequently manifested the precocious
pluck and sturdiness so greatly admired by the Romanys of the road; and when he would take a whip and
lead the horse, or in other ways show his courage,
the delight of his parents was in its turn delightful.
They would look at the child as if charmed, and then
at one another with feelings too deep for words, and
then at me for sympathetic admiration.

The keeper of the house where they lodged was
in his way a character and a linguist. Welsh was
his native tongue and English his second best. He
also knew others, such as Romany, of which he was
proud, and the Shelta or Minklas of the tinkers, of
which he was not. The only language which he
knew of which he was really ashamed was Italian,
and though he could maintain a common conversation in it he always denied that he remembered more
than a few words. For it was not as the tongue of
Dante, but as the lingo of organ-grinders and such
"catenone" that he knew it, and I think that the
Palmer and I lost dignity in his eyes by inadvertently
admitting that it was familiar to us. "I should n't
have thought it," was all his comment on the discovery, but I knew his thought, and it was that we
had made ourselves unnecessarily familiar with vulgarity.

It is not every one who is aware of the extent to
which Italian is known by the lower orders in London. It is not spoken as a language; but many of
its words, sadly mangled, are mixed with English as
a jargon. Thus the Italian *scappare*, to escape, or
run away, has become *scarper;* and a dweller in the

Seven Dials has been heard to say he would "*scarper* with the *feele* of the *donna* of the *cassey;*" which means, run away with the daughter of the landlady of the house, and which, as the editor of the Slang Dictionary pens, is almost pure Italian, — *scappare colla figlia della donna della casa.* Most costermongers call a penny a *saltee,* from *soldo ;* a crown, a *caroon ;* and one half, *madza,* from *mezza.* They count as follows : —

	ITALIAN.
Oney saltee, a penny	Uno soldo.
Dooey saltee, twopence	Dui soldi.
Tray saltee, threepence	Tre soldi.
Quarterer saltee, fourpence	Quattro soldi.
Chinker saltee, fivepence	Cinque soldi.
Say saltee, sixpence	Sei soldi.
Say oney saltee, or setter saltee, seven-pence	Sette soldi.
Say dooee saltee, or otter saltee, eight-pence	Otto soldi.
Say tray saltee, or nobba saltee, nine-pence	Nove soldi.
Say quarterer saltee, or dacha (datsha) saltee, tenpence	Dieci soldi.
Say chinker saltee, or dacha one saltee, elevenpence	Dieci uno soldi
Oney beong, one shilling	Uno bianco.
A beong say saltee, one shilling and sixpence	Uno bianco sei soldi.
Madza caroon, half a crown	Mezza corona.

Mr. Hotten says that he could never discover the derivation of *beong,* or *beonk.* It is very plainly the Italian *bianco,* white, which, like *blanc* in French and *blank* in German, is often applied slangily to a silver coin. It is as if one had said, "a shiner." Apropos

of which word there is something curious to be noted.
It came forth in evidence, a few years ago in England,
that burglars or other thieves always carried with
them a piece of coal ; and on this disclosure, a certain
writer, in his printed collection of curiosities, comments as if it were a superstition, remarking that the
coal is carried for an amulet. But the truth is that
the thief has no such idea. The coal is simply a
sign for money ; and when the bearer meets with a
man whom he thinks may be a " fence," or a purchaser of stolen goods, he shows the coal, which is
as much as to say, Have you money ? Money, in
vulgar gypsy, is *wongur*, a corruption of the better
word *angar*, which also means a hot coal; and *braise*,
in French *argôt*, has the same double meaning. I
may be wrong, but I suspect that *rat*, a dollar in
Hebrew, or at least in Schmussen, has its root in
common with *ratzafim*, coals, and possibly *poschit*, a
farthing, with *pecham*, coal. In the six kinds of fire
mentioned in the Talmud,[1] there is no identification
of coals with money ; but in the German legends of
Rubezahl, there is a tale of a charcoal-burner who
found them changed to gold. Coins are called shiners
because they shine like glowing coals, and I dare say
that the simile exists in many more languages.

One twilight we found in the public sitting-room
of the lodging-house a couple whom I can never forget. It was an elderly gypsy and his wife. The
husband was himself characteristic ; the wife was
more than merely picturesque. I have never met
such a superb old Romany as she was ; indeed, I doubt
if I ever saw any woman of her age, in any land or
any range of life, with a more magnificently proud

[1] *Yoma*, fol. 21, col. 2.

expression or such unaffected dignity. It was the whole poem of " Crescentius " living in modern time in other form.

When a scholar associates much with gypsies there is developed in him in due time a perception or intuition of certain kinds of men or minds, which it is as difficult to describe as it is wonderful. He who has read Matthew Arnold's " Gipsy Scholar " may, however, find therein many apt words for it. I mean very seriously what I say ; I mean that through the Romany the demon of Socrates acquires distinctness ; I mean that a faculty is developed which is as strange as divination, and which is greatly akin to it. The gypsies themselves apply it directly to palmistry ; were they well educated they would feel it in higher forms. It may be reached among other races and in other modes, and Nature is always offering it to us freely ; but it seems to live, or at least to be most developed, among the Romany. It comes upon the possessor far more powerfully when in contact with certain lives than with others, and with the sympathetic it takes in at a glance that which may employ it at intervals for years to think out.

And by this *dūk* I read in a few words in the Romany woman an eagle soul, caged between the bars of poverty, ignorance, and custom ; but a great soul for all that. Both she and her husband were of the old type of their race, now so rare in England, though commoner in America. They spoke Romany with inflection and conjugation ; they remembered the old rhymes and old words, which I quoted freely, with the Palmer. Little by little, the old man seemed to be deeply impressed, indeed awed, by our utterly inexplicable knowledge. I wore a velveteen coat, and had on a broad, soft felt hat.

"You talk as the old Romanys did," said the old man. "I hear you use words which I once heard from old men who died when I was a boy. I thought those words were lying in graves which have long been green. I hear songs and sayings which I never expected to hear again. You talk like gypsies, and such gypsies as I never meet now; and you look like Gorgios. But when I was still young, a few of the oldest Romany *chals* still wore hats such as you have; and when I first looked at you, I thought of them. I don't understand you. It is strange, very strange."

"It is the Romany *soul*," said his wife. "People take to what is in them; if a bird were born a fox, it would love to fly."

I wondered what flights she would have taken if she had wings. But I understood why the old man had spoken as he did; for, knowing that we had intelligent listeners, the Palmer and I had brought forth all our best and quaintest Romany curios, and these rural Welsh wanderers were not, like their English pals, familiar with Romany ryes. And I was moved to like them, and nobody perceives this sooner than a gypsy. The old couple were the parents of young Lee, and said they had come to visit him; but I think that it was rather to see us that we owed their presence in Aberystwith. For the tinker and Anselo were at this time engaged, in their secret and owl-like manner, as befitted men who were up to all manner of ways that were dark, in collecting the most interesting specimens of Romanys, for our especial study; and whenever this could be managed so that it appeared entirely accidental and a surprise, then they retired into their shadowed souls and chuckled with fiendish glee at having managed things so charmingly. But it will be long ere I forget how the old man's eye looked into the past as he recalled, —

> "The hat of antique shape and coat of gray,
> The same the gypsies wore,"

and went far away back through my words to words heard in the olden time, by fires long since burnt out, beneath the flame-gilt branches of forests which have sailed away as ships, farther than woods e'er went from Dunsinane, and been wrecked in Southern seas. But though I could not tell exactly what was in every room, I knew into what house his soul had gone ; and it was for this that the scholar-gypsy went from Oxford halls "to learn strange arts and join a gypsy tribe." His friends had gone from earth long since, and were laid to sleep ; some, perhaps, far in the wold and wild, amid the rocks, where fox and wild bird were their visitors ; but for an instant they rose again from their graves, and I knew them.

"They could do wonders by the power of the imagination," says Glanvil of the gypsies ; "their fancy binding that of others." Understand by imagination and fancy all that Glanvil really meant, and I agree with him. It is a matter of history that, since the Aryan morning of mankind, the Romanys have been chiromancing, and, following it, trying to read people's minds and bind them to belief. Thousands of years of transmitted hereditary influences always result in something ; it has really resulted with the gypsies in an instinctive, though undeveloped, intuitive

15

perception, which a sympathetic mind acquires from them, — nay, is compelled to acquire, out of mere self-defense; and when gained, it manifests itself in many forms,

"But it needs heaven-sent moments for this skill."

AMERICAN GYPSIES.

I.

GYPSIES IN PHILADELPHIA.

I⊤ is true that the American gypsy has grown more
vigorous in this country, and, like many plants, has
thriven better for being trans — I was about to write
incautiously *ported*, but, on second thought, say
planted. Strangely enough, he is more Romany than
ever. I have had many opportunities of studying
both the elders from England and the younger gypsies, born of English parents, and I have found that
there is unquestionably a great improvement in the
race here, even from a gypsy stand-point. The young
sapling, under more favorable influences, has pushed
out from the old root, and grown stronger. The
causes for this are varied. Gypsies, like peacocks,
thrive best when allowed to range afar. *Il faut leur
donner le clef des champs* (you must give them the
key of the fields), as I once heard an old Frenchman,
employed on Delmonico's Long Island farm, lang
syne, say of that splendid poultry. And what a
range they have, from the Atlantic to the Pacific!
Marry, sir, 't is like roaming from sunrise to sunset,
east and west, "and from the aurora borealis to a
Southern blue-jay," and no man shall make them
afraid. Wood! " Well, 't is a *kushto tem for kāsht*"

(a fair land for timber), as a very decent *Romani-chal* said to me one afternoon. It was thinking of him which led me to these remarks.

I had gone with my niece — who speaks Romany — out to a gypsyry by Oaklands Park, and found there one of our good people, with his wife and chil dren, in a tent. Hard by was the wagon and the horse, and, after the usual initiatory amazement at being accosted in the *kālo jib*, or black language, had been survived, we settled down into conversation. It was a fine autumnal day, Indian-summery, — the many in one of all that is fine in weather all the world over, put into a single glorious sense, — a sense of bracing air and sunshine not over-bold or bright, and purple, tawny hues in western skies, and dim, sweet feelings of the olden time. And as we sat lounging in lowly seats, and talked about the people and their ways, it seemed to me as if I were again in Devonshire or Surrey. Our host — for every gypsy who is visited treats you as a guest, thus much Oriental politeness being deeply set in him — had been in America from boyhood, but he seemed to be perfectly acquainted with all whom I had known over the sea. Only one thing he had not heard, the death of old Gentilla Cooper, of the Devil's Dyke, near Brighton, for I had just received a letter from England announcing the sad news.

" Yes, this America is a good country for travelers. *We can go South in winter.* Aye, the land is big enough to go to a warm side in winter, and a cool one in summer. But I don't go South, because I don't like the people ; I don't get along with them. *Some Romanys do.* Yes, but I 'm not on that horse. I hear that the old country 's getting to be a hard

place for our people. Yes, just as you say, there's
no *tan to hatch*, no place to stay in there, unless you
pay as much as if you went to a hotel. 'T is n't so
here. Some places they 're uncivil, but mostly we
can get wood and water, and a place for a tent, and
a bite for the old *gry* [horse]. The country people
like to see us come, in many places. They 're more
high-minded and hon'rable here than they are in
England. If we can cheat them in horse-dealin' they
stand it as gentlemen always ought to do among
themselves in such games. Horse-dealin' is horse-
stealin', in a way, among real gentlemen. If I can
Jew you or you do me, it's all square in gamblin',
and nobody has any call to complain. Therefore, I
allow that Americans are higher up as gentlemen
than what they are in England. It is not all of one
side, like a jug-handle, either. Many of these American farmers can cheat me, and have done it, and are
proud of it. Oh, yes; they 're much higher toned
here. In England, if you put off a *bavolengro* [broken-
winded horse] on a fellow he comes after you with a
chinamāngri [writ]. Here he goes like a man and
swindles somebody else with the *gry*, instead of sneak-
ing off to a magistrate.

"Yes," he continued, "England's a little country, very little, indeed, but it is astonishing how many
Romanys come out of it over here. *Do I notice any
change in them after coming?* I do. When they
first come, they drink liquor or beer all the time.
After a while they stop heavy drinking."

I may here observe that even in England the gypsy, although his getting drunk is too often regulated
or limited simply by his means, seldom shows in his
person the results of long-continued intemperance.

Living in the open air, taking much exercise, constantly practicing boxing, rough riding, and other manly sports, he is " as hard as nails," and generally lives to a hearty old age.   As he very much prefers beer to spirits, it may be a question whether excess in such drinking is really any serious injury to him. The ancestors of the common English peasants have for a thousand, it may be for two thousand, years or more all got drunk on beer, whenever they could afford it, and yet a more powerful human being than the English peasant does not exist.   It may be that the weaklings all die at an early age.   This I cannot deny, nor that those who survive are simply so tough that beer cannot kill them.   What this gypsy said of the impartial and liberal manner in which he and his kind are received by the farmers is also true.   I once conversed on this subject with a gentleman farmer, and his remarks were much like those of the Rom. I inferred from what he said that the coming of a party of gypsy horse-dealers into his neighborhood was welcomed much as the passengers on a Southern steamboat were wont of old to welcome the proprietor of a portable faro bank.   " I think," said he, " that the last time the gypsies were here they left more than they took away."   An old Rom told me once that in some parts of New Jersey they were obliged to watch their tents and wagons very carefully for fear of the country people.   I do not answer for the truth of this.   It speaks vast volumes for the cleverness of gypsies that they can actually make a living by trading horses in New Spain.

It is very true that in many parts of America the wanderers are welcomed with *feux de joie*, or with salutes of shot-guns, — the guns, unfortunately, being shotted and aimed at them. I have mentioned in another chapter, on a Gypsy Magic Spell, that once in Tennessee, when an old Romany mother had succeeded in hoaxing a farmer's wife out of all she had in the world, the neighboring farmers took the witch, and, with a view to preventing effectually further depredation, caused her to pass " through flames material and temporal unto flames immaterial and eternal ; " that is to say, they burned her alive. But the gypsy would much prefer having to deal with lynchers than with lawyers. Like the hedge-hog, which is typically a gypsy animal, he likes better to be eaten by those of his own kind than to be crushed into dirt by those who do not understand him. This story of the hedge-hog was cited from my first gypsy book by Sir Charles Dilke, in a speech in which he made an application of it to certain conservatives who remained blindly suffering by their own party. It will hold good forever. Gypsies never flourished so in Europe as during the days when every man's hand was against them. It is said that they raided and plundered about Scotland for fifty years before they were definitely discovered to be mere marauders, for the Scots themselves were so much given up to similar pursuits that the gypsies passed unnoticed.

The American gypsies do not beg, like their English brothers, and particularly their English sisters. This fact speaks volumes for their greater prosperity and for the influence which association with a proud race has on the poorest people. Our friends at Oaklands always welcomed us as guests. On another occasion when we went there, I said to my niece, " If we find strangers who do not know us, do not speak at first in Romany. Let us astonish them." We came to a tent, before which sat a very dark, old-fashioned gypsy woman. I paused before her, and said in English, —

" Can you tell a fortune for a young lady? "

" She don't want her fortune told," replied the old woman, suspiciously and cautiously, or it may be with a view of drawing us on. "No, I can't tell fortunes."

At this the young lady was so astonished that, without thinking of what she was saying, or in what language, she cried, —

" *Dordi! Can't tute pen dukkerin?* " (Look! Can't you tell fortunes?)

This unaffected outburst had a greater effect than the most deeply studied theatrical situation could have brought about. The old dame stared at me and at the lady as if bewildered, and cried, —

" In the name of God, what kind of gypsies are *you?* "

" Oh! *mendui shom bori chovihani!* " cried L., laughing; "we are a great witch and a wizard, and if you can't tell me my fortune, I'll tell yours. Hold out your hand, and cross mine with a dollar, and I'll tell you as big a lie as you ever *penned* a *galderli Gorgio* [a green Gentile]."

"Well," exclaimed the gypsy, "I'll believe that you can tell fortunes or do anything! *Dordi! dordi!* but this is wonderful. Yet you 're not the first Romany *rāni* [lady] I ever met. There 's one in Delaware: a *boridiri* [very great] lady she is, and true Romany, —*flick o the jib te rinkeni adosta* [quick of tongue and fair of face]. Well, I am glad to see you."

" Who is that talking there? " cried a man's voice

from within the tent. He had heard Romany, and he spoke it, and came out expecting to see familiar faces. His own was a study, as his glance encountered mine. As soon as he understood that I came as a friend, he gave way to infinite joy, mingled with sincerest grief that he had not at hand the means of displaying hospitality to such distinguished Romanys as we evidently were. He bewailed the absence of strong drink. Would we have some tea made? Would I accompany him to the next tavern, and have some beer? All at once a happy thought struck him. He went into the tent and brought out a piece of tobacco, which I was compelled to accept. Refusal would have been unkind, for it was given from the very heart. George Borrow tells us that, in Spain, a poor gypsy once brought him a pomegranate as a first acquaintanceship token. A gypsy is a gypsy wherever you find him.

These were very nice people. The old dame took a great liking to L., and showed it in pleasant manners. The couple were both English, and liked to talk with me of the old country and the many mutual friends whom we had left behind. On another visit, L. brought a scarlet silk handkerchief, which she had bound round her head and tied under her chin in a very gypsy manner. It excited, as I anticipated, great admiration from the old dame.

"*Ah kennā tute dikks rinkeni*—now you look nice. That's the way a Romany lady ought to wear it! Don't she look just as Alfi used to look?" she cried to her husband. "Just such eyes and hair!"

Here L. took off the *diklo*, or handkerchief, and passed it round the gypsy woman's head, and tied it under her chin, saying, —

"I am sure it becomes you much more than it does me. Now you look nice : —

"'Red and yellow for Romany,
And blue and pink for the Gorgiee.'"

We rose to depart, the old dame offered back to L. her handkerchief, and, on being told to keep it, was greatly pleased. I saw that the way in which it was given had won her heart.

"Did you hear what the old woman said while she was telling your fortune?" asked L., after we had left the tent.

"Now, I think of it, I remember that she or you had hold of my hand, while I was talking with the old man, and he was making merry with my whisky. I was turned away, and around so that I never noticed what you two were saying."

"She *penned* your *dukkerin*, and it was wonderful. She said that she must tell it."

And here L. told me what the old *dye* had insisted on reading in my hand. It was simply very remarkable, and embraced an apparent knowledge of the past, which would make any credulous person believe in her happy predictions of the future.

"Ah, well," I said, "I suppose the *dukk* told it to her. She may be an eye-reader. A hint dropped here and there, unconsciously, the expression of the face, and a life's practice will make anybody a witch. And if there ever was a witch's eye, she has it."

"I would like to have her picture," said L., "in that *lullo diklo* [red handkerchief]. She looked like all the sorceresses of Thessaly and Egypt in one, and, as Bulwer says of the Witch of Vesuvius, was all the more terrible for having been beautiful."

Some time after this we went, with Britannia Lee,

a-gypsying, not figuratively, but literally, over the river into New Jersey. And our first greeting, as we touched the ground, was of good omen, and from a great man, for it was Walt Whitman. It is not often that even a poet meets with three sincerer admirers than the venerable bard encountered on this occasion ; so, of course, we stopped and talked, and L. had the pleasure of being the first to communicate to Bon Gualtier certain pleasant things which had recently been printed of him by a distinguished English author, which is always an agreeable task. Blessed upon the mountains, or at the Camden ferryboat, or anywhere, are the feet of anybody who bringeth glad tidings.

"Well, are you going to see gypsies?"

"We are. We three gypsies be. By the abattoir. *Au revoir.*"

And on we went to the place where I had first found gypsies in America. All was at first so still that it seemed if no one could be camped in the spot.

"*Se kekno adoi.*" (There's nobody there.)

"*Dordi!*" cried Britannia, "*Dikkava me o tuv te tan te wardo.*] [I see a smoke, a tent, a wagon.] I declare, it is my *puro pal*, my old friend, W."

And we drew near the tent and greeted its owner, who was equally astonished and delighted at seeing such distinguished Romany *tāni rānis*, or gypsy young ladies, and brought forth his wife and three really beautiful children to do the honors. W. was a good specimen of an American-born gypsy, strong, healthy, clean, and temperate, none the worse for wear in out-of-dooring, through tropical summers and terrible winters. Like all American Romanys, he was more

straightforward than most of his race in Europe.
All Romanys are polite, but many of the European
kind are most uncomfortably and unconsciously naïve.
Strange that the most innocent people should be
those who most offend morality. I knew a lady
once — Heaven grant that I may never meet with
such another! — who had been perfectly educated
in entire purity of soul. And I never knew any
devergondée who could so shock, shame, and pain
decent people as this Agnes did in her sweet ignorance.

"I shall never forget the first day you came to my
camp," said W. to Britannia. "Ah, you astonished
me then. You might have knocked me down with a
feather. And I did n't know what to say. You
came in a carriage with two other ladies. And you
jumped out first, and walked up to me, and cried,
'*Sa'shān!*' That stunned me, but I answered,
'*Sa'shān*.' Then I did n't speak Romanes to you,
for I did n't know but what you kept it a secret
from the other two ladies, and I did n't wish to be-
tray you. And when you began to talk it as deep as
any old Romany I ever heard, and pronounced it so
rich and beautiful, I thought I 'd never heard the
like. I thought you must be a witch."

"*Awer me shom chovihani*" (but I am a witch),
cried the lady. "*Mukka men jā adré o tan.*" (Let
us go into the tent.) So we entered, and sat round the
fire, and asked news of all the wanderers of the roads,
and the young ladies, having filled their pockets with
sweets, produced them for the children, and we were
as much at home as we had ever been in any salon ;
for it was a familiar scene to us all, though it would,
perhaps, have been a strange one to the reader, had

he by chance, walking that lonely way in the twilight, looked into the tent and asked his way, and
there found two young ladies — *bien mises* — with
their escort, all very much at their ease, and talking
Romany as if they had never known any other tongue
from the cradle.

"What is the charm of all this?" It is that if one
has a soul, and does not live entirely reflected from
the little thoughts and little ways of a thousand other
little people, it is well to have at all times in his
heart some strong hold of nature. No matter how
much we may be lost in society, dinners, balls, business, we should never forget that there is an eternal
sky with stars over it all, a vast, mysterious earth with
terrible secrets beneath us, seas, mountains, rivers,
and forests away and around ; and that it is from
these and what is theirs, and not from gas-lit, stifling
follies, that all strength and true beauty must come.
To this life, odd as he is, the gypsy belongs, and to be
sometimes at home with him by wood and wold takes
us for a time from "the world." If I express myself vaguely and imperfectly, it is only to those who
know not the charm of nature, its ineffable soothing
sympathy, — its life, its love. Gypsies, like children,
feel this enchantment as the older grown do not. To
them it is a song without words ; would they be happier if the world brought them to know it as words
without song, without music or melody? I never read
a right old English ballad of sumere when the leaves
are grene or the not-broune maid, with its rustling as
of sprays quivering to the song of the wode-wale, without thinking or feeling deeply how those who wrote
them would have been bound to the Romany. It is
ridiculous to say that gypsies are not "educated"

to nature and art, when, in fact, they live it. I sometimes suspect that æsthetic culture takes more true love of nature out of the soul than it inspires. One would not say anything of a wild bird or deer being deficient in a sense of that beauty of which it is a part. There are infinite grades, kinds, or varieties of feeling of nature, and every man is perfectly satisfied that his is the true one. For my own part, I am not sure that a rabbit, in the dewy grass, does not feel the beauty of nature quite as much as Mr. Ruskin, and much more than I do.

No poet has so far set forth the charm of gypsy life better than Lenau has done, in his highly-colored, quickly-expressive ballad of " Die drei Zigeuner," of which I here give a translation into English and another into Anglo-American Romany.

THE THREE GYPSIES.

I saw three gypsy men, one day,
    Camped in a field together,
As my wagon went its weary way,
    All over the sand and heather.

And one of the three whom I saw there
    Had his fiddle just before him,
And played for himself a stormy air,
    While the evening-red shone o'er him.

And the second puffed his pipe again
    Serenely and undaunted,
As if he at least of earthly men
    Had all the luck that he wanted.

In sleep and comfort the last was laid,
    In a tree his cymbal [1] lying,
Over its strings the breezes played,
    O'er his heart a dream went flying.

---

[1] *Zimbel.* The cymbal of the Austrian gypsies is a stringed instrument, like the zitter.

Ragged enough were all the three,
　Their garments in holes and tatters ;
But they seemed to defy right sturdily
　The world and all worldly matters.

Thrice to the soul they seemed to say,
　When earthly trouble tries it,
How to fiddle, sleep it, and smoke it away,
　And so in three ways despise it.

And ever anon I look around,
　As my wagon onward presses,
At the gypsy faces darkly browned,
　And the long black flying tresses.

TRIN ROMANI CHALIA.

Dikdom me trin geeria
　Sār yeckno a tacho Rom,
Sā miro wardo ghias adūr
　Apré a wafedo drom.

O yeckto sos boshengero,
　Yuv kellde pes-kokero,
O kamlo-dūd te perelé
　Sos lullo apré lo.

O duito sār a swägele
　Dikde 'pré lestes tūv,
Ne kamde kūmi, penava mé
　'Dré sār o midúvels pūv.

O triuto sovadé kushto-bāk
　. Lest 'zimbel adré rukk se,
O bavol kelld' pré i tavia,
　O sutto 'pré leskro zī.

Te sār i lenghcri rūdaben
　Shan katterdi-chingerdo
Awer me penav' i Romani chals
　Ne kesserden chi pā lo.

Trin dromia leude sikkerden, kau
  Sār dikela wafedo,
Ta bosher, tuver te sove-a-lé
  Ajā sā bachtalo.

Dikdom palal, sā ghiom adūr
  Talla yeckno Romani chal
'Pré lengheri kāli-brauni mūi,
  Te lengheri kāli bal.

II.

THE CROCUS-PITCHER.[1]

(PHILADELPHIA.)

IT was a fine spring noon, and the corner of Fourth and Library streets in Philadelphia was like a rock in the turn of a rapid river, so great was the crowd of busy business men which flowed past. Just out of the current a man paused, put down a parcel which he carried, turned it into a table, placed on it several vials, produced a bundle of hand-bills, and began, in the language of his tribe, to *cant* — that is, *cantare*, to sing — the virtues of a medicine which was certainly *patent* in being spread out by him to extremest thinness. In an instant there were a hundred people round him. He seemed to be well known and waited for. I saw at a glance what he was. The dark eye and brown face indicated a touch of the *diddikai*, or one with a little gypsy blood in his veins, while his fluent patter and unabashed boldness showed a long familiarity with race-grounds and the road, or with the Cheap-Jack and Dutch auction business, and other pursuits requiring unlimited eloquence and impudence. How many a man of learning, nay of genius, might have paused and envied that vagabond the gifts which were worth so little to their possessor! But what was remarkable about him was that instead of endeavoring to conceal any gypsy

---

[1] *Crocus*, in common slang an itinerant quack, mountebank, or seller of medicine; *Pitcher*, a street dealer.

16

indications, they were manifestly exaggerated. He wore a broad-brimmed hat and ear-rings and a red embroidered waistcoat of the most forcible old Romany pattern, which was soon explained by his words.

"Sorry to keep you waiting," he said. "I am always sorry to detain a select and genteel audience. But I was detained myself by a very interesting incident. I was invited to lunch with a wealthy German gentleman ; a very wealthy German, I say, one of the pillars of your city and front door-step of your council, and who would be the steeple of your exchange, if it had one. And on arriving at his house he remarked, ' Toctor, by tam you koom yust in goot dime, for mine frau und die cook ish bote fall sick mit someding in a hoory, und I kess she 'll die pooty quick-sudden.' Unfortunately I had with me, gentlemen, but a single dose of my world-famous Gypsy's Elixir and Romany Pharmacopheionepenthé. (That is the name, gentlemen, but as I detest quackery I term it simply the Gypsy's Elixir.) When the German gentleman learned that in all probability but one life could be saved he said, ' Vell, denn, doctor, subbose you gifes dat dose to de cook. For mine frau ish so goot dat it 's all right mit her. She 's reaty to tie. But de boor gook ish a sinner, ash I knows, und not reaty for de next world. And dere ish no vomans in town dat can gook mine sauer-kraut ash she do.' Fortunately, gentlemen, I found in an unknown corner of a forgotten pocket an unsuspected bottle of the Gypsy's Elixir, and both interesting lives were saved with such promptitude, punctuality, neatness and dispatch that the cook proceeded immediately to conclude the preparation of our meal — (thank you, sir, — one dollar, if you please, sir. You say I only

charged half a dollar yesterday! That was for a
smaller bottle, sir. Same size, as this, was it? Ah,
yes, I gave you a large bottle by mistake, — so you
owe me fifty cents. Never mind, don't give it back.
I 'll take the half dollar.")

All of this had been spoken with the utmost volu-
bility. As I listened I almost fancied myself again
in England, and at a country fair. Taking in his
audience at a glance, I saw his eye rest on me ere it
flitted, and he resumed, —

"We gypsies are, as you know, a remarkable race,
and possessed of certain rare secrets, which have all
been formulated, concentrated, dictated, and plenipo-
tentiarated into this idealized Elixir. If I were a
mountebank or a charlatan I would claim that it
cures a hundred diseases. Charlatan is a French
word for a quack. I speak French, gentlemen; I
speak nine languages, and can tell you the Hebrew
for an old umbrella. The Gypsy's Elixir cures colds,
gout, all nervous affections, with such cutaneous disor-
ders as are diseases of the skin, debility, sterility,
hostility, and all the illities that flesh is heir to except
what it can't, such as small-pox and cholera. It has
cured cholera, but it don't claim to do it. Others
claim to cure, but can't. I am not a charlatan, but an
Ann-Eliza. That is the difference between me and a
lady, as the pig said when he astonished his missus
by blushing at her remarks to the postman. (*Better
have another bottle, sir. Have n't you the change?
Never mind, you can owe me fifty cents. I know a
gentleman when I see one.*) I was recently Down East
in Maine, where they are so patriotic, they all put the
stars and stripes into their beds for sheets, have the
Fourth of July three hundred and sixty-five times in

the year, and eat the Declaration of Independence for breakfast. And they would n't buy a bottle of my Gypsy's Elixir till they heard it was good for the Constitution, whereupon they immediately purchased my entire stock. Don't lose time in securing this invaluable blessing to those who feel occasional pains in the lungs. This is not taradiddle. I am engaged to lecture this afternoon before the Medical Association of Germantown, as on Wednesday before the University of Baltimore; for though I sell medicine here in the streets, it is only, upon my word of honor, that the poor may benefit, and the lowly as well as the learned know how to prize the philanthropic and eccentric gypsy."

He run on with his patter for some time in this vein, and sold several vials of his panacea, and then in due time ceased, and went into a bar-room, which I also entered. I found him in what looked like prospective trouble, for a policeman was insisting on purchasing his medicine, and on having one of his hand-bills. He was remonstrating, when I quietly said to him in Romany, "Don't trouble yourself; you were not making any disturbance." He took no apparent notice of what I said beyond an almost imperceptible wink, but soon left the room, and when I had followed him into the street, and we were out of ear-shot, he suddenly turned on me and said, —

"Well, you *are* a swell, for a Romany. How do you do it up to such a high peg?"

"Do what?"

"Do the whole lay, — look so gorgeous?"

"Why, I'm no better dressed than you are, — not so well, if you come to that *vongree*" (waistcoat).

"'T is n't *that*, — 't is n't the clothes. It's the air

and the style. Anybody 'd believe you 'd had no end
of an education. I could make ten dollars a patter if
I could do it as natural as you do. Perhaps you 'd
like to come in on halves with me as a bonnet. *No?*
Well, I suppose you have a better line. You 've been
lucky. I tell you, you astonished me when you *rakkered*, though I spotted you in the crowd for one who
was off the color of the common Gorgios, — or, as the
Yahudi say, the *Goyim*. No, I carn't *rakker*, or none
to speak of, and noways as deep as you, though I was
born in a tent on Battersea Common and grew up a
fly fakir. What 's the drab made of that I sell in
these bottles? Why, the old fake, of course, — you
need n't say *you* don't know that. *I talk good English.*
Yes, I know I do. A fakir is bothered out of his life
and chaffed out of half his business when he drops his
h's. A man can do anything when he must, and I
must talk fluently and correctly to succeed in such a
business. *Would I like a drop of something?* You
paid for the last, now you must take a drop with me.
Do I know of any Romanys in town? Lots of them.
There is a ken in Lombard Street with a regular fly
mort, — but on second thoughts we won't go there, —
and — oh, I say — a very nice place in —— Street.
The landlord is a Yahud; his wife can *rakker* you,
I 'm sure. *She 's a good lot, too.*"

And while on the way I will explain that my acquaintance was not to be regarded as a real gypsy.
He was one of that large nomadic class with a tinge
of gypsy blood who have grown up as waifs and strays,
and who, having some innate cleverness, do the best
they can to live without breaking the law — much.
They deserve pity, for they have never been cared
for; they owe nothing to society for kindness, and

yet they are held even more strictly to account by the law than if they had been regularly Sunday-schooled from babyhood. This man when he spoke of Romanys did not mean real gypsies; he used the word as it occurs in Ainsworth's song of

> "Nix my dolly, pals fake away.
> And here I am both tight and free,
> A regular rollicking Romany."

For he meant *Bohemian* in its widest and wildest sense, and to him all that was apart from the world was *his* world, whether it was Rom or Yahudi, and whether it conversed in Romany or Schmussen, or any other tongue unknown to the Gentiles. He had indeed no home, and had never known one.

It was not difficult to perceive that the place to which he led me was devoted in the off hours to some other business besides the selling of liquor. It was neat and quiet, in fact rather sleepy; but its card, which was handed to me, stated in a large capital head-line that it was OPEN ALL NIGHT, and that there was pool at all hours. I conjectured that a little game might also be performed there at all hours, and that, like the fountain of Jupiter Ammon, it became livelier as it grew later, and that it certainly would not be on the full boil before midnight.

"*Scheiker für mich, der Isch will jain soreff shaske-nen*" (Beer for me and brandy for him), I said to the landlord, who at once shook my hand and saluted me with *Sholem!* Even so did Ben Daoud of Jerusalem, not long ago. Ben knew me not, and I was buying a pocket-book of him at his open-air stand in Market Street, and talking German, while he was endeavoring to convince me that I ought to give five cents more for it than I had given for a similar case the

day before, on the ground that it was of a different
color, or under color that the leather had a different
ground, I forget which. In talking I let fall the word
kesef (silver). In an instant Ben had taken my hand,
and said *Sholem aleichum*, and " Can you talk Spanish ? " — which was to show that he was superfine
Sephardi, and not common Ashkenaz.

" Yes," resumed the crocus-fakir ; " a man must be
able to talk English very fluently, pronounce it correctly, and, above all things, keep his temper, if he
would do anything that requires chanting or patter-
ing. *How did I learn it?* A man can learn to do
anything when it 's business and his living depends on
it. The people who crowd around me in the streets
cannot pronounce English decently ; not one in a
thousand here can say *laugh*, except as a sheep says
it. Suppose that you are a Cheap Jack selling things
from a van. About once in an hour some tipsy fellow tries to chaff you. He hears your tongue going,
and that sets his off. He hears the people laugh at
your jokes, and he wants them to laugh at his. When
you say you 're selling to raise money for a burned-
out widow, he asks if she is n't your wife. Then you
answer him, ' No, but the kind-hearted old woman
who found you on the door-step and brought you up
to the begging business.' If you say you are selling
goods under cost, it 's very likely some yokel will cry
out, ' Stolen, hey ? ' And you patter as quick as lightning, ' Very likely ; I thought your wife sold 'em to
me too cheap for the good of somebody's clothes-line.'.
If you show yourself his superior in language and wit,
the people will buy better ; they always prefer a gentleman to a cad. Bless me ! why, a swell in a dress-
coat and kid gloves, with good patter and hatter, can

sell a hundred rat-traps while a dusty cad in a flash
kingsman would sell one.   As for the replies, most
of them are old ones.   As the men who interrupt you
are nearly all of the same kind, and have heads of
very much the same make, with an equal number of
corners, it follows that they all say nearly the same
things.   Why, I 've heard two duffers cry out the
same thing at once to me.   So you soon have answers
cut and dried for them.   We call 'em *cocks*, because
they 're just like half-penny ballads, all ready printed,
while the pitcher always has the one you want ready
at his finger-ends.   It is the same in all canting.   I
knew a man once who got his living by singing of
evenings in the gaffs to the piano, and making up
verses on the gentlemen and ladies as they came in;
and very nice verses he made, too, — always as smooth
as butter.   *How do you do it?*   I asked him one day.
'Well, you would n't believe it,' said he; 'but they 're
mostly cocks.   The best ones I buy for a tanner [six-
pence] apiece.   If a tall gentleman with a big beard
comes in, I strike a deep chord and sing, —

> " ' This tall and handsome party,
>   With such a lot of hair,
> Who seems so grand and hearty,
>   Must be a *militaire ;*
> We like to see a swell come
>   Who looks so *distingué*,
> So let us bid him welcome,
>   And hope he 'll find us gay.'

" The last half can be used for anybody.   That 's
the way the improvisatory business is managed for
visitors.   Why, it 's the same with fortune-telling.
You have noticed that.   Well, if the Gorgios had, it
would have been all up with the fake long ago.   The
old woman has the same sort of girls come to her

with the same old stories, over and over again, and she has a hundred dodges and gets a hundred straight tips where nobody else would see anything; and of course she has the same replies all ready. There is nothing like being glib. And there's really a great deal of the same in the regular doctor business, as I know, coming close on to it and calling myself one. Why, I've been called into a regular consultation in Chicago, where I had an office, — 'pon my honor I was, and no great honor neither. It was all patter, and I pattered 'em dumb."

I began to think that the fakir could talk forever and ever faster. If he excelled in his business, he evidently practiced at all times to do so. I intimated as much, and he at once proceeded fluently to illustrate this point also.

"You hear men say every day that if they only had an education they would do great things. What it would all come to with most of them is that they would *talk* so as to shut other men up and astonish 'em. They have not an idea above that. I never had any schooling but the roads and race-grounds, but I can talk the hat off a lawyer, and that's all I can do. Any man of them could talk well if he tried; but none of them will try, and so they go through life, telling you how clever they'd have been if somebody else had only done something for them, instead of doing something for themselves. So you must be going. Well, I hope I shall see you again. Just come up when you're going by and say that your wife was raised from the dead by my Elixir, and that it's the best medicine you ever had. And if you want to see some regular tent gypsies, there's a camp of them now just four miles from here; real old style

Romanys. Go out on the road four miles, and you 'll find them just off the side, — anybody will show you the place. *Sarishan !* "

I was sorry to read in the newspaper, a few days after, that the fakir had been really arrested and imprisoned for selling a quack medicine. For in this land of liberty it makes an enormous difference whether you sell by advertisement in the newspapers or on the sidewalk, which shows that there is one law for the rich and another for the poor, even in a republic.

III.

GYPSIES IN CAMP.

(NEW JERSEY.)

THE Weather had put on his very worst clothes, and was never so hard at work for the agricultural interests, or so little inclined to see visitors, as on the Sunday afternoon when I started gypsying. The rain and the wind were fighting one with another, and both with the mud, even as the Jews in Jerusalem fought with themselves, and both with the Romans, — which was the time when the *Shaket*, or butcher, killed the ox who drank the water which quenched the fire which the reader has often heard all about, yet not knowing, perhaps, that the house which Jack built was the Holy Temple of Jerusalem. It was with such reflections that I beguiled time on a long walk, for which I was not unfitly equipped in corduroy trousers, with a long Ulster and a most disreputable cap befitting a stable-boy. The rig, however, kept out the wet, and I was too recently from England to care much that it was raining. I had seen the sun on color about thirty times altogether during the past year, and so had not as yet learned to miss him. It is on record that when the Shah was in England a lady said to him, " Can it be possible, your highness, that there are in your dominions people who worship the sun ? " " Yes," replied the monarch, musingly ; " and so would you, if you could only see him."

The houses became fewer as I went on, till at last I reached the place near which I knew the gypsies must be camped. As is their custom in England, they had so established themselves as not to be seen from the road. The instinct which they display in thus getting near people, and yet keeping out of their sight, even as rats do, is remarkable. I thought I knew the town of Brighton, in England, thoroughly, and had explored all its nooks, and wondered that I had never found any gypsies there. One day I went out with a Romany acquaintance, who, in a short time, took me to half a dozen tenting-places, round corners in mysterious by-ways. It often happens that the spots which they select to *hatch the tan*, or pitch the tent, are picturesque bits, such as artists love, and all gypsies are fully appreciative of beauty in this respect. It is not a week, as I write, since I heard an old horse-dealing veteran of the roads apologize to me with real feeling for the want of a view near his tent, just as any other man might have excused the absence of pictures from his walls. The most beautiful spot for miles around Williamsport, in Pennsylvania, a river dell, which any artist would give a day to visit, is the favorite camping-ground of the Romany. Woods and water, rocks and loneliness, make it lovely by day, and when, at eventide, the fire of the wanderers lights up the scene, it also lights up in the soul many a memory of tents in the wilderness, of pictures in the Louvre, of Arabs and of Wouvermanns and belated walks by the Thames, and of Salvator Rosa. Ask me why I haunt gypsydom! It has put me into a thousand sympathies with nature and art, which I had never known without it. The Romany, like the red Indian, and all who dwell

by wood and wold as outlawes wont to do, are the
best human links to bind us to their home-scenery,
and lead us into its inner life. What constitutes the
antithetic charm of those wonderful lines,

> " Afar in the desert, I love to ride,
>   With the silent bush-boy alone by my side,"

but the presence of the savage who belongs to the
scene, and whose *being* binds the poet to it, and
blends him with it as the flux causes the fire to melt
the gold ?

I left the road, turned the corner, and saw before
me the low, round tents, with smoke rising from the
tops, dark at first and spreading into light gray, like
scalp-locks and feathers upon Indian heads. Near
them were the gayly-painted vans, in which I at once
observed a difference from the more substantial-look-
ing old-country *vardo*. The whole scene was so English that I felt a flutter at the heart : it was a bit
from over the sea ; it seemed as if hedge-rows should
have been round, and an old Gothic steeple looking
over the trees. I thought of the last gypsy camp I
had seen near Henley-on-Thames, and wished Plato
Buckland were with me to share the fun which one
was always sure to have on such an occasion in his
eccentric company. But now Plato was, like his father in the song,

> " *Duro pardel the boro pani*,"
>   Far away over the broad-rolling sea,

and I must introduce myself. There was not a sign
of life about, save in a sorrowful hen, who looked
as if she felt bitterly what it was to be a Pariah
among poultry and a down-pin, and who cluttered as
if she might have had a history of being borne from
her bower in the dark midnight by desperate African

reivers, of a wild moonlit flitting and crossing black roaring torrents, drawn all the while by the neck, as a Turcoman pulls a Persian prisoner on an "alaman," with a rope, into captivity, and finally of being sold unto the Egyptians. I drew near a tent: all was silent, as it always is in a *tan* when the foot-fall of the stranger is heard ; but I knew that it was packed with inhabitants.

I called in Romany my greeting, and badé somebody come out. And there appeared a powerfully built, dark-browed, good-looking man of thirty, who was as gypsy as Plato himself. He greeted me very civilly, but with some surprise, and asked me what he could do for me.

" Ask me in out of the rain, pal," I replied. " You don't suppose I 've come four miles to see you and stop out here, do you ? "

This was, indeed, reasonable, and I was invited to enter, which I did, and found myself in a scene which would have charmed Callot or Goya. There was no door or window to the black tent ; what light there was came through a few rifts and rents and mingled with the dull gleam of a smoldering fire, producing a perfect Rembrandt blending of rosy-red with dreamy half-darkness. It was a real witch-aura, and the denizens were worthy of it. As my eyes gradually grew to the gloom, I saw that on one side four brown old Romany sorceresses were " *beshing apré ye pus* " (sitting on the straw), as the song has it, with deeper masses of darkness behind them, in which other forms were barely visible. Their black eyes all flashed up together at me, like those of a row of eagles in a cage ; and I saw in a second that, with men and all, I was in a party who were anything but milksops in fact, with as regularly determined a lot of hard old Romanys as ever battered a policeman. I confess that a feeling like a thrill of joy came over me — a memory of old days and by-gone scenes over the sea — when I saw this, and knew they were not *diddikais*, or half-breed mumpers. On the other side, several young people, among them three or four good-looking girls, were eating their four-o'clock meal from a canvas spread on the ground. There were perhaps twenty persons in the place, including the children who swarmed about.

Even in a gypsy tent something depends on the style of a self-introduction by a perfect stranger. Stepping forward, I · divested myself of my Ulster, and handed it to a nice damsel, giving her special injunction to fold it up and lay it by. My *mise en scène* appeared to meet with approbation, and I stood forth and remarked, —

" Here I am, glad to see you; and if you want to see a regular *Romany rye* [gypsy gentleman], just over from England, now 's your chance. *Sarishan!* "

And I received, as I expected, a cordial welcome. I was invited to sit down and eat, but excused myself as having just come from *hābben*, or food, and settled myself to a cigar. But while everybody was polite, I felt that under it all there was a reserve, a chill. I was altogether too heavy a mystery. I knew my friends, and they did not know me. Something, however, now took place which went far to promote conviviality. The tent-flap was lifted, and there entered an elderly woman, who, as a gypsy, might have been the other four in one, she was so quadruply dark, so fourfold uncanny, so too-too witch-like in her eyes. The others had so far been reserved as to speaking

Romany; she, glancing at me keenly, began at once to talk it very fluently, without a word of English, with the intention of testing me ; but as I understood her perfectly, and replied with a burning gush of the same language, being, indeed, glad to have at last "got into my plate," we were friends in a minute. I did not know then that I was talking with a celeb· rity whose name has even been groomily recorded in an English book ; but I found at once that she was truly "a character." She had manifestly been sent for to test the stranger, and I knew this, and made myself agreeable, and was evidently found *tacho*, or all right. It being a rule, in fact, with few exceptions, that when you really like people, in a friendly way, and are glad to be among them, they never fail to find it out, and the jury always comes to a favorable verdict.

And so we sat and talked on in the monotone in which Romany is generally spoken, like an Indian song, while, like an Indian drum, the rain pattered an accompaniment on the tightly drawn tent. Those who live in cities, and who are always realizing self, and thinking how they think, and are while awake given up to introverting vanity, never *live* in song. To do this one must be a child, an Indian, a dweller in fields and green forests, a brother of the rain and road-puddles and rolling streams, and a friend of the rustling leaves and the summer orchestra of frogs and crickets and rippling grass. Those who hear this music and think to it never think about it; those who live only in books never sing to it in soul. As there are dreams which *will not* be remembered or known to *reason*, so this music shrinks from it. It is wonderful how beauty perishes like a shade-grown flower before the sunlight of analysis. It is dying out all the world over in women, under the influence of cleverness and "style;" it is perishing in poetry and art before criticism; it is wearing away from manliness, through priggishness; it is being crushed out of true gentleness of heart and nobility of soul by the pessimist puppyism of miching Mallockos. But nature is eternal and will return. When man has run one of his phases of culture fairly to the end, and when the fruit is followed by a rattling rococo husk, then comes a winter sleep, from which he awakens to grow again as a child-flower. We are at the very worst of such a time; but there is a morning redness far away, which shows that the darkness is ending, the winter past, the rain is over and gone. Arise, and come away!

"Sossi kair'd tute to av'akai pardel o boro pāni?" (And what made you come here across the broad water?) said the good old dame confidentially and kindly, in the same low monotone. "Si lesti chorin a gry?" (Was it stealing a horse?)

Dum, dum, dum, patter, patter, dum! played the rain.

"Avali I dikked your romus kaliko" (I saw your husband yesterday), remarked some one aside to a girl.

Dum, dum, dum, patter, patter, dum!

"No, mother deari, it was not a horse, for I am on a better, higher lay."

Dum, dum, dum, patter, patter, dum!

"He is a first-rate dog, but mine 's as good."

Dum, dum, dum, patter, dum!

"Tacho! There 's money to be made by a gentleman like you by telling fortunes."

17

Dum, dum, dum, patter, dum!

" Yes, a five-hundred-dollar hit sometimes.   But, *dye,* I work upon a better lay."

Dum, dum, dum, patter, dum!

" Perhaps you are *a boro drabengro* " (a great physician).

Dum, dum, dum, patter, dum!

" It was away among the rocks that he fell into the reeds, half in the water, and kept still till they went by."

" If any one is ill among you, I may be of use."

Dum, dum, dum, patter, dum!

" And what a wind!   It blows as if the good Lord were singing!   Kushti chirus se atch a-kerri." (This is a pleasant day to be at home.)

Dum, dum, dum, patter, dum!

" I thought you were a doctor, for you were going about in the town with the one who sells medicine. I heard of it."

Dum, dum, dum, patter, dum!

" Do not hurry away!   Come again and see us.   I think the Coopers are all out in Ohio."

Dum, dum, dum, patter, dum!

The cold wind and slight rain seemed refreshing and even welcome, as I went out into the cold air. The captain showed me his stock of fourteen horses and mules, and we interchanged views as to the best method of managing certain maladies in such stock. I had been most kindly entertained ; indeed, with the home kindliness which good people in the country show to some hitherto unseen and unknown relative who descends to them from the great world of the city.   Not but that my friends did not know cities and men as well as Ulysses, but even Ulysses sometimes met with a marvel. In after days I became quite familiar with the several families who made the camp, and visited them in sunshine. But they always occur to me in memory as in a deep Rembrandt picture, a wonderful picture, and their voices as in vocal chiaroscuro ; singing to the wind without and the rain on the tent, —

Dum, dum, dum, patter, dum !

IV.

HOUSE GYPSIES IN PHLADELPHIA.

THIS chapter was written by my niece through marriage, Miss Elizabeth Robins. It is a part of an article which was published in " The Century," and it sets forth certain wanderings in seeking old houses in the city of Philadelphia.

All along the lower part of Race Street, saith the lady, are wholesale stores and warehouses of every description. Some carts belonging to one of them had just been unloaded. The stevedores who do this — all negroes — were resting while they waited for the next load. They were great powerful men, selected for their strength, and were of many hues, from *café au lait*, or coffee much milked, up to the browned or black-scorched berry itself, while the very *athletæ* were coal-black. They wore blue overalls, and on their heads they had thrown old coffee-bags, which, resting on their foreheads, passed behind their ears and hung loosely down their backs. It was in fact the *haik* or bag-cloak of the East, and it made a wonderfully effective Arab costume. One of them was half leaning, half sitting, on a pile of bags ; his Herculean arms were folded, and he had unconsciously assumed an air of dignity and defiance. He might have passed for an African chief. When we see such men in Egypt or other sunny countries *outre mer*, we become artistically eloquent ; but it rarely occurs

to sketchers and word-painters to do much business
in the home-market.

The mixture of races in our cities is rapidly increasing, and we hardly notice it. Yet it is coming to pass
that a large part of our population is German and
Irish, and that our streets within ten years have become fuller of Italian fruit dealers and organ-grinders,
so that *Cives sum Romanus* (I am a Roman citizen),
when abroad, now means either " I possess a monkey "
or " I sell pea-nuts." Jews from Jerusalem peddle
pocket-books on our sidewalks, Chinamen are monop-
lizing our washing and ironing, while among labor-
ing classes are thousands of Scandinavians, Bohemians, and other Slaves. The prim provincial element
which predominated in my younger years is yielding
before this influx of foreigners, and Quaker monotony
and stern conservatism are vanishing, while Philadelphia becomes year by year more cosmopolite.

As we left the handsome negroes and continued
our walk on Water Street an Italian passed us. He
was indeed very dirty and dilapidated; his clothes
were of the poorest, and he carried a rag-picker's bag
over his shoulder; but his face, as he turned it towards
us, was really beautiful.

" *Siete Italiano ?* " (Are you an Italian ?) asked
my uncle.

" *Si, signore* " (Yes, sir), he answered, showing all
his white teeth, and opening his big brown eyes very
wide.

" *E come lei piace questo paese ?* " (And how do
you like this country ?)

"Not at all. It is too cold," was his frank answer,
and laughing good-humoredly he continued his search
through the gutters. He would have made a good

model for an artist, for he had what we do not always
see in Italians, the real southern beauty of face and
expression. Two or three weeks after this encounter,
we were astonished at meeting on Chestnut Street a
little man, decently dressed, who at once manifested
the most extraordinary and extravagant symptoms of
delighted recognition. Never saw I mortal so grin-full,
so bowing. As we went on and crossed the street,
and looked back, he was waving his hat in the air
with one hand, while he made gestures of delight
with the other. It was the little Italian rag-picker.

Then along and afar, till we met a woman, decently
enough dressed, with jet-black eyes and hair, and looking not unlike a gypsy. "A Romany!" I cried
with delight. Her red shawl made me think of gypsies, and when I caught her eye I saw the indescrib-
ble flash of the *kālorat*, or black blood. It is very
curious that Hindus, Persians, and gypsies have in
common an expression of the eye which distinguishes
them from all other Oriental races, and chief in this
expression is the Romany. Captain Newbold, who
first investigated the gypsies of Egypt, declares that,
however disguised, he could always detect them by
their glance, which is unlike that of any other human
being, though something resembling it is often seen
in the ruder type of the rural American. I believe
myself that there is something in the gypsy eye which
is inexplicable, and which enables its possessor to see
farther through that strange mill-stone, the human
soul, than I can explain. Any one who has ever seen
an old fortune-teller of "the people" keeping some
simple-minded maiden by the hand, while she holds her
by her glittering eye, like the Ancient Mariner, with
a basilisk stare, will agree with me. As Scheele de

Vere writes, "It must not be forgotten that the human eye has, beyond question, often a power which far transcends the ordinary purposes of sight, and approaches the boundaries of magic."

But one glance, and my companion whispered, "Answer me in Romany when I speak, and don't seem to notice her." And then, in loud tone, he remarked, while looking across the street, —

"*Adovo's a kushto puro rinkeno kér adoi.*" (That is a nice old pretty house there.)

"*Avali, rya*" (Yes, sir), I replied.

There was a perceptible movement by the woman in the red shawl to keep within ear-shot of us. Mine uncle resumed, —

"*Boro kushto covva se ta rakker a jib te kek Gorgio iinella.*" (It's nice to talk a language that no Gentile knows.)

The red shawl was on the trail. "*Je crois que ça mord,*" remarked my uncle. We allowed our artist guide to pass on, when, as I expected, I felt a twitch at my outer garment. I turned, and the witch eyes, distended with awe and amazement, were glaring into mine, while she said, in a hurried whisper, —

"Was n't it Romanes?"

"*Avah,*" I replied, "*mendui rakker sarja adovo jib. Būtikūmi ryeskro lis se denna Gorgines.*" (Yes, we always talk that language. Much more genteel it is than English.)

"*Te adovo wavero rye?*" (And that *other* gentleman?) with a glance of suspicion at our artist friend.

"*Sar tacho*" (He's all right), remarked mine uncle, which I greatly fear meant, when correctly translated in a Christian sense, "He's all wrong." But there is a natural sympathy and intelligence between Bohemians of every grade, all the world over, and I never knew a gypsy who did not understand an artist. One glance satisfied her that he was quite worthy of our society.

"And where are you *tannin kennā?*" (tenting now), I inquired.

"We are not tenting at this time of year; we 're *kairin*," i. e., house-ing, or home-ing. It is a good verb, and might be introduced into English.

"And where is your house?"

"There, right by Mammy Sauerkraut's Row. Come in and sit down."

I need not give the Romany which was spoken, but will simply translate. The house was like all the others. We passed through a close, dark passage, in which lay canvas and poles, a kettle and a *sarshta*, or the iron which is stuck into the ground, and by which a kettle hangs. The old-fashioned tripod, popularly supposed to be used by gypsies, in all probability never existed, since the Roms of India to-day use the *sarshta*, as mine uncle tells me he learned from a *ci-devant* Indian gypsy Dacoit, or wandering thief, who was one of his intimates in London.

We entered an inner room, and I was at once struck by its general indescribable unlikeness to ordinary rooms. Architects declare that the type of the tent is to be distinctly found in all Chinese and Arab or Turkish architecture; it is also as marked in a gypsy's house — when he gets one. This room, which was evidently the common home of a large family, suggested, in its arrangement of furniture and the manner in which its occupants sat around, the tent and the wagon. There was a bed, it is true, but there was a roll of sail-cloth, which evidently did duty for sleeping on at night, but which now, rolled up, acted the part described by Goldsmith : —

> " A thing contrived a double part to play,
> A bed by night, a sofa during day."

There was one chair and a saddle, a stove and a chest of drawers. I observed an engraving hanging up which I have several times seen in gypsy tents. It represents a very dark Italian youth. It is a favorite also with Roman Catholics, because the boy has a consecrated medal. The gypsies, however, believe that the boy stole the medal. The Catholics think the picture is that of a Roman boy, because the inscription says so ; and the gypsies call it a Romany, so that all are satisfied. There were some eight or nine children in the room, and among them more than one whose resemblance to the dark-skinned saint might have given color enough to the theory that he was

> " One whose blood
> Had rolled through gypsies ever since the flood."

There was also a girl, of the pantherine type, and one damsel of about ten, who had light hair and fair complexion, but whose air was gypsy and whose youthful countenance suggested not the golden, but the brazenest, age of life. Scarcely was I seated in the only chair, when this little maiden, after keenly scrutinizing my appearance, and apparently taking in the situation, came up to me and said, —

" Yer come here to have yer fortune told. I 'll tell it to yer for five cents."

" *Can tute pen dukkerin aja ?* " (Can you tell fortunes already ?) I inquired. And if that damsel had been lifted at that instant by the hair into the infi-

nite glory of the seventh sphere, her countenance
could not have manifested more amazement. She
stood *bouche beante*, stock still staring, open-mouthed
wide. I believe one might have put a brandy ball
into it, or a "bull's eye," without her jaws closing
on the dainty. It was a stare of twenty-four carats,
and fourth proof.

" This here *rye*," remarked mine uncle, affably, in
middle English, " is a hartist. He puts 'is heart into
all he does; *that's* why. He ain't Romanes, but he
may be trusted. He's come here, that wot he has,
to draw this 'ere Mammy Sauerkraut's Row, because
it's interestin'. He ain't a tax-gatherer. *We* don't
approve o' payin' taxes, none of hus. We practices
heconomy, and dislike the po-lice. Who was Mammy
Sauerkraut ? "

" I know ! " cried the youthful would-be fortune-
teller. " She was a witch."

" *Tool yer chib !* " (Hold your tongue !) cried the
parent. " Don't bother the lady with stories about
chovihanis " (witches).

" But that's just what I want to hear ! " I cried.
" Go on, my little dear, about Mammy Sauerkraut,
and you will get your five cents yet, if you only give
me enough of it."

" Well, then, Mammy Sauerkraut was a witch, and
a little black girl who lives next door told me so.
And Mammy Sauerkraut used to change herself into
a pig of nights, and that's why they called her
Sauerkraut. This was because they had pig ketchers
going about in those times, and once they ketched
a pig that belonged to her, and to be revenged on
them she used to look like a pig, and they would
follow her clear out of town way up the river, and

she'd run, and they'd run after her, till by and by fire would begin to fly out of her bristles, and she jumped into the river and sizzed."

This I thought worthy of the five cents. Then my uncle began to put questions in Romany.

" Where is Anselo W.? He that was *staruben* for a *gry?*" (imprisoned for a horse).

" *Staruben apopli.*" (Imprisoned again.)

" I am sorry for it, sister Nell. He used to play the fiddle well. I wot he was a canty chiel', and dearly lo'ed the whisky, oh !"

" Yes, he was too fond of that. How well he could play !"

" Yes," said my uncle, " he could. And I have sung to his fiddling when the *tatto-pāni* [hot water, *i. e.*, spirits] boiled within us, and made us gay, oh, my golden sister! That's the way we Hungarian gypsy gentlemen always call the ladies of our people. I sang in Romany."

" I 'd like to hear you sing now," remarked a dark, handsome young man, who had just made a mysterious appearance out of the surrounding shadows.

" It 's a *kamaben gilli* " (a love-song), said the *rye ;* " and it is beautiful, deep old Romanes, — enough to make you cry."

There was the long sound of a violin, clear as the note of a horn. I had not observed that the dark young man had found one to his hand, and, as he accompanied, my uncle sang; and I give the lyric as he afterwards gave it to me, both in Romany and English. As he frankly admitted, it was his own composition.

KE TRINALI.

Tu shan miri pireni
  Me kamāva tute,
Kamlidiri, rinkeni,
  Kāmes maude buti ?

Sa o miro kūshto gry
  'Taders miri wardi, —
Sa o boro būno rye
  Rikkers lesto stardi.

Sa o bokro dré o char
  Hawala adovo, —
Sa i choramengeri
  Lels o ryas luvoo, —

Sa o sasto levinor
  Kairs amandy mātto, —
Sa o yag adré o tan
  Kairs o geero tātto, —

Sa i pūri Romni chai
  Pens o kushto dukkrin, —
Sa i Gorgi dinneli,
  Patsers lākis pukkrin, —

Tute taders tiro rom,
  Sims o gry, o wardi,
Tute chores o zī adrom
  Rikkers sā i stardi.

Tute haws te chores m'ri zē,
  Tutes dukkered būti
Tu shan miro jivaben
  Me t'vel paller tute.

Paller tute sarasa
  Pardel pūv te pāni,
Trinali — o krallisa !
  Miri chovihāni !

TO TRINALI.

Now thou art my darling girl,
    And I love thee dearly ;
Oh, beloved and my fair,
    Lov'st thou me sincerely ?

As my good old trusty horse
    Draws his load or bears it ;
As a gallant cavalier
    Cocks his hat and wears it ;

As a sheep devours the grass
    When the day is sunny ;
As a thief who has the chance
    Takes away our money ;

As strong ale when taken down
    Makes the strongest tipsy ;
As a fire within a tent
    Warms a shivering gypsy ;

As a gypsy grandmother
    Tells a fortune neatly ;
As the Gentile trusts in her,
    And is done completely, —

So you draw me here and there,
    Where you like you take me ;
Or you sport me like a hat, —
    What you will you make me.

So you steal and gnaw my heart,
    For to that I 'm fated !
And by you, my gypsy Kate,
    I 'm intoxicated.

And I own you are a witch,
    I am beaten hollow ;
Where thou goest in this world
    I am bound to follow, —

Follow thee, where'er it be,
    Over land and water,

Trinali, my gypsy queen!
Witch and witch's daughter!

"Well, that *is* deep Romanes," said the woman, admiringly. "It 's beautiful."

"*I* should think it was," remarked the violinist. "Why, I did n't understand more than one half of it. But what I caught I understood." Which, I reflected, as he uttered it, is perhaps exactly the case with far more than half the readers of all poetry. They run on in a semi-sensuous mental condition, soothed by cadence and lulled by rhyme, reading as they run for want of thought. Are there not poets of the present day who mean that you shall read them thus, and who cast their gold ornaments hollow, as jewelers do, lest they should be too heavy?

"My children," said Meister Karl, "I could go on all day with Romany songs; and I can count up to a hundred in the black language. I know three words for a mouse, three for a monkey, and three for the shadow which falleth at noonday. And I know how to *pen dukkerin, lel dūdikabin te chiv o manzin apré latti.*"[1]

"Well, the man who knows *that* is up to *drab* [medicine], and has n't much more to learn," said the young man. "When a *rye 's* a Rom he 's anywhere at home."

"So *kushto bak!*" (Good luck!) I said, rising to go. "We will come again!"

"Yes, we will come again," said Meister Karl. "Look for me with the roses at the races, and tell me the horse to bet on. You'll find my *patteran* [a

[1] A brief *résumé* of the most characteristic gypsy mode of obtaining property.

mark or sign to show which way a gypsy has traveled] at the next church-door, or may be on the public-house step. Child of the old Egyptians, mother of all the witches, sister of the stars, daughter of darkness, farewell!"

This bewildering speech was received with admiring awe, and we departed. I should have liked to hear the comments on us which passed that evening among the gypsy denizens of Mammy Sauerkraut's Row.

V.

A GYPSY LETTER.

ALL the gypsies in the country are not upon the roads. Many of them live in houses, and that very respectably, nay, even aristocratically. Yea, and it may be, O reader, that thou hast met them and knowest them not, any more than thou knowest many other deep secrets of the hearts and lives of those who live around thee. Dark are the ways of the Romany, strange his paths, even when reclaimed from the tent and the van. It is, however, intelligible enough that the Rom converted to the true faith of broadcloth garments by Poole, or dresses by Worth, as well as to the holy gospel of daily baths and *savon au violet*, should say as little as possible of his origin. For the majority of the world being snobs, they continually insist that all blood unlike their own is base, and the child of the *kālorat*, knowing this, sayeth naught, and ever carefully keeps the lid of silence on the pot of his birth. And as no being that ever was, is, or will be ever enjoyed holding a secret, playing a part, or otherwise entering into the deepest mystery of life — which is to make a joke of it — so thoroughly as a gypsy, it follows that the being respectable has to him a raciness and drollery and pungency and point which passeth faith. It has often occurred to me, and the older I grow the more I find it true, that the *real* pleasure which bank presidents, moral politicians, not a few clergymen, and most other highly representative good men take in having a high character is the exquisite secret consciousness of its being utterly undeserved. They love acting. Let no man say that the love of the drama is founded on the artificial or sham. I have heard the Reverend Histrio-mastix war and batter this on the pulpit; but the utterance *per se* was an actual, living lie. He was acting while he preached. Love or hunger is not more an innate passion than acting. The child in the nursery, the savage by the Nyanza or in Alaska, the multitude of great cities, all love to bemask and seem what they are not. Crush out carnivals and masked balls and theatres, and lo, you! the disguising and acting and masking show themselves in the whole community. Mawworm and Aminidab Sleek then play a rôle in every household, and every child becomes a wretched little Roscius. Verily I say unto you, the fewer actors the more acting; the fewer theatres the more stages, and the worse. Lay it to heart, study it deeply, you who believe that the stage is an open door to hell, for the chances are ninety and nine to one that if this be true *you* will end by consciously or unconsciously keeping a private little gate thereunto. Beloved, put this in thy pipe and fumigate it, that acting in some form is a human instinct which cannot be extinguished, which never has been and never will be; and this being so, is it not better, with Dr. Bellows, to try to put it into proper form than to crush it? Truly it has been proved that with this, as with a certain other unquenchable penchant of humanity, when you suppress a score of professionals you create a thousand zealous amateurs. There was never in this world a stage on which mere acting was

18

more skillfully carried out than in all England under Cromwell, or in Philadelphia under the Quakers. Eccentric dresses, artificial forms of language, separate and "peculiar" expressions of character unlike those of "the world," were all only giving a form to that craving for being odd and queer which forms the soul of masking and acting. Of course people who act all the time object to the stage. *Le diable ne veut pas de miroir.*

The gypsy of society not always, but yet frequently, retains a keen interest in his wild ancestry. He keeps up the language; it is a delightful secret; he loves now and then to take a look at "the old thing." Closely allied to the converted sinners are the *aficionados*, or the ladies and gentlemen born with unconquerable Bohemian tastes, which may be accounted for by their having been themselves gypsies in preëxistent lives. No one can explain how or why it is that the *aficion* comes upon them. It is *in* them. I know a very learned man in England, a gentleman of high position, one whose name is familiar to my readers. He could never explain or understand why from early childhood he had felt himself drawn towards the wanderers. When he was only ten years old he saved up all his little store of pence wherewith to pay a tinker to give him lessons in Romany, in which tongue he is now a Past Grand. I know ladies in England and in America, both of the blood and otherwise, who would give up a ball of the highest flight in society, to sit an hour in a gypsy tent, and on whom a whispered word of Romany acts like wild-fire. Great as my experience has been I can really no more explain the intensity of this yearning, this *rapport*, than I can fly. My own fancy for gypsydom is faint and feeble compared

to what I have found in many others. It is in them
like the love for opium, for music, for love itself, or
for acting. I confess that there is to me a nameless
charm in the strangely, softly flowing language, which
gives a sweeter sound to every foreign word which it
adopts, just as the melody of a forest stream is said
to make more musical the songs of the birds who
dwell beside it. Thus Wentzel becomes Wenselo and
Anselo; Arthur, Artaros; London, Lundra; Sylvester,
Westaros. Such a phrase as "*Dordi! dovelo adoi?*"
(See! what is that there?) could not be surpassed
for mere beauty of sound.

It is apropos of living double lives, and playing
parts, and the charm of stealing away unseen, like
naughty children, to romp with the tabooed offspring
of outlawed neighbors, that I write this, to introduce
a letter from a lady, who has kindly permitted me to
publish it. It tells its own story of two existences,
two souls in one. I give it as it was written, first in
Romany, and then in English : —

Febmunti 1st.

MIRO KAMLO PAL, — Tu tevel mishto ta shun te latcher-
dum me akovo kūrikus tacho Romany tan akai adré o gav.
Buti kāmaben lis sas ta dikk mori foki apopli; buti kushti
ta shun moro jib. Mi-duvel atch apā mande, sī ne shomas
pash naflo o Gorginess, vonk' akovo vias. O waver divvus
sa me viom fon a swell saleskro hāben, dikdom me dui
Romani chia beshin alay apré a longo skamin adré ——
Square. Kālor yākkor, kālor balyor, lūllo ,diklas apré i
sherria, te lender trushnia aglal lender piria. Mi-duvel,
shomas pāsh divio sār kamaben ta dikav lender! Avo!
kairdum o wardomengro hatch i graia te sheldom avrī,
" *Come here!* " Yon penden te me sos a rāni ta dūkker,
te vian sig adosta. Awer me saldom te pendom adré
Romanis ; " Sarishān miri dearis! Tute don't jin mandy's a

Romany!" Yon nastis patser lende kania nera yakkor. "Mi-duvel! Sā se tiro nav? putchdo yeck. "Miro nav se Britannia Lee." Kenna-sig yon diktas te me sos tachi, te penden amengi lender navia shanas M. te D. Lis sos duro pā lende ta jin sā a Romani rāni astis jiv amen Gorgios, te dikk sa Gorgious, awer te vel kushti Romani ajā, te tevel buoino lakis kāloratt. Buti rakkerdém apré mori foki, buti nevvi. buti savo sos rumado, te beeno, te puredo, savo sos vino fon o puro tem, te būtikumi aja kekkeno sos rakkerbcu sa gudli. M. pende amengi, "Mandy don't jin how tute can jiv among dem Gorgics." Pukerdom anpāli: " Mandy dont jiv, mandy mérs kairin amen lender." Yon mangades mande ta well ta dikk a len, adré lendes kér apré o chūmba kai atchena pa o wen. Pende M., " Av miri pen ta hā a bitti sār mendi. Tute jins the chais are only kérri arātti te Kūrrkus."

Sunday sala miri pen te me ghion adoi te latchedon o ker. O tan sos bitto, awer sā i Romanis pende, dikde boro adosta paller jivin adré o wardo. M. sos adoi te lakis roms dye, a kūshti pūri chai. A. sar shtor chavia. M. kerde hāben sā mendui viom adoi. I pūri dye sos mishto ta dikk mande, yoi kāmde ta jin sār trūstal mande. Rakkerdem buti ajā, te yoi pende te yoi né kekker latchde a Romani rāni denna mande. Pendom me ke laki shan adré society kūmi Romani rānia, awer i galderli Gorgios ne jinena lis.

Yoi pende sā miri pen dikde simlo Lusha Cooper, te siggerde lākis kāloratt būtider denna me. " Tute don't favor the Coopers, miri dearie! Tute pens tiri dye rummerd a mush navvered Smith. Wās adovo the Smith as lelled kellin te kurin booths pāsher Lundra Bridge? Sos tute beeno adré Anglaterra?" Pūkkerdom me ke puri dye sār jināv me trūstal miri kokeri te simensi. Tu jinsa shan kek Gorgies sā longi-bavoli apré genealogies, sā i puri Romani dyia. Vonka foki nāstis chin lende adré lilia, rikkerena lende aduro adré lendros sherria. *Que la main droit perd recueille la gauche.*

" Does tute jin any of the ——'s?" pende M. " Tute

dikks sim ta ——'s juva." "Ne kekker, yois too pauno,"
pens A. "It's chomani adré the look of her," pende M.
Dikkpáli miro pal. Tu jinsa te —— sos i chi savo dudi-
kabinde mānūsh, navdo —— būti wongur. Vānka yoi sos
lino apré, o Beshomengro pende ta kér laki chiv apré a
shuba sims Gorgios te adenne lelled lāki adré a tan sar
desh te dui gorgi chaia. —— astissa pen i chai savo chordé
lestis lovvo. Vanka yoi vias adré o tan, yoi ghias sig keti
laki, te pende : "Jināva me lāki talla lākis longi vangusti,
te rinkeni mui. Yoi sos stardi dui beshya, awer o Gorgio
kekker las leski vongur pāli."

Savo-chirus mendi rākkerden o wuder pirido, te trin·
manushia vian adré. . . . Pali lenders sarishans, M. shelde
avrī : "Av ta misali, rikker yer skammins longo tute !
Mrs. Lee, why didn't tute bring yer rom ? " " Adenna me
shom kek rumadi." " Mi-duvel, Britannia ! " pende ——.
" M. pende amengy te tu sos rumado." " M. didn't dukker
tacho vonka yoi dukkerd adovo. Yois a dinneli," pendom
me. Te adenne sar mendi saden atūt M. Hāben sos kushto,
liom a kani, ballovas te puvengros, te kushto curro levina.
Liom mendi kushto paiass dré moro pūro Romany dromus.
Rinkenodiro sos, kérde mande pāsh ta ruv, shomas sā kūshto-bākno ta atch yecker apopli men mori foki. Sos " Britannia ! " akai, te " Britannia ! " doi, te sār sā adré o pūro
cheirus, vonka chavi shomas. Ne patserava me ta Dante
chinde : —

> " Nessun maggior dolore
> Che ricordarsi dei tempi felici."

Talla me shomas kūshto-bākno ta pen apré o puro chirus.
Sar lende piden miro kāmaben Romaneskaes, sar gudlo ;
talla H. Yov pende nastis kér lis, pā yuv kennā lias tabūti.
Kushto dikin Romnichal yuv. Tu tevel jin lesti sārakai pā
Romani, yuv se sa kālo. Te *avec l'air indefinnissable du
vrai Bohemien.* Yuv patserde me ta piav miro sastopen
wavescro chirus. Kanā shomas pā misali, geero vias keti
tan ; dukkeriben kamde yov. Hunali sos i pūri dye te

pendes amergi, " Beng lel o pūro jūkel for welliu vānka
mendi shom hāin, te kennā tu shan akai, miri Britannia.
Yov ne tevel lel kek kūshto bak.   Mandy'll pen leste a
wafedo dukkerin."   Adoi A. putcherde mengy, " Does tute
dūkker or sā does tute kér."   " Miri pen, mandy'll pen tute
tacho.   Mandy dukkers te dudikabins te kérs būti covvas.
Shom a tachi Romani chovihani."   "Tacho ! tacho ! " saden
butider.   Miri pen te me rikkerdem a boro matto-morricley
pā i chavis.   Yon beshden alay apré o purj. hāis lis.   Rinkeno
picture sas, pendom dikkav mande te miri penia te pralia
kennā shomas bitti.   Latcherdom me a tāni kāli chavi of
panj besh chorin levina avrī miro curro.   Dikde, sār lakis
bori kāli yakka te kāli balia simno tikno Bacchante, sa yoi
prasterde adrom.

Pendom parako pā moro kūshto-bākeno chirus — " kushto
bak " te " kūshto divvus."   Mendi diom moro tachopen ta
well apopli, te kān viom kérri.   Patserāva dikk tute akai
tallā o prasteriu o ye graia.   Kūshto bāk te kūshto rātti.

Sarja tiro pen,   BRITANNIA LEE.

TRANSLATION.

February 1st.

MY DEAR FRIEND, — You will be glad to learn that I,
within the week, found a real Romany family (place) here
in this town.   Charming it was to find our folk again ;
pleasant it was to listen to our tongue.   The Lord be on
me ! but I was half sick of Gentiles and their ways till this
occurred.   The other day, as I was returning from a highly
aristocratic breakfast, where we had winter strawberries
with the *crème de la crème*, I saw two gypsy women sitting
on a bench in —— Square.   Black eyes, black hair, red ker-
chiefs on their heads, their baskets on the ground before
their feet.   Dear Lord ! but I was half wild with delight at
seeing them.   Aye, I made the coachman stop the horses,
and cried aloud, " Come here ! "   They thought I was a
lady to fortune-tell, and came quickly.   But I laughed, and
said in Romany, " How are you, my dears ?   You don't

know that I am a gypsy." They could not trust their very
ears or eyes! At length one said, "My God! what *is*
your name?" "My name's Britannia Lee," and, at a
glance, they saw that I was to be trusted, and a Romany.
Their names, they said, were M. and D. It was hard (far)
for them to understand how a Romany lady *could* live
among Gentiles, and look so Gorgious, and yet be a true
gypsy withal, and proud of her dark blood. Much they
talked about our people; much news I heard, — much as to
who was married and born and buried, who was come from
the old country, and much more. Oh, *never* was such news
so sweet to me! M. said, "I don't know how you *can*
live among the Gentiles." I answered, "I don't live; I *die*,
living in their houses with them." They begged me then
to come and see them in their home, upon the hill, where
they are wintering. M. said, "Come, my sister, and eat
a little with us. You know that the women are only at
home at night and on Sunday."

Sunday morning, sister and I went there, and found the
house. It was a little place, but, as they said, after the life
in wagons it seemed large. M. was there, and her husband's mother, a nice old woman; also A., with four children. M. was cooking as we entered. The old mother
was glad to see us; she wished to know all about us. All
talked, indeed, and that quite rapidly, and she said that I
was the first Romany lady[1] she had ever seen. I said to
her that in society are many gypsy ladies to be found, but
that the wretched Gentiles do not know it.

She said that my sister looked like Lusha Cooper, and
showed her dark blood more than I do. "You don't favor
the Coopers, my dearie. You say your mother married a
Smith. Was that the Smith who kept a dancing and box-

---

[1] Lady, in gypsy *rāni*. The process of degradation is curiously
marked in this language. *Rāni* (*rawnee*), in Hindi, is a queen. *Rye*,
or *rae*, a gentleman, in its native land, is applicable to a nobleman,
while *rashai*, a clergyman, even of the smallest dissenting type, rises
in the original *rishi* to a saint of the highest order.

ing place near London Bridge? Were you born in England?" I told the old mother all I knew about myself and my relations. You know that no Gorgios are so long, winded on genealogies as old mothers in Rom. When people don't write them down in their family Bibles, they carry them, extended, in their heads. *Que la main droit perd recueille la gauche.*

" Do you know any of the ——'s?" said M. " You look like ——'s wife." " No ; she's too pale," said A. " It's something in the look of her," said M.

Reflect, my brother. You know that —— was the woman who " cleaned out " a man named —— of a very large sum [1] by " dukkeripen " and " dudikabin." " When she was arrested, the justice made her dress like any Gorgio, and placed her among twelve Gentile women. The man who had been robbed was to point out who among them had stolen his money. When she came into the room, he went at once to her, and said, ' I know her by her long skinny fingers and handsome face.' She was imprisoned for two years, but the Gorgio never recovered his money."

What time we reasoned thus, the door undid, and three men entered. After their greetings, M. cried, " Come to table ; bring your chairs with you ! " " Mrs. Lee, why did n't you bring your husband ? " " Because I am not married." " Lord ! Britannia ! Why, M. told me that you were." " Ah, M. did n't fortune right when she fortuned that. She's a fool," quoth I. And then we all laughed like children. The food was good : chickens and ham and fried potatoes, with a glass of sound ale. We were gay as flies in summer, in the real old Romany way. 'T was " Britannia " here, " Britannia " there, as in the merry days when we were young. · Little do I believe in Dante's words, —

---

[1] This was the very same affair and the same gypsies described and mentioned on page 383 of *In Gypsy Tents*, by Francis Hindes Groome, Edinburgh, 1880. I am well acquainted with them.

> "Nessun maggior dolore,
> Che ricordarsi dei tempi felici."

> "There is no greater grief
> Than to remember by-gone happy days."

For it is always happiness to me to think of good old times when I was glad. All drank my health, *Romanes-kaes*, together, with a shout, — all save H., who said he had already had too much. Good-looking gypsy, that! You 'd know him anywhere for Romany, he is so dark, — *avec l'air indéfinissable du vrai Bohemien.* He promised to drink my health another time.

As we sat, a gentleman came in below, wishing to have his fortune told. I remember to have read that the Pythoness of Delphian oracle prepared herself for *dukkerin*, or presaging, by taking a few drops of cherry-laurel water. (I have had it prescribed for my eyes as R̃ *aq. laur. cerasi. fiat lotio,* — possibly to enable me to see into the future.) Perhaps it was the cherry-brandy beloved of British matrons and Brighton school-girls, taken at Mutton's. *Mais revenons à nos moutons.* The old mother had taken, not cherry-laurel water, nor even cherry-brandy, but joly good ale, and olde, which, far from fitting her to reveal the darksome lore of futurity, had rendered her loath to leave the festive board of the present. Wrathful was the sybil, furious as the Vala when waked by Odin, angry as Thor when he missed his hammer, to miss her merriment. "May the devil take the old dog for coming when we are eating, and when thou art here, my Britannia! Little good fortune will he hear this day. Evil shall be the best I 'll promise him." Thus spake the sorceress, and out she went to keep her word. Truly it was a splendid picture this of "The Enraged Witch," as painted by Hexenmeister von Teufel, of Höllenstadt, — her viper eyes flashing infernal light and most unchristian fire, shaking *les noirs serpents de ses cheveux,* as she went forth. I know how, in an instant, her face was beautiful with welcome, smiling like a Neapolitan at a cent;

but the poor believer caught it hot, all the same, and had a sleepless night over his future fate. I wonder if the Pythoness of old, when summoned from a *petit souper*, or a holy prophet called out of bed of a cold night, to decide by royal command on the fate of Israel, ever "took it out" on the untimely king by promising him a lively, unhappy time of it. Truly it is fine to be behind the scenes and see how they work the oracle. For the gentleman who came to consult my witch was a man of might in the secrets of state, and one whom I have met in high society. And, oh! *if* he had known who it was that was up-stairs, laughing at him for a fool!

While she was forth, A. asked me, "Do you tell fortunes, or *what*?" "My sister," I replied, "I'll tell thee the truth. I do tell fortunes. I keep a house for the purchase of stolen goods. I am largely engaged in making counterfeit money and all kinds of forgery. I am interested in burglary. I lie, swear, cheat, and steal, and get drunk on Sunday. And I do many other things. I am a real Romany witch." This little confession of faith brought down the house. "Bravo! bravo!" they cried, laughing.

Sister and I had brought a great tipsy-cake for the children, and they were all sitting under a table, eating it. It was a pretty picture. I thought I saw in it myself and all my sisters and brothers as we were once. Just such little gypsies and duckling Romanys! And now! And then! What a comedy some lives are, — yea, such lives as mine! And now it is *you* who are behind the scenes; anon, I shall change with you. *Va Pierre, vient Pierette.* Then I surprised a little brown maiden imp of five summers stealing my beer, and as she was caught in the act, and tore away shrieking with laughter, she looked, with her great black eyes and flowing jetty curling locks, like a perfect little Bacchante.

Then we said, "Thank you for the happy time!" "Good

luck!" and "Good day!" giving our promises to come again. So we went home all well. I hope to see you at the races here. Good luck and good-night also to you.

Always your friend,   Britannia Lee.

I have somewhat abbreviated the Romany text of this letter, and Miss Lee herself has somewhat polished and enlarged the translation, which is strictly fit and proper, she being a very different person in English from what she is in gypsy, as are most of her kind. This letter may be, to many, a strange lesson, a quaint essay, a social problem, a fable, an epigram, or a frolic, — just as they choose to take it. To me it is a poem. Thou, my friend, canst easily understand why all that is wild and strange, out-of-doors, far away by night, is worthy of being Tennysoned or Whitmanned. If there be given unto thee stupendous blasted trees, looking in the moonlight like the pillars of a vast and ghostly temple; the fall of cataracts down awful rocks; the wind wailing in wondrous language or whistling Indian melody all night on heath, rocks, and hills, over ancient graves and through lonely caves, bearing with it the hoot of the night-owl; while over all the stars look down in eternal mystery, like eyes reading the great riddle of the night which thou knowest not, — this is to thee like Ariel's song. To me and to us there are men and women who are in life as the wild river and the night-owl, as the blasted tree and the wind over ancient graves. No man is educated until he has arrived at that state of thought when a picture is quite the same as a book, an old gray-beard jug as a manuscript, men, women, and children as libraries. It was but yester morn that I read a cuneiform inscription printed by doves' feet in the snow, finding a meaning where in by-gone years I should have seen only a quaint resemblance. For in this by the *ornithomanteia* known of old to the Chaldean sages I saw that it was neither from arrow-heads or wedges which gave the letters to the old Assyrians. When thou art at this point, then Nature is equal in all her types, and the city, as the forest, full of endless beauty and piquancy, — *in sæcula sæculorum*.

I had written the foregoing, and had enveloped and directed it to be mailed, when I met in a lady-book entitled " Magyarland " with the following passages : —

" The gypsy girl in this family was a pretty young woman, with masses of raven hair and a clear skin, but, notwithstanding her neat dress and civilized surroundings, we recognized her immediately. It is, in truth, not until one sees the Romany translated to an entirely new form of existence, and under circumstances inconsistent with their ordinary lives, that one realizes how completely different they are from the rest of mankind in form and feature. Instead of disguising, the garb of civilization only enhances the type, and renders it the more apparent. No matter what dress they may assume, no matter what may be their calling, no matter whether they are dwellers in tents or houses, it is impossible for gypsies to disguise their origin. Taken from their customary surroundings, they become at once an anomaly and an anachronism, and present such an instance of the absurdity of attempting to invert the order of nature that we feel more than ever how utterly different they are from the human race; that there is a key to their strange life which we do not possess, — a secret freemasonry that renders them more isolated than the veriest savages dwelling in the African wilds, — and a hidden mystery hanging over them and their origin that we shall never comprehend. They are indeed a people so entirely separate and distinct that, in whatever clime or quarter of the globe they may be met with, they are instantly recognized; for with them forty centuries of association with civilized races have not succeeded in obliterating one single sign."

"Alas!" cried the princess; "I can never, never find the door of the enchanted cavern, nor enter the golden cavern, nor solve its wonderful mystery. It has been closed for thousands of years, and it will remain closed forever."

"What flowers are those which thou holdest?" asked the hermit.

"Only primroses or Mary's-keys,[1] and tulips," replied the princess.

"Touch the rock with them," said the hermit, "and the door will open."

The lady writer of "Magyarland" held in her hand all the while, and knew it not, a beautiful primrose, which might have opened for her the mysterious Romany cavern. On a Danube steamboat she saw a little blind boy sitting all day all alone: only a little Slavonian peasant boy, "an odd, quaint little specimen of humanity, with loose brown garments, cut precisely like those of a grown-up man, and his bits of feet in little raw-hide moccasins." However, with a

---

[1] *Primulaveris:* in German *Schlüssel blume*, that is, key flowers; also Mary's-keys and keys of heaven. Both the primrose and tulip are believed in South Germany to be an Open Sesame to hidden treasure.

tender, gentle heart she began to pet the little waif. And the captain told her what the boy was. " He is a *guslar*, or minstrel, as they call them in Croatia. The Yougo-Slavs dedicate all male children who are born blind, from infancy, to the Muses. As soon as they are old enough to handle anything, a small mandolin is given them, which they are taught to play ; after which they are taken every day into the woods, where they are left till evening to commune in their little hearts with nature. In due time they become poets, or at any rate rhapsodists, singing of the things they never saw, and when grown up are sent forth to earn their livelihood, like the troubadours of old, by singing from place to place, and asking alms by the wayside.

" It is not difficult for a Slav to become a poet ; he takes in poetic sentiment as a river does water from its source. The first sounds he is conscious of are the words of his mother singing to him as she rocks his cradle. Then, as she watches the dawning of intelligence in his infant face, her mother language is that of poetry, which she improvises at the moment, and though he never saw the flowers nor the snow-capped mountains, nor the flowing streams and rivers, he describes them out of his inner consciousness, and the influence which the varied sounds of nature have upon his mind."

Rock and river and greenwood tree, sweet-spiced spring flower, rustling grass, and bird-singing nature and freedom, — this is the secret of the poets' song and of the Romany, and there is no other mystery in either. He who sleeps on graves rises mad or a poet; all who lie on the earth, which is the grave and cradle of nature, and who live *al fresco*, understand gyp-

sies as well as my lady Britannia Lee. Nay, when
some natures take to the Romany they become like
the Norman knights of the Pale, who were more Pad-
dyfied than the Paddies themselves. These become
leaders among the gypsies, who recognize the fact
that one renegade is more zealous than ten Turks.
As for the " mystery " of the history of the gypsies,
it is time, sweet friends, that 't were ended. When
we know that there is to-day, in India, a sect and set
of Vauriens, who are there considered Gipsissimæ,
and who call themselves, with their wives and language and being, Rom, Romni, and Romnipana, even
as they do in England ; and when we know, moreover, that their faces proclaim them to be Indian, and
that they have been a wandering caste since the dawn
of Hindu history, we have, I trow, little more to
seek. As for the rest, you may read it in the great
book of Out-of Doors, *capitulo nullo folio nigro*, or
wherever you choose to open it, written as distinctly,
plainly, and sweetly as the imprint of a school-boy's
knife and fork on a mince-pie, or in the uprolled
rapture of the eyes of Britannia when she inhaleth
the perfume of a fresh bunch of Florentine violets.
Ite missa est.

GYPSIES IN THE EAST.

Noon in Cairo.

A silent old court-yard, half sun and half shadow, in which quaintly graceful, strangely curving columns seem to have taken from long companionship with trees something of their inner life, while the palms, their neighbors, from long in-door existence, look as if they had in turn acquired household or animal instincts, if not human sympathies. And as the younger the race the more it seeks for poets and orators to express in thought what it only feels, so these dumb pillars and plants found their poet and orator in the fountain which sang or spoke for them strangely and sweetly all night and day, uttering for them not only their waking thoughts, but their dreams. It gave a voice, too, to the ancient Persian tiles and the Cufic inscriptions which had seen the caliphs, and it told endless stories of Zobeide and Mesrour and Haroun al Raschid.

Beyond the door which, when opened, gave this sight was a dark ancient archway twenty yards long, which opened on the glaring, dusty street, where camels with their drivers and screaming *sais*, or carriage-runners and donkey-boys and crying venders, kept up the wonted Oriental din. But just within the archway, in its duskiest corner, there sat all day a living picture, a dark and handsome woman, apparently

thirty years old, who was unveiled. She had before
her a cloth and a few shells; sometimes an Egyptian
of the lower class stopped, and there would be a grave
consultation, and the shells would be thrown, and
then further solemn conference and a payment of
money and a departure. And it was world-old Egyptian, or Chaldean, as to custom, for the woman was a
Rhagarin, or gypsy, and she was one of the diviners
who sit by the wayside, casting shells for auspices,
even as shells and arrows were cast of old, to be cursed
by Israel.

It is not remarkable that among the myriad *man-
teias* of olden days there should have been one by
shells. The sound of the sea as heard in the nautilus
or conch, when

> " It remembers its august abode
> And murmurs as the ocean murmurs there,"

is very strange to children, and I can remember
how in childhood I listened with perfect faith to the
distant roaring, and marveled at the mystery of the
ocean song being thus forever kept alive, inland.
Shells seem so much like work of human hands, and
are often so marked as with letters, that it is not
strange that faith soon found the supernatural in
them. The magic shell of all others is the cowrie.
Why the Roman ladies called it *porcella*, or little pig,
because it has a pig's back, is the objective explanation of its name, and how from its gloss that name,
or porcellana, was transferred to porcelain, is in
books. But there is another side to the shell, and
another or esoteric meaning to " piggy," which was
also known to the *dames du temps jadis*, to Archi-
piada and Thais, *qui fut la belle Romaine*, — and this
inner meaning makes of it a type of birth or creation.

19

Now all that symbolizes fertility, birth, pleasure, warmth, light, and love is opposed to barrenness, cold, death, and evil; whence it follows that the very sight of a shell, and especially of a cowrie, frightens away the devils as well as a horse-shoe, which by the way has also its cryptic meaning. Hence it was selected to cast for luck, a world-old custom, which still lingers in the game of props ; and for the same reason it is hung on donkeys, the devil being still scared away by the sight of a cowrie, even as he was scared away of old by its prototype, as told by Rabelais.

As the sibyls sat in caves, so the sorceress sat in the dark archway, immovable when not sought, mysterious as are all her kind, and something to wonder at. It was after passing her, and feeling by quick intuition what she was, that the court-yard became a fairy-land, and the fountain its poet, and the palm-trees Tamar maids. There are people who believe there is no mystery, that an analysis of the gypsy sorceress would have shown an ignorant outcast; but while nature gives chiaro-oscuro and beauty, and while God is the Unknown, I believe that the more light there is cast by science the more stupendous will be the new abysses of darkness revealed. These natures must be taken with the *life* in them, not dead, — and their life is mystery. The Hungarian gypsy lives in an intense mystery, yes, in true magic in his singing. You may say that he cannot, like Orpheus, move rocks or tame beasts with his music. If he could he could do no more than astonish and move us, and he does that now, and the *why* is as deep a mystery as that would be.

So far is it from being only a degrading superstition in those who believe that mortals like themselves can predict the future, that it seems, on the contrary, ennobling. It is precisely because man feels a mystery within himself that he admits it may be higher in others; if spirits whisper to him in dreams and airy passages of trembling light, or in the music never heard but ever felt below, what may not be revealed to others? You may tell me if you will that prophecies are all rubbish and magic a lie, and it may be so, — nay, *is* so, but the awful mystery of the Unknown without a name and the yearning to penetrate it *is*, and is all the more, because I have found all prophecies and jugglings and thaumaturgy fail to bridge over the abyss. It is since I have read with love and faith the evolutionists and physiologists of the most advanced type that the Unknown has become to me most wonderful, and that I have seen the light which never shone on sea or land as I never saw it before. And therefore to me the gypsy and all the races who live in freedom and near to nature are more poetic than ever. For which reason, after the laws of acoustics have fully explained to me why the nautilus sounds like a far off-ocean dirge, the unutterable longing *to know more* seizes upon me,

> " Till my heart is full of longing
> For the secret of the sea,
> And the heart of the great ocean
> Sends a thrilling pulse through me."

That gypsy fortune-teller, sitting in the shadow, is, moreover, interesting as a living manifestation of a dead past. As in one of her own shells when petrified we should have the ancient form without its color, all the old elements being displaced by new ones, so we have the old magic shape, though every atom in it is different; the same, yet not the same.

Life in the future, and the divination thereof, was a
stupendous, ever-present reality to the ancient Egyptian, and the sole inspiration of humanity when it
produced few but tremendous results.   It is when we
see it in such living forms that it is most interesting.   As in Western wilds we can tell exactly by the
outline of the forests where the borders of ancient
inland seas once ran, so in the great greenwood of
history we can trace by the richness or absence of
foliage and flower the vanished landmarks of poetry,
or perceive where the enchantment whose charm has
now flown like the snow of the foregone year once
reigned in beauty.   So a line of lilies has shown me
where the sea-foam once fell, and pine-trees sang of
masts preceding them.

> " I sometimes think that never blows so red
> The rose as where some buried Cæsar bled ;
> That every hyacinth the garden wears
> Dropt in her lap from some once lovely head." [1]

The memory of that court-yard reminds me that I
possess two Persian tiles, each with a story.   There is
a house in Cairo which is said to be more or less
contemporary with the prophet, and it is inhabited by
an old white-bearded emir, more or less a descendant of the prophet.   This old gentleman once gave
as a precious souvenir to an American lady two of
the beautiful old tiles from his house, whereof I had
one.   In the eyes of a Muslim there is a degree of
sanctity attached to this tile, as one on which the
eyes of the prophet may have rested, — or at least
the eyes of those who were nearer to him than we
are.   Long after I returned from Cairo I wrote and

---

[1] Omar Khayyám, *Rubaiyat.*

GYPSIES IN THE EAST.

published a fairy-book called Johnnykin,[1] in which
occurred the following lines: —

> Trust not the Ghoul, love,
> Heed not his smile ;
> *Out of the Mosque, love,*
> *He stole the tile.*

One day my friend the Palmer from over the sea
came to me with a present. It was a beautiful Persian tile.

"Where did you get it?" I asked.

"I stole it out of a mosque in Syria."

"Did you ever read my Johnnykin?"

"Of course not."

"I know you never did." Here I repeated the verse.
"But you remember what the Persian poet says:—

> "'And never since the vine-clad earth was young
> Was some great crime committed on the earth,
> But that some poet prophesied the deed.'"

"True, and also what the great Tsigane poet
sang : —

> "'O manush te lela sossi choredó,
> Wafodiro se te choramengró.'
>
> "He who takes the stolen ring,
> Is worse than he who stole the thing."

"And it would have been better for you, while you
were *dukkerin* or prophesying, to have prophesied
about something more valuable than a tile."

And so it came to pass that the two Persian tiles,
one given by a descendant of the Prophet, and the
other the subject of a prophecy, rest in my cabinet
side by side.

In Egypt, as in Austria, or Syria, or Persia, or India, the gypsies are the popular musicians. I had long

---

[1] *Johnnykin and the Goblins.* London : Macmillan.

sought for the derivation of the word *banjo*, and one day I found that the Oriental gypsies called a gourd by that name. Walking one day with the Palmer in Cambridge, we saw in a window a very fine Hindu lute, or in fact a real banjo made of a gourd. We inquired, and found that it belonged to a mutual friend, Mr. Charles Brookfield, one of the best fellows living, and who, on being forthwith "requisitioned" by the unanimous voice of all who sympathized with me in my need, sent me the instrument. "He did not think it right," he said, "to keep it, when Philology wanted it. If it had been any other party, — but he always had a particular respect and awe of her." I do not assert that this discovery settles the origin of the word *banjo*, but the coincidence is, to say the least, remarkable.

I saw many gypsies in Egypt, but learned little from them. What I found I stated in a work called the "Egyptian Sketch Book." It was to this effect: My first information was derived from the late Khedivé Ismael, who during an interview with me said, "There are in Egypt many people known as Rhagarin, or Ghagarin, who are probably the same as the gypsies of Europe. They are wanderers, who live in tents, and are regarded with contempt even by the peasantry. Their women tell fortunes, tattoo, and sell small wares; the men work in iron. They are all adroit thieves, and noted as such. The men may sometimes be seen going round the country with monkeys. In fact, they appear to be in all respects the same people as the gypsies of Europe."

I habitually employed, while in Cairo, the same donkey-driver, an intelligent and well-behaved man named Mahomet, who spoke English fairly. On ask-

ing him if he could show me any Rhagarin, he replied
that there was a fair or market held every Saturday at Boulac, where I would be sure to meet with
women of the tribe. The men, he said, seldom ventured into the city, because they were subject to much
insult and ill-treatment from the common people.

On the day appointed I rode to Boulac. The market was very interesting. I saw no European or
Frangi there, except my companion, Baron de Cosson,
who afterwards traveled far into the White Nile country, and who had with his brother Edward many remarkable adventures in Abyssinia, which were well
recorded by the latter in a book. All around were
thousands of blue-skirted and red-tarbouched or white-
turbaned Egyptians, buying or selling, or else amusing themselves, but with an excess of outcry and
hallo which indicates their grown child character.
There were dealers in donkeys and horses roaring
aloud, "He is for ten napoleons! Had I asked twenty
you would have gladly given me fifteen!" "O true
believers, here is a Syrian steed which will give
renown to the purchaser!" Strolling loosely about
were dealers in sugar-cane and pea-nuts, which are
called gooba in Africa as in America, pipe peddlers
and venders of rosaries, jugglers and minstrels. At
last we came to a middle-aged woman seated on the
ground behind a basket containing beads, glass armlets, and such trinkets. She was dressed like any
Arab-woman of the lower class, but was not veiled,
and on her chin blue lines were tattooed. Her features and expression were, however, gypsy, and not
Egyptian. And as she sat there quietly I wondered
how a woman could feel in her heart who was looked
down upon with infinite scorn by an Egyptian, who

might justly be looked down on in his turn with sublime contempt by an average American Methodist colored whitewasher who "took de ' Ledger.' " Yet there was in the woman the quiet expression which associates itself with respectability, and it is worth remarking that whenever a race is greatly looked down on by another from the stand-point of mere color, as in America, or mere religion, as in Mahometan lands, it always contains proportionally a larger number of *decent* people than are to be found among those who immediately oppress it. An average Chinese is as a human being far superior to a hoodlum, and a man of color to the white man who cannot speak of him or to him except as a "naygur" or a "nigger." It is when a man realizes that he is superior in *nothing* else save race, color, religion, family, inherited fortune, and their contingent advantages that he develops most readily into the prig and snob.

I spoke to the woman in Romany, using such words as would have been intelligible to any of her race in any other country; but she did not understand me, and declared that she could speak nothing but Arabic. At my request Mahomet explained to her that I had come from a distant country in Orobba, or Europe, where there were many Rhagarin, who said that their fathers came from Egypt, and that I wished to know if any in the old country could speak the old language. She replied that the Rhagarin of Montesinos could still speak it; but that her people in Egypt had lost the tongue. Mahomet, in translating, here remarked that Montesinos meant Mount Sinai or Syria. I then asked her if the Rhagarin had no peculiar name for themselves, and she answered, "Yes; we call ourselves Tatâren."

This at least was satisfactory. All over Southern Germany and in Norway the gypsies are called Tartaren, and though the word means Tartars, and is misapplied, it indicates the race. The woman seemed to be much gratified at the interest I manifested in her people. I gave her a double piaster, and asked for its value in blue glass armlets. She gave me four, and as I turned to depart called me back, and with a good-natured smile handed me four more as a present. This generosity was very gypsy-like, and very unlike the habitual meanness of the ordinary Egyptian.

After this Mahomet took me to a number of Rhagarin. They all resembled the one whom I had seen, and all were sellers of small articles and fortune-tellers. They all differed slightly from common Egyptians in appearance, and were more unlike them in not being importunate for money, nor disagreeable in their manners. But though they were as certainly gypsies as old Charlotte Cooper herself, none of them could speak Romany. I used to amuse myself by imagining what some of my English gypsy friends would have done if turned loose in Cairo among their cousins. How naturally old Charlotte would have waylaid and "dukkered" and amazed the English ladies in the Muskee, and how easily that reprobate old amiable cosmopolite, the Windsor Frog, would have mingled with the motley mob of donkey-boys and tourists before Shepherd's Hotel, and appointed himself an *attaché* to their excursions to the Pyramids, and drunk their pale ale or anything else to their healths, and then at the end of the day have claimed a wage for his politeness! And how well the climate would have agreed with them, and how they would have agreed that it was of all lands the best for *tannin*, or tenting out, in the world!

The gypsiest-looking gypsy in Cairo, with whom
I became somewhat familiar, was a boy of sixteen, a
snake-charmer; a dark and even handsome youth,
but with eyes of such wild wickedness that no one
who had ever seen him excited could hope that he
would ever become as other human beings. I believe
that he had come, as do all of his calling, from a
snake-catching line of ancestors, and that he had taken
in from them, as did Elsie Venner, the serpent nature.
They had gone snaking, generation after generation,
from the days of the serpent worship of old, it may
be back to the old Serpent himself; and this tawny,
sinuous, active thing of evil, this boy, without the
least sense of sympathy for any pain, who devoured a
cobra alive with as much indifference as he had just
shown in petting it, was the result. He was a human
snake. I had long before reading the wonderfully
original work of Doctor Holmes reflected deeply on
the moral and immoral influences which serpent worship of old, in Syria and other lands, must have had
upon its followers. But Elsie Venner sets forth the
serpent nature as benumbed or suspended by cold
New England winters and New England religions,
moral and social influences; the Ophites of old and
the Cairene gypsy showed the boy as warmed to life in
lands whose winters are as burning summers. Elsie
Venner is not sensual, and sensuality is the leading
trait of the human-serpent nature. Herein lies an
error, just as a sculptor would err who should present
Lady Godiva as fully draped, or Sappho merely as a
sweet singer of Lesbos, or Antinous only as a fine
young man. He who would harrow hell and rake
out the devil, and then exhibit to us an ordinary sinner, or an *opera bouffe* " Mefistofele," as the result,

reminds one of the seven Suabians who went to hunt
a monster, — " *ä Ungeheuer*," — and returned with a
hare. Elsie Venner is not a hare ; she is a wonderful
creation; but she is a winter-snake. I confess that I
have no patience, however, with those who pretend
to show us summer-snakes, and would fain dabble with
vice ; who are amateurs in the diabolical, and drawing-room dilettanti in damnation. Such, as I have
said before, are the æsthetic adorers of Villon, whom
the old *roué* himself would have most despised, and
the admirers of " Faustine," whom Faustina would
have picked up between her thumb and finger, and
eyed with serene contempt before throwing them out
of the window. A future age will have for these
would-be wickeds, who are only monks half turned
inside out, more laughter than we now indulge in at
Chloe and Strephon.

I always regarded my young friend Abdullah as a
natural child of the devil and a serpent-souled young
sinner, and he never disappointed me in my opinion
of him. I never in my life felt any antipathy to serpents, and he evidently regarded me as a *sapengro,* or
snake-master. The first day I met him he put into
my hands a cobra which had the fangs extracted, and
then handled an asp which still had its poison teeth.
On his asking me if I was afraid of it, and my telling
him " No," he gave it to me, and after I had petted
it, he always manifested an understanding, — I cannot say sympathy. I should have liked to see that
boy's sister, if he ever had one, and was not hatched
out from some egg found in the desert by an Egyptian incubus or incubator. She must have been a
charming young lady, and his mother must have
been a beauty, especially when in court-dress, — with

her broom *et præterea nihil.* But neither, alas, could
be ever seen by me, for it is written in the " Gittin "
that there are three hundred species of male demons,
but what the female herself is like is known to no
one.

Abdullah first made his appearance before me at
Shepherd's Hotel, and despite his amazing natural impudence, which appeared to such splendid advantage
in the street that I always thought he must be a lin-
eal descendant of the brazen serpent himself, he
evinced a certain timidity which was to me inexplicable, until I recalled that the big snake of Irish
legends had shown the same modesty when Saint
Patrick wanted him to enter the chest which he had
prepared for his prison.   "Sure, it's a nate little
house I've made for yees," said the saint, " wid an
iligant parlor."   " I don't like the look av it at all, at
all," says the sarpent, as he squinted at it suspiciously,
" and I'm loath to *inter* it."

Abdullah looked at the parlor as if he too were loath
to "inter " it; but he was in charge of one in whom
his race instinctively trust, so I led him in.   His apparel was simple : it consisted of a coarse shirt, very
short, with a belt around the waist, and an old tar-
bouch on his head.   Between the shirt and his bare
skin, as in a bag, was about a half peck of cobras,
asps, vipers, and similar squirming property; while
between his cap and his hair were generally stowed
one or two enormous living scorpions, and any small
serpents that he could not trust to dwell with the
larger ones.   When I asked Abdullah where he contrived to get such vast scorpions and such lively serpents, he replied, " Out in the desert."   I arranged,
in fact, to go out with him some day a-snaking and

scorp'ing, and have ever since regretted that I did not avail myself of the opportunity. He showed off his snakes to the ladies, and concluded by offering to eat the largest one alive before our eyes for a dollar, which price he speedily reduced to a half. There was a young New England lady present who was very anxious to witness this performance; but as I informed Abdullah that if he attempted anything of the kind I would kick him out-of-doors, snakes and all, he ceased to offer to show himself a cannibal. Perhaps he had learned what Rabbi Simon ben Yochai taught, that it is a good deed to smash the heads of the best of serpents, even as it is a duty to kill the best of Goyim. And if by Goyim he meant Philistines, I agree with him.

I often met Abdullah after that, and helped him to several very good exhibitions. Two or three things I learned from him. One was that the cobra, when wide awake, yet not too violently excited, lifts its head and maintains a curious swaying motion, which, when accompanied by music, may readily be mistaken for dancing acquired from a teacher. The Hindu *sappa-wallahs* make people believe that this "dancing" is really the result of tuition, and that it is influenced by music. Later, I found that the common people in Egypt continue to believe that the snakes which Abdullah and his tribe exhibit are as dangerous and deadly as can be, and that they are managed by magic. Whether they believe, as it was held of old by the Rabbis, that serpents are to be tamed by sorcery only on the Sabbath, I never learned.

Abdullah was crafty enough for a whole generation of snakes, but in the wisdom attributed to serpents he was woefully wanting. He would run by my side

in the street as I rode, expecting that I would pause
to accept a large wiggling scorpion as a gift, or purchase a viper, I suppose for a riding-whip or a neck-
tie.   One day when I was in a jam of about a hundred donkey-boys, trying to outride the roaring mob,
and all of a fever with heat and dust, Abdullah spied
me, and, joining the mob, kept running by my side,
crying in maddening monotony, " Snake, sah! Scorpion, sah! Very fine snake to-day, sah!"—just as
if his serpents were edible delicacies, which were for
that day particularly fresh and nice.

There are three kinds of gypsies in Egypt,—the
Rhagarin, the Helebis, and the Nauar.   They have
secret jargons among themselves; but as I ascertained
subsequently from specimens given by Captain New-
boldt[1] and Seetzen, as quoted by Pott,[2] their language
is made up of Arabic " back-slang, Turkish and
Greek, with a very little Romany,—so little that it
is not wonderful that I could not converse with them
in it.   The Syrian gypsies, or Nuri, who are seen
with bears and monkeys in Cairo, are strangers in the
land.   With them a conversation is not difficult.   It
is remarkable that while English, German, and Turkish or Syrian gypsy look so different and difficult as
printed in books, it is on the whole an easy matter to
get on with them in conversation.   The roots being
the same, a little management soon supplies the rest.

Abdullah was a Helebi.   The last time I saw him
I was sitting on the balcony of Shepherd's Hotel, in
the early evening, with an American, who had never
seen a snake-charmer.   I called the boy, and inad-

---

[1] Vide *Journal of the Royal Asiatic Society*, vol. xvi. part 2, 1856
p. 285.
[2] *Die Zigeuner.*

vertently gave him his pay in advance, telling him to show all his stock in trade. But the temptation to swindle was too great, and seizing the coin he rushed back into the darkness. From that hour I beheld him no more. I think I can see that last gleam of his demon eyes as he turned and fled. I met in after-days with other snake-boys, but for an eye which indicated an unadulterated child of the devil, and for general blackguardly behavior to match, I never found anybody like my young friend Abdullah.

The last snake-masters whom I came across were two sailors at the Oriental Seamen's Home in London. And strangely enough, on the day of my visit they had obtained in London, of all places, a very large and profitable job; for they had been employed to draw the teeth of all the poisonous serpents in the Zoölogical Garden. Whether these practitioners ever applied for or received positions as members of the Dental College I do not know, any more than if they were entitled to practice as surgeons without licenses. Like all the Hindu *sappa-wallahs*, or snake-men, they are what in Europe would be called gypsies.

GYPSY NAMES AND FAMILY CHARAC-
TERISTICS.

———◆———

THE following list gives the names of the principal gypsy
families in England, with their characteristics. It was prepared for me by an old, well-known Romany, of full blood.
Those which have (A) appended to them are known to have
representatives in America. For myself, I believe that gypsies bearing all these names are to be found in both countries. I would also state that the personal characteristics
attributed to certain families are by no means very strictly
applicable, neither do any of them confine themselves rigidly
to any particular part of England. I have met, for instance,
with Bosvilles, Lees, Coopers, Smiths, Bucklands, etc., in
every part of England as well as Wales. I am aware that
the list is imperfect in all respects.

AYRES.
BAILEY (A). Half-bloods. Also called rich. **Roam** in
    Sussex.
BARTON. Lower Wiltshire.
BLACK. Hampshire.
BOSVILLE (A). Generally spread, but are specially to be
    found in Devonshire. I have found several fine speci-
    mens of real Romanys among the American Bosvilles.
    In Romany, *Chumomishto*, that is, Buss (or Kiss) well.
BROADWAY (A). Somerset.
BUCKLAND. In Gloucestershire, but abounding over Eng-
    land. Sometimes called *Chokamengro*, that is. Tailor.

BURTON (A). Wiltshire.

CHAPMAN (A). Half-blood, and are commonly spoken of as a rich clan. Travel all over England.

CHILCOTT (vul. CHILCOCK).

CLARKE. Half-blood. Portsmouth.

COOPER (A). Chiefly found in Berkshire and Windsor. In Romany, *Vardo mescro.*

DAVIES.

DICKENS. Half-blood.

DIGHTON. Blackheath.

DRAPER. Hertfordshire.

FINCH.

FULLER. Hardly half-blood, but talk Romany.

GRAY. Essex. In Romany, *Gry*, or horse.

HARE (A). Chiefly in Hampshire.

HAZARD. Half-blood. Windsor.

HERNE. Oxfordshire and London. "Of this name there are," says Borrow (Romano Lavo-Lil), "two gypsy renderings: (1.) Rosar-mescro or Ratzie-mescro, that is, *duck-fellow*; the duck being substituted for the *heron*, for which there is no word in Romany, this being done because there is a resemblance in the sound of Heron and Herne. (2.) Balor-engre, or Hairy People, the translator having confounded Herne with Haaren, Old English for hairs."

HICKS. Half-blood. Berkshire.

HUGHES. Wiltshire.

INGRAHAM (A). Wales and Birmingham, or in the Kálo tem or Black Country.

JAMES. Half-blood.

JENKINS. Wiltshire.

JONES. Half-blood. Headquarters at Battersea, near London.

LEE (A). The same in most respects as the Smiths, but are even more widely extended. I have met with several of the most decided type of pure-blooded, old-fashioned gypsies among Lees in America. They are sometimes

20

among themselves called *purum*, a *lee-k*, from the fancied resemblance of the words.

LEWIS. Hampshire.

LOCKE. Somerset and Gloucestershire.

LOVEL. Known in Romany as Kamlo, or Kamescro, that is, lover. London, but are found everywhere.

LOVERIDGE. Travel in Oxfordshire; are in London at Shepherd's Bush.

MARSHALL. As much Scotch as English, especially in Dumfriesshire and Galloway, in which latter region, in Saint Cuthbert's church-yard, lies buried the "old man" of the race, who died at the age of one hundred and seven. In Romany Makkado-tan-engree, that is, Fellows of the Marshes. Also known as Bungoror, cork-fellows and Chikkenemengree, china or earthenware (lit. dirt or clay) men, from their cutting corks, and peddling pottery, or mending china.

MATTHEWS. Half-blood. Surrey.

NORTH.

PETULENGRO, or SMITH. The Romany name Petulengro means Master of the Horseshoe; that is, Smith. The gypsy who made this list declared that he had been acquainted with Jasper Petulengro, of Borrow's Lavengro, and that he died near Norwich about sixty years ago. The Smiths are general as travelers, but are chiefly to be found in the East of England.

PIKE. Berkshire.

PINFOLD, or PENFOLD. Half and quarter blood. Widely extended, but most at home in London.

RÓLLIN (ROLAND ?). Half-blood. Chiefly about London.

SCAMP. Chiefly in Kent. A small clan. Mr. Borrow derives this name from the Sanskrit Ksump, to go. I trust that it has not a more recent and purely English derivation.

SHAW.

SMALL (A). Found in West England, chiefly in Somerset and Devonshire.

STANLEY (A). One of the most extended clans, but said to be chiefly found in Devonshire. They sometimes call themselves in joke Beshalay, that is, Sit-Down, from the word *stan*, suggesting standing up in connection with lay. Also Bangor, or Baromescre, that is, Stone (stan) people. Thus "Stony-lea" was probably their first name. Also called Kashtengrees, Woodmen, from the New Forest.

TAYLOR. A clan described as *diddikai*, or half-bloods. Chiefly in London. This clan should be the only one known as *Chokamengro*.

TURNER.

WALKER. Half-blood. Travel about Surrey.

WELLS (A). Half-blood. Somerset.

WHARTON. WORTON. I have only met the Whartons in America.

WHEELER. Pure and half-blood. Battersea.

WHITE.

"Adré o Lavines tem o Romanies see WOODS, ROBERTS, WILLIAMS, and JONES. In Wales the gypsies are Woods, Roberts, Williams, and Jones."[1]

CHARACTERISTICS.[2]

Of these gypsies the BAILIES are fair.

The BIRDS are in Norfolk and Suffolk.

The BLACKS are dark, stout, and strong.

The BOSVILLES are rather short, fair, stout, and heavy.

The BROADWAYS are fair, of medium height and good figures.

The BUCKLANDS are thin, dark, and tallish.

The BUNCES travel in the South of England.

The BURTONS are short, dark, and very active.

The CHAPMANS are fair.

---

[1] *The Dialect of the English Gypsies.*

[2] I beg the reader to bear it in mind that all this is literally as it was given by an old gypsy, and that I am not responsible for its accuracy or inaccuracy.

The CLARKES are fair and well-sized men.

The COOPERS are short, dark, and very active.

The DIGHTONS are very dark and stout.

The DRAPERS are very tall and large and dark.

The FAAS are at Kirk Yetholm, in Scotland.

The GRAYS are very large and fair.

The GREENES are small and dark.

The GREGORIES range from Surrey to Suffolk.

The HARES are large, stout, and dark.

The HAZARDS are tall and fair.

The HERNES (Herons) are very large and dark.

The HICKS are very large, strong, and fair.

The HUGHES are short, stubby, and dark.

The INGRAHAMS are fair and all of medium height.

The JENKINS are dark, not large, and active.

The JONES are fair and of middling height.

The LANES are fair and of medium height.

The LEES are dark, tall, and stout.

The LEWIS are dark and of medium height.

The LIGHTS are half-bloods, and travel in Middlesex.

The LOCKES are shortish, dark, and large.

The LOVELLS are dark and large.

The MACES are about Norwich.

The MATTHEWS are thick, short, and stout, fair, and good fighters.

The MILLERS are at Battersea.

NORTH. Are to be found at Shepherd's Bush.

The OLIVERS are in Kent.

The PIKES are light and very tall.

The PINFOLDS are light, rather tall, not heavy. (Are really a Norfolk family. F. Groome.)

The ROLANDS are rather large and dark.

The SCAMPS are very dark and stout.

The SHAWS travel in Middlesex.

The SMALLS are tall, stout, and fair.

The SMITHS are dark, rather tall, slender, and active.

The STANLEYS are tall, dark, and handsome.

The TAYLORS are short, stout, and dark.

The TURNERS are also in Norfolk and Suffolk.

The WALKERS are stout and fair.

The WELLS are very light and tall.

The WHEELERS are thin and fair.

The WHITES are short and light.

The YOUNGS are very dark. They travel in the northern counties, and belong both to Scotland and England.

The following is a collection of the more remarkable "fore" or Christian names of Romanys : —

MASCULINE NAMES.

Opi Boswell.

Wanselo, or Anselo. I was once of the opinion that this name was originally Lancelot, but as Mr. Borrow has found Wentzlow, *i. e.*, Wenceslas, in England, the latter is probably the original. I have found it changed to Onslow, as the name painted on a Romany van in Aberystwith, but it was pronounced Anselo.

Pastor-rumis.

Spico.

Jineral, *i. e.*, General Cooper.

Horferus and Horfer. Either Arthur or Orpheus. His name was then changed to Wacker-doll, and finally settled into Wacker.

Plato or Platos Buckland.

Wine-Vinegar Cooper. The original name of the child bearing this extraordinary name was Owen. He died soon after birth, and was in consequence always spoken of as Wine-Vinegar, — Wine for the joy which his parents had at his birth, and Vinegar to signify their grief at his loss.

Gilderoy Buckland.	Silvanus Boswell.
Lancelot Cooper.	Sylvester, Vester, Wester,
Oscar Buckland.	Westarus and 'Starus.
Dimiti Buckland.	Liberty.
Piramus Boswell.	Goliath.

Reconcile.

Justerinus.

Faunio.

Shek-ésu. I am assured on good authority that a gypsy had a child baptized by this name.

Artaros.

Culvato (Claude).

Divervus.

Lasho, *i. e.*, Louis.

Vesuvius. I do not know whether any child was actually called by this burning cognomen, but I remember that a gypsy, hearing two gentlemen talking about Mount Vesuvius, was greatly impressed by the name, and consulted with them as to the propriety of giving it to his little boy.

Wisdom.

Inverto.

Studaveres Lovel.

Octavius.

Render Smith.

Sacki.

Spysell.

Spico.

Loverin.

Mantis.

Happy Boswell.

FEMININE NAMES.

Selinda, Slinda, Linda, Slindi.

Mia.

Mizelia, Mizelli, Mizela.

Lina.

Pendivella.

Jewránum, *i. e.*, Geranium.

Virginta.

Suby, Azuba.

Isaia.

Richenda.

Kiomi.

Liberina.

Malindi.

Otchamé.

Renée.

Sinaminta.

Y-yra or Yeira.

Delira, Delcera.

Delilah.

Prudence.

Providence.

Eve.

Athaliah.

Gentilla, Gentie.

Synfie. Probably Cynthia.

Sybie. Probably from Sibyl.

Canairis.

Fenella.

Floure, Flower, Flora.

Kisaiya.

Orlenda.

Reyora, Regina.

Syeira. Probably Cyra.

Truffeni.

Ocean Solis.

Marili Stanley.

Britannia.

Glani.

Zuba.

Sybarini Cooper.

Esmeralda Locke.

Penti.

Reservi. This extraordinary name was derived from a reservoir, by which some gypsies were camped, and where a child was born.

Lementina.

Rodi.

Alabīna.

Dosia.

Lavi.

Silvina.

Richenda.

Marbelenni.

Ashena.

Vashti.

Youregh.

Penelli. Possibly from Fenella.

Ségel Buckland.

Morella Knightly.

Eza.

Lenda.

Collia.

Casello (Celia).

Catseye.

Trainette.

Perpinia.

Dora.

Starlina.

Bazena.

Bena.

Ewri.

Koket.

Lusho.

GYPSY STORIES.

IN ROMANY, WITH TRANSLATION.

———◆———

MERLINOS TE TRINALI.

"Miro koko, pen mandy a rinkeno gudlo?"
Avali miri chavi. Me 'tvel pen tute dui te
shyan trin, vonka tute 'atches sār pūkeno. Shūn
amengi. Yeckorus adré o Làvines tem sos a boro
chovihan, navdo Merlinos. Gusvero mush sos Merlinos, būti seeri covva yuv asti kair. Jindás yuv ta
pūr yeck jivnipen adré o waver, saster adré o rūpp,
te o rūpp adré sonakai. Finō covva sos adovo te sos
miro. Te longoduro fon leste jivdes a bori chovihani,
Trinali sos lākis nav. Boridiri chovihani sos Trinali,
būti manushe seerdas yoi, būti ryor pūrdas yoi adré
mylia te bālor, te né kesserdas yeck haura pā sār
lender dush.

Yeck divvus Merlinos liás lester chovihaneskro ran
te jas adūro ta latcher i chovihanī te pessur lāki
drován pā sār lākis wafropen. Te pā adovo tacho
dívvus i rāni Trinali shūndas sa Merlinos boro ruslo
sorelo chovihan se, te pendas, "Sossi ajafra mush?
Me dukkerāva leste or yuv tevel mer mande, s'up
mi o beng! me shom te seer leste. Mukkamen dikk
savo lela kūmi shūnaben, te savo sē o jinescrodiro?"
Te adoi o Merlinos jās apré o dromus, sārodívvus
akonyo, sarja adré o kamescro dūd, te Trinali jās

adré o wesh sarjā adré o rātinus, o tam, o kālopen,
o shure, denne yoi sos chovihāni. Kennāsig, yān
latcherde yeckawaver, awer Merlinos né jindas yoi
sos Trinali, te Trinali né jindas adovo manush se
Merlinos. Te yuv sos būti kamelo ke laki, te yoi
apopli ; kennāsig yāndūi ankairde ta kām yeckawaver butidiro. Vonka yeck jinella adovo te o waver
jinella lis, kek boro chirus tvel i duī sosti jinavit.
Merlinos te Trinali pende " me kamava tute," sig
ketenes, te chūmerde yeckawaver, te beshde alay
rikkerend adré o simno pelashta te rakkerde kūshto
bāk.

Te adenna Merlinos pūkkerdas lāki, yuv jas ta
dusher a būti wafodi chovihani, te Trinali pendas
lesko o simno covva, sā yoi sos ruzno ta kair o sīmno
keti a boro chovihano. Te i dūi ankairede ta mān-
ger yeckawāver ta mūkk o covva jā, te yoi te yuv
shomas atrash o nasherin lende pireno te pirenī.
Awer Merlinos pendas, " Mandy sovahalldom pā o
kam ta pur lāki pā sār lākis jivaben adré o wāver
trūppo." Te yoi ruvvedas te pendas, " Sovahalldas
me pā o chone ta pūr adovo chovihano adré a wavero,
sim's tute." Denna Merlinos putcherdas, " Sāsi les-
ters nav ? " Yoi pendas, " Merlinos." Yuv rakkere-
das palall, " Me shom leste, sāsī tiro nav ? " Yoi
shelledas avrī, " Trinali ! "

Kennā vānka chovihanis sovahallan chumeny apré
o kam te i choni, yān sosti keravit or mér. Te denna
Merlinos pendas, " Jinesa tu sā ta kair akovo pennis
sār kūshto te tacho ? " " Kekker mīro kāmlo pireno,"
pendas i chori chovihanī sā yoi ruvdas." " Denna
me shom kūmi jinescro, ne tute," pendas Merlinos.
" Shukar te kūshto covva se akovo, miri romni. Me
tevel pūr tute adré mande, te mande adré tute. Te
vonka mendui shom romadi mendui tevel yeck."

Sā yeck mush ta dívvus kennā penella yoi siggerdas leste, te awavero pens yuv siggerdas lāki. Ne jināva me miri kāmeli. Ne dikkdas tu kekker a dui sheres-cro haura? Avali! Wūsser lis uppar, te vānka lis pellalay pūkk amengy savo rikk se alay. Welsher pendas man adovo. Welsheri pennena sarja tacho-pen.

MERLIN AND TRINALI.

" My uncle, tell me a pretty story! "

Yes, my child. I will tell you two, and perhaps three, if you keep very quiet. Listen to me. Once in Wales there was a great wizard named Merlin. Many magic things he could do. He knew how to change one living being into another, iron into silver, and silver into gold. A fine thing that would be if it were mine. And afar from him lived a great witch. Trinali was her name. A great witch was Trinali. Many men did she enchant, many gentlemen did she change into asses and pigs, and never cared a copper for all their sufferings.

One day Merlin took his magic rod, and went afar to find the witch, and pay her severely for all her wickedness. And on that very [true] day the lady Trinali heard how Merlin was [is] a great, powerful wizard, and said, " What sort of a man is this? I will punish him or he shall kill me, deuce help me! I will bewitch him. Let us see who has the most cleverness and who is the most knowing. " And then Merlin went on the road all day alone, always in sunshine; and Trinali went in the forest, always in the shade, the darkness, the gloom, for she was a black witch. Soon they found one another, but Merlin did not know [that] she was Trinali, and Trinali

did not know that man was [is to be] Merlin. And
he was very pleasant to her, and she to him again.
Very soon the two began to love one another very
much. When one knows that and the other knows
it, both will soon know it. Merlin and Trinali said
" I love thee " both together, and kissed one another,
and sat down wrapped in the same cloak, and conversed happily.

Then Merlin told her he was going to punish a
very wicked witch; and Trinali told him the same
thing, how she was bold [daring] to do the same
thing to a great wizard. And the two began to beg
one another to let the thing go, and she and he were
afraid of losing lover and sweetheart. But Merlin
said, " I swore by the sun to change her for her
whole life into another form " [body] ; and she wept
and said, " I swore by the moon to change that wizard into another [person] even as you did." Then
Merlin inquired, " What is his name ? " She said,
" Merlin." He replied, " I am he ; what is your
name ? " She cried aloud, " Trinali."

Now when witches swear anything on the sun or
the moon, they must do it or die. Then Merlin said,
" Do you know how to make this business all nice
and right ? " " Not at all, my dear love," said the
poor witch, as she wept. " Then I am cleverer than
you," said Merlin. " An easy and nice thing it is,
my bride. For I will change you into me, and myself
into you. And when we are married we two will be
one."

So one man says nowadays that she conquered
him, and another that he conquered her. I do not
know [which it was], my dear. Did you ever see a
two-headed halfpenny ? *Yes?* Throw it up, and

when it falls down ask me which side is under. A
Welsher told me that story. Welshers always tell
the truth.

O PŪV-SŪVER.

Yeckorus sims būti kedivvus, sos rakli, te yoi sos
kushti partanengrī, te yoi astis kair a rinkeno plāchta,
yeck sār dívvus. Te covakai chi kamdas rye butidiro,
awer yeck dívvus lākis pīreno sos stardo adré staruben. Te vonka yoi shundas lis, yoi hushtiedas apré
te jas keti krallis te mangerdas leste choruknes ta
mūkk lākis pīreno jā pīro. Te krallis patserdas lāki
tevel yoi kairdas leste a rinkeno plāchta, yeck sār
divvus pā kūrikus, hafta plāchta pā hafta dívvus, yuv
tvel ferdel leste, te dé leste tachaben ta jā 'vrī. I
tāni rāni siggerdas ta keravit, te pā shov dívvus yoi
táderedas adrom, kūshti zī, pā lis te sārkon chirus
adré o shab yoi bítcherdas plāchta keta krallis. Awer
avella yeck dívvus yoi sos kinlo, te pendes yoi néi
kamdas kair būtsi 'dovo dívvus sī sos brishnū te yoi
nestis shīri a sappa dré o kamlo dūd. Adenn' o krallis
pendas te yoi nestis kair būtsi hafta dívvus lava lakis
pīreno, o rye sosti hatch staramescro te yoi ne mūkk-
das kāmaben adosta pā leste. Te i rakli sos sā hún-
nalo te tukno dré lakis zī yoi merdas o rúvvin te lias
pūraben adré o pūv-sūver. Te keti dívvus kennā yoi
pandella apré lakris tavia, vonka kam peshella, te i
cuttor pāni tu dikess' apré lende shan o panni fon
lākis yākka yoi ruvdas pā lākris pīreno.

Te tu vel hatch kaulo yeck lilieskro dívvus tu astis
nasher sār o kairoben fon o chollo kūrikus, miri chavi.
Tu peness' tu kāmess' to shūn waveri gudli. Sār
tacho. Me tevel pūker tute rinkno gudlo apré kāli
foki. Repper tute sārkon me penāva sā me repper-
das lis fon miro bābus.

THE SPIDER.[1]

Once there was a girl, as there are many to-day, and she was a good needle-worker, and could make a beautiful cloak in one day. And that [there] girl loved a gentleman very much; but one day her sweetheart was shut up in prison, and when she heard it she hastened and went to the king, and begged him humbly to let her love go free. And the king promised her if she would make him a fine cloak, — one every day for a week, seven cloaks for seven days, — he would forgive him, and give him leave to go free. The young lady hastened to do it, and for six days she worked hard [lit. pulled away] cheerfully at it, and always in the evening she sent a cloak to the king. But it came [happened] one day that she was tired, and said [that] she did not wish to work because it was rainy, and she could not dry or bleach the cloth [?] in the sunlight. Then the king said that if she could not work seven days to get her lover the gentleman must remain imprisoned, for she did not love him as she should [did not let love enough on him]. And the maid was so angry and vexed in her heart [or soul] that she died of grief, and was changed into a spider. And to this day she spreads out her threads when the sun shines, and the dewdrops which you see on them are the tears which she has wept for her lover.

If you remain idle one summer day you may lose a whole week's work, my dear. You say that you would like to hear more stories! All right. I will tell you a nice story about lazy people.[2] Remember

---

[1] Literally, the earth-sewer.

[2] *Kāli foki. Kālo* means, as in Hindustani, not only black, but also lazy. Pronounced *kaw-lo.*

all I tell you, as I remembered it from my grandfather.

GORGIO, KALO-MANUSH, TE ROM.

Yeckorus pā ankairoben, kon i manūshia nanei la-
via, o boro Dúvel jas pirián. Sā sī asar? Shūn miri
chavi, me givellis tute : —

> Būti beshia kedivvus kennā
> Adré o tem ankairoben,
> O boro Dúvel jās 'vrī ajā,
> Ta dikk i mushia miraben.

Sa yuv pirridas, dikkdas trin mūshia pāsh o dromes-
cro rikk, hatchin keti chomano mūsh te vel dé lendis
navia, te len putcherde o boro Dúvel ta navver lende.
Dordi, o yeckto mush sos pāno, te o boro Dúvel pūkkerdas kavodoi, "Gorgio." Te yuv sikkerdas leste
kokero keti dovo, te sūderdas leste būti kāmeli sā
jewries, te rinkeni rūdaben, te jās *gorgeous.* Te o
wavescro geero sos kālo sā skunya, te o boro Dúvel
pendas, "Nigger!" te yuv *nikkeredas* adrom, sā
sūjery te mūzhili, te yuv se *nikkerin* sarjā keti kennā,
adré o kamescro dūd, te yuv's kālo-kālo ta kair būtsi,
naneí tu serbers leste keti lis, te tazzers lis. Te o
trinto mush sos brauno, te yuv beshdas pūkeno, tūvin
leste's swägler, keti o boro Dúvel rākkerdas, "Rom!"
te adenna o mūsh hatchedas apré, te pendas būti
kāmelo, "Parraco Rya tiro kūshtaben ; me te vel
mishto piav tiro sastopen!" Te jās romeli a *roamin*
langs i lescro romni, te kekker dukkerdas lester koke-
rus, né kesserdas pa chichi fon adennadoi keti kennā,
te jās adral o sweti, te kekker hatchedas pūkenus, te
nanei hudder ta kéravit ket' o boro Dúvel penell' o
lav. Tacho adovo se sā tiri yakka, miri kāmli.

GORGIO,[1] BLACK MAN, AND GYPSY.

Once in the creation, when men had no names, the Lord went walking. How was that? Listen, my child, I will sing it to you: —

> Many a year has passed away
> Since the world was first begun,
> That the great Lord went out one day
> To see how men's lives went on.

As he walked along he saw three men by the roadside, waiting till some man would give them names; and they asked the Lord to name them. See! the first man was white, and the Lord called him Gorgio. Then he adapted himself to that name, and adorned himself with jewelry and fine clothes, and went *gorgeous*. And the other man was black and the Lord called him Nigger, and he lounged away [*nikker*, to lounge, loiter; an attempted pun], so idle and foul; and he is always lounging till now in the sunshine, and he is too lazy [*kalo-kalo*, black-black, or lazy-lazy, that is, too black or too lazy] to work unless you compel and punish him. And the third man was brown, and he sat quiet, smoking his pipe, till the Lord said, Rom! [gypsy, or " roam "]; and then that man arose and said, very politely, " Thank you, Lord, for your kindness. I 'd be glad to drink your health." And he went, Romany fashion, a-roaming [2] with his romni [wife], and never troubled himself about anything from that time till to-day, and went through the world, and never rested and never wished

---

[1] *Gorgio.* Gentile; any man not a gypsy. Possibly from *ghora aji*, " Master white man," Hindu. Used as *goi* is applied by Hebrews to the unbelievers.

[2] *Romeli, rom'ni.* Wandering, gypsying. It is remarkable that *rumna*, in Hindu, means to roam.

to until the Lord speaks the word. That is all as
true as your eyes, my dear!

YAG–BAR TE SASTER.

SĀ O KAM SOS ANKERDO.

" Pen mandy a waver gudlo trūstal o ankairoben!"
Né shomas adoi, awer shūndom būti apā lis fon miro
bābus. Foki pende mengy sā o chollo-tem [1] sos kérdo
fon o kam, awer i Romany chalia savo keren sār
chingernes, pen o kam sos kérdo fon o boro tem.
Wafedo gry se adovo te nestis ja sigan te anpāli o
kūshto drom. Yeckorus 'dré o pūro chirus, te kennā,
sos a bori pūreni chovihāni te kérdas sīrīni covvas,
te jivdas sār akonyo adré o heb adré o rātti. Yeck
dívvus yoi latchedas yāg-bar adré o pūv, te tilldas es
apré te pūkkeredas lestes nav pāle, " Yāg-bar." Te
pāsh a bittus yoi latchedas a bitto kūshto-saster, te
haderdas lis apré te putchedas lestis nav, te lis rak-
kerdas apopli, " Saster." Chivdási dui 'dré lākis
pūtsī, te pendas Yāg-bar, " Tu sosti rummer o rye,
Saster!" Te yān kérdavit, awer yeck dívvus i dui
ankairede ta chinger, te Saster dés lestis jūva Yag-
bar a tatto-yek adré o yakk, te kairedas i chingari ta
mūkker avri, te hotcher i pūri jūva's pūtsī. Sā yoi
wūsserdas hotcherni putsī adré o hev, te pendas lis ta
kessur adrom keti avenna o mūsh sāri jūva kun kekker chingerd chichi. I chingari shan staria, te dovo
yāg sē o kam, te lis nanei jillo avrī keti kennā, te lis
tevel hotcher andūro būti beshia pā sār jinova mé
keti chingerben. Tacho sī? Né shomas adoi.

[1] *Chollo-tem.* Whole country, world.

FLINT AND STEEL.

OR HOW THE SUN WAS CREATED.

" Tell me another story about the creation !"

I was not there at the time, but I heard a great deal about it from my grandfather. All he did there was to turn the wheel. People tell me that the world was made from the sun, but gypsies, who do everything all contrary, say that the sun was made from the earth. A bad horse is that which will not travel either way on a road. Once in the old time, as [there may be] now. was a great old witch, who made enchantments, and lived all alone in the sky in the night. One day she found a flint in a field, and picked her up, and the stone told her that her name was Flint. And after a bit she found a small piece of steel, and picked him up, and asked his name, and he replied, " Steel " [iron]. She put the two in her pocket, and said to Flint, " You must marry Master Steel." So they did, but one day the two began to quarrel, and Steel gave his wife Flint a hot one [a severe blow] in the eye, and made sparks fly, and set fire to the old woman's pocket. So she threw the burning pocket up into the sky, and told it to stay there until a man and his wife who had never quarreled should come there. The sparks [from Flint's eye] are the stars, and the fire is the sun, and it has not gone out as yet, and it will burn on many a year, for all I know to the contrary. Is it true ? I was not there.

21

O MANŪSH KON JIVDAS ADRÉ O CHONE (SHONE).

"Pen mandy a wāver gudlo apā o chone?"

Avali miri deari. Adré o pūro chirus būtidosta manushia jivvede kūshti-bākeno 'dré o chone, sār chichi ta kair awer ta rikker āp o yāg so kérela o dūd. Awer, amen i foki jivdas būti wafodo mūleno manush, kon dusherdas te lias witchaben atūt sār i waveri deari manushia, te yuv kairedas lis sā's ta shikker lende sār adrom, te chivdas len avrī o chone. Te kennā o sig o i foki shan jillo, yuv pendas: "Kennā akovi dinneli juckalis shan jillo, me te vel jiv mashni te kūshto, sār akonyus." Awer pāsh o bitto, o yāg ankairdas ta hátch alay, te akovo geero latchdas se yuv né kāmdas ta hatch adré o rātti te merav shillino, yuv sosti jā sarja pā kosht. Te kanna i waveri foki shanas adoi, yān né kerden o rikkaben te wadderiu i kāshta adré o dívvusko chirus, awer kennā asti lel lis sār apré sustis pikkia, sār i rātti, te sār o divvus. Sā i foki akai apré o chollo-tem dikena adovo manush keti dívvus kennā, sar pordo o koshter te bittered, te mūserd te gūmeri, te gūberin keti leskro noko kokero, te kūnerin akonyus pāsh lestis yāg. Te i chori mushia te yuv badderedas adrom, yul [yān] jassed sār atūt te trūstal o hev akai, te adoi, te hatchede up būti pā lender kokeros; te adovi shan i starya, te chirkia, te bitti dūdapen tu díkessa sārakai.

"Se adovo sār tacho?" Akovi se kūmi te me jinova. Awer kanna sā tu penessa mé astis dikk o manush dré o chone savo rikkela kāsht apré lestes dūmo, yuv sosti keravit ta chiv adré o yāg, te yuv ne tevel dukker lestes kokero ta kair adovo te yuv sus rumado or lias palyor, sā lis se kāmmaben adosta o mūsh chingerd lestis palya te nassered lende sār andūro. Tacho.

THE MAN WHO LIVED IN THE MOON.

"Tell me another story about the moon."

Yes, my dear. In the old time many men lived happily in the moon, with nothing to do but keep up the fire which makes the light. But among the folk lived a very wicked, obstinate man, who troubled and hated all the other nice [dear] people, and he managed it so as to drive them all away, and put them out of the moon. And when the mass of the folk were gone, he said, "Now those stupid dogs have gone, I will live comfortably and well, all alone." But after a bit the fire began to burn down, and that man found that if he did not want to be in the darkness [night] and die of cold he must go all the time for wood. And when the other people were there, they never did any carrying or splitting wood in the day-time, but now he had to take it all on his shoulders, all night and all day. So the people here on our earth see that man to this day all burdened [full] of wood, and bitter and grumbling to himself, and lurking alone by his fire. And the poor people whom he had driven away went all across and around heaven, here and there, and set up in business for themselves, and they are the stars and planets and lesser lights which you see all about.

ROMANY TACHIPEN.

Taken down accurately from an old gypsy. Common dialect, or "half-and-half" language.

"Rya, tute kāms mandy to pukker tute the tachopen — āwo? Se's a boro or a kūsi covva, mandy 'll rakker tacho, s'up mi-duvel, apré mi meriben,

bengis adré man'nys see if mandy pens a bitto huckaben ! An' sā se adduvvel ? Did mandy ever chore
a kāni adré mi jiv ? and what do the Romany chals
kair o' the poris, 'cause kekker ever dikked chīchī
pāsh of a Romany tan ? Kek rya, — mandy *never*
chored a kāni an' adré sixty beshes kennā 'at mandy's
been apré the drumyors, an' sār dovo chirus mandy
never dikked or shūned or jinned of a Romany chal's
chorin yeck. What 's adduvel tute pens ? — that
Petulengro kāliko dívvus penned tute yuv rikkered
a yāgengeree to muller kānis ! Avali rya — tacho
se ajā — the mush penned adré his kokero see *weshni*
kanis. But kek *kairescro* kānis. Romanis kekker
chores lendy."

GYPSY TRUTH.

" Master, you want me to tell you all the truth,
— yes ? If it 's a big or a little thing, I 'll tell the
truth, so help me God, upon my life ! The devil be
in my soul if I tell the least lie ! And what is it ?
Did I ever in all my life steal a chicken ? and what
do the gypsies do with the feathers, because nobody
ever saw any near a gypsy tent ? Never, sir, — I *never*
stole a chicken ; and in all the sixty years that I 've
been on the roads, in all that time I never saw or
heard or knew of a gypsy's stealing one. What 's
that you say ? — that Petulengro told you yesterday
that he carried a gun to kill *chickens!* Ah yes,
sir, — that is true, too. The man meant in his heart
wood chickens [that is, pheasants]. But not *domestic*
chickens. Gypsies never steal *them.*[1] "

---

[1] There is a great moral difference, not only in the gypsy mind, but
in that of the peasant, between stealing and poaching. But in fact, as
regards the appropriation of poultry of any kind, a young English
gypsy has neither more nor less scruple than other poor people of his
class.

CHOVIHANIPEN.

" Miri diri bībī, me kamāva butidiro tevel chovi-hani. Kāmāva ta dukker geeris te ta jin kūnjerni cola. Tu sosti sikker mengi sārakovi."

" Oh miri kāmli ! vonka tu vissa te vel chovihani, te i Gorgie jinena lis, tu lesa buti tugnus. Sār i chavi tevel shellavrī, te kair a gudli te wūsser baria kánna dikena tute, te shyan i bori foki mérena tute. Awer kūshti se ta jin garini covva, kushti se vonka chori churkni jūva te sār i sweti chungen' apré, jinela sā ta kair lende wafodopen ta pessur sār lenghis dūsh. Te man tevel sikker tute chomany chovihaneskes. Shun ! Vonka tu kamesa pen o dukkerin, lesa tu sār tiro man [1] ta latcher ajafera a manush te manushī lis se. Dé lende o yack, chiv lis drováŋ opā lakis yakka tevel se rakli. Vonka se pash trasherdo yoi tevel pen būti talla jinaben. Kánna tu sos kédo lis sórkon chérus tu astis risser buti dinneli chaia sa tav trūstal tiro āngushtri. Kennā-sig tiri yakka dikena pensa sappa, te vonka tu shan boïni tu tevel dikk pens' o puro beng. O pāshno covva mīri deari se ta jin sā ta plasser, te kāmer, te masher foki. Vanka rakli lela chumeni kek-siglo adré lakis mūi, tu sastis pen laki adovo sikerela buti bāk. Kánna lela lulli te safráni balia, pen lāki adovo se tatcho sigaben yoi sasti lel buti sonakei. Kánna lakis koria wena kete-nes, dovo sikerela yoi tevel ketni buti barveli rya. Pen sarjā vonka tu dikesa o latch apré lākis cham, talla lakis kor, te vaniso, adovos sigaben yoi tevel a bori rāni. Mā kessur tu ki lo se, 'pré o truppo te pré o bull, pen lāki sarjā o latch adoi se sigaben o

---

[1] *Man lana*, Hindostani : to set the heart upon. *Manner*, Eng. Gyp. : t ɔ encourage ; also, to forbid.

boridirines. Hammer laki apré. Te dikessa tu yoi
lela bitti wastia te bitti piria, pen lāki trūstal a rye
ko se divius pā rinkeni pīria, te sā o rinkeno wast
anela kūmi bacht te rinkno mūi. Hammerin te
kāmerin te masherin te shorin shan o pāsh o dukkerin. Se kek rakli te kekno mush adré mi duvel's
chollo-tem savo ne se boïno te hunkari pā chomani,
te sī tu astis latcher sā se tu susti lel lender wongur.
Stastis, latcher sār o rakkerben apré foki.

"Awer miri bibi, adovos sar hokkanipen. Me kamāva buti ta sikker tachni chovihanipen. Pen mandy
sī nanei tachi chovahanis, te sā yol dikena."

"O tachi chovihani miri chavi, lela yakka pensa
chiriclo, o kunsus se rikkeredo apré pensa bongo chiv.
Buti Yahūdi, te nebollongeri lena jafri yakka. Te
cho'hani balia shan rikkerdi pa lākis ankairoben te
surri, te adenna risserdi. Vonka Gorgikani cho'hani
lena shelni yākka, adulli shan i trasheni.

"Me penava tuki chomani sirines. Vonka tu latchesa o pori te o sasterni krafni, te anpāli tu latchesa
cuttor fon papiros, tu sastis chin apré lis sār o pori
savo tu kamesa, te hā lis te tu lesa lis. Awer tu
sasti chin sār tīro noko rātt. Sī tu latchessa pāsh o
lon-doeyav o boro matcheskro-bar, te o puro curro,
chiv lis keti kan, shunesa godli. Tevel tastis kana
pordo chone peshela, besh sar nangi adré lakis dūd
hefta ratti, te shundes adré lis, sarrāti o gudli te vel
tachodiro, te anpāle tu shunesa i feris rakerena sig
adosta. Vonka tu keresa hev sār o bar adré o mulleskri-tan, jasa tu adoi yeck ratti pāsh a wāver te
kennā-sig tu shunesa sā i mūlia rakerena. Sorkon-
chirus penena ki lovo se garrido. Sastis lel o bar te
risser lis apré o mulleskri-tan, talla hev si kédo.

"Me penāva tūki apopli chomani cho'haunes. Lel

vini o sar covva te suverena apré o pani, pā lenia,
pā doeyav. Te asar i paneskri mullos kon jivena
adré o pani rakkerena keti pūveskri chovihanīs. Si
manūsh dikela pāno panna, te partan te diklo apré o
pāni te lela lis, adovo sikela astis lel a pireni, o yuzhior
te o kushtidir o partan se, o kushtidir i rakli. Sī
latchesa ran apré o pani, dovo sikela sastis kūr tiro
wafedo geero. Chokka or curro apré o pāni penela
tu tevel sig atch kāmelo sar tiri pīreni, te pīreno.
Te safrāni rūzhia pā pāni dukerena sonaki, te pauni,
rupp, te loli, kammaben."

"Kána latchesa klisin, dovo se būti bacht. Vonka
haderesa lis apré, pen o manusheskro te rakleskri nav,
te yān wena kamlo o tute. Butidir bacht sī lullo dori
te tav. Rikker lis, sikela kushti kāmaben. Mān
nasher lis avrī tiro zī miri chavi."

" Nanei, bībī, kekker."

WITCHCRAFT.[1]

" My dear aunt, I wish very much to be a witch.
I would like to enchant people and to know secret
things. You can teach me all that."

" Oh, my darling! if you come to be a witch, and
the Gentiles know it, you will have much trouble.
All the children will cry aloud, and make a noise and
throw stones at you when they see you, and perhaps
the grown-up people will kill you. But it is nice to
know secret things; pleasant for a poor old humble
woman whom all the world spits upon to know how
to do them evil and pay them for their cruelty. And
I *will* teach you something of witchcraft. Listen!

---

[1] *Chovihan*, m., *chovihanī*, fem., often *cho'ian* or *cho'ani*, a witch.
Probably from the Hindu *'toanee*, a witch, which has nearly the same
pronunciation as the English gypsy word.

When thou wilt tell a fortune, put all thy heart into finding out what kind of a man or woman thou hast to deal with. Look [keenly], fix thy glance sharply, especially if it be a girl. When she is half-frightened, she will tell you much without knowing it. When thou shalt have often done this thou wilt be able to twist many a silly girl like twine around thy fingers. Soon thy eyes will look like a snake's, and when thou art angry thou wilt look like the old devil. Half the business, my dear, is to know how to please and flatter and allure people. When a girl has anything unusual in her face, you must tell her that it signifies extraordinary luck. If she have red or yellow hair, tell her that is a true sign that she will have much gold. When her eyebrows meet, that shows she will be united to many rich gentlemen. Tell her always, when you see a mole on her cheek or her forehead or anything, that is a sign she will become a great lady. Never mind where it is, on her body, — tell her always that a mole or fleck is a sign of greatness. *Praise her up.* And if you see that she has small hands or feet, tell her about a gentleman who is wild about pretty feet, and how a pretty hand brings more luck than a pretty face. Praising and petting and alluring and crying-up are half of fortune-telling. There is no girl and no man in all the Lord's earth who is not proud and vain about something, and if you can find it out you can get their money. If you can, pick up all the gossip about people."

"But, my aunt, that is all humbug. I wish much to learn real witchcraft. Tell me if there are no real witches, and how they look."

"A real witch, my child, has eyes like a bird, the corner turned up like the point of a curved pointed knife. Many Jews and un-Christians have such eyes. And witches' hairs are drawn out from the beginning [roots] and straight, and then curled [at the ends]. When Gentile witches have green eyes they are the most [to be] dreaded.

" I will tell you something magical. When you find a pen or an iron nail, and then a piece of paper, you should write on it with the pen all thou wishest, and eat it, and thou wilt get thy wish. But thou must write all in thy own blood. If thou findest by the sea a great shell or an old pitcher [cup, etc.], put it to your ear: you will hear a noise. If you can, when the full moon shines sit quite naked in her light and listen to it; every night the noise will become more distinct, and then thou wilt hear the fairies talking plainly enough. When you make a hole with a stone in a tomb go there night after night, and erelong thou wilt hear what the dead are saying. Often they tell where money is buried. You must take a stone and turn it around in the tomb till a hole is there.

" I will tell you something more witchly. Observe [take care] of everything that swims on water, on rivers or the sea. For so the water-spirits who live in the water speak to the earth's witches. If a man sees cloth on the water and gets it, that shows he will get a sweetheart; the cleaner and nicer the cloth, the better the maid. If you find a staff [stick or rod] on the water, that shows you will beat your enemy. A shoe or cup floating on the water means that you will soon be loved by your sweetheart. And yellow flowers [floating] on the water foretell gold, and white, silver, and red, love.

" When you find a key, that is much luck. When you pick [lift it] up, utter a male or female name, and the person will become your own. Very lucky is a red string or ribbon. Keep it. It foretells happy love. Do not let this run away from thy soul, my child."

"No, aunt, never."

THE ORIGIN OF THE GYPSIES.

This chapter contains in abridged form the substance of papers on the origin of the gypsies and their language, read before the London Philological Society; also of another paper read before the Oriental Congress at Florence in 1878; and a *résumé* of these published in the London *Saturday Review*.

It has been repeated until the remark has become accepted as a sort of truism, that the gypsies are a mysterious race, and that nothing is known of their origin. And a few years ago this was true; but within those years so much has been discovered that at present there is really no more mystery attached to the beginning of these nomads than is peculiar to many other peoples. What these discoveries or grounds of belief are I shall proceed to give briefly, my limits not permitting the detailed citation of authorities. First, then, there appears to be every reason for believing with Captain Richard Burton that the Jāts of Northwestern India furnished so large a proportion of the emigrants or exiles who, from the tenth century, went out of India westward, that there is very little risk in assuming it as an hypothesis, at least, that they formed the *Hauptstamm* of the gypsies of Europe. What other elements entered into these, with whom we are all familiar, will be considered presently. These gypsies came from India, where caste is established and callings are hereditary even among out-castes. It is not assuming too much to suppose that, as they evinced a marked aptitude for certain pursuits and an inveterate attachment to certain habits, their ancestors had in these respects resembled them for ages. These pursuits and habits were that

They were tinkers, smiths, and farriers.

They dealt in horses, and were naturally familiar with them.

They were without religion.

They were unscrupulous thieves.

Their women were fortune-tellers, especially by chiromancy.

They ate without scruple animals which had died a natural death, being especially fond of the pig, which, when it has thus been "butchered by God," is still regarded even by prosperous gypsies in England as a delicacy.

They flayed animals, carried corpses, and showed such aptness for these and similar detested callings that in several European countries they long monopolized them.

They made and sold mats, baskets, and small articles of wood.

They have shown great skill as dancers, musicians, singers, acrobats; and it is a rule almost without exception that there is hardly a traveling company of such performers or a theatre, in Europe or America, in which there is not at least one person with some Romany blood.

Their hair remains black to advanced age, and they retain it longer than do Europeans or ordinary Orientals.

They speak an Aryan tongue, which agrees in the

main with that of the Jāts, but which contains words
gathered from other Indian sources. This is a con-
sideration of the utmost importance, as by it alone
can we determine what was the agglomeration of
tribes in India which formed the Western gypsy.

Admitting these as the peculiar pursuits of the
race, the next step should be to consider what are
the principal nomadic tribes of gypsies in India and
Persia, and how far their occupations agree with those
of the Romany of Europe. That the Jāts probably
supplied the main stock has been admitted. This
was a bold race of Northwestern India, which at one
time had such power as to obtain important victories
over the caliphs. They were broken and dispersed
in the eleventh century by Mahmoud, many thousands of them wandering to the West. They were
without religion, " of the horse, horsey," and notorious thieves. In this they agree with the European
gypsy. But they are not habitual eaters of *mullo
bālor*, or "dead pork;" they do not devour everything like dogs. We cannot ascertain that the Jāt
is specially a musician, a dancer, a mat and basket
maker, a rope-dancer, a bear-leader, or a peddler.
We do not know whether they are peculiar in India
among the Indians for keeping their hair unchanged
to old age, as do pure-blood English gypsies. All of
these things are, however, markedly characteristic of
certain different kinds of wanderers, or gypsies, in
India. From this we conclude, hypothetically, that
the Jāt warriors were supplemented by other tribes,
—chief among these may have been the Dom,—
and that the Jāt element has at present disappeared,
and been supplanted by the lower type.

The Doms are a race of gypsies found from Central India to the far northern frontier, where a portion of their early ancestry appears as the Domarr, and are supposed to be pre-Aryan. In "The People of India," edited by J. Forbes Watson and J. W. Kaye (India Museum, 1868), we are told that the appearance and modes of life of the Doms indicate a marked difference from those of the people who surround them (in Behar). The Hindus admit their claim to antiquity. Their designation in the Shastras is Sopuckh, meaning dog-eater. They are wanderers; they make baskets and mats, and are inveterate drinkers of spirits, spending all their earnings on it. They have almost a monopoly as to burning corpses and handling all dead bodies. They eat all animals which have died a natural death, and are particularly fond of pork of this description. "Notwithstanding profligate habits, many of them attain the age of eighty or ninety; and it is not till sixty or sixty-five that their hair begins to get white." The Domarr are a mountain race, nomads, shepherds, and robbers. Travelers speak of them as "gypsies." A specimen which we have of their language would, with the exception of one word, which is probably an error of the transcriber, be intelligible to any English gypsy, and be called pure Romany. Finally, the ordinary Dom calls himself a Dom, his wife a Domni, and the being a Dom, or the collective gypsydom, Domnipana. *D* in Hindustani is found as *r* in English gypsy speech, — *e. g.*, *doi*, a wooden spoon, is known in Europe as *roi*. Now in common Romany we have, even in London, —

Rom . . . . . A gypsy.
Romni . . . . A gypsy wife.
Romnipen . . . Gypsydom.

Of this word *rom* I shall have more to say. It may be observed that there are in the Indian *Dom* certain distinctly-marked and degrading features, characteristic of the European gypsy, which are out of keeping with the habits of warriors, and of a daring Aryan race which withstood the caliphs. Grubbing in filth as if by instinct, handling corpses, making baskets, eating carrion, being given to drunkenness, does not agree with anything we can learn of the Jāts. Yet the European gypsies are all this, and at the same time "horsey" like the Jāts. Is it not extremely probable that during the "out-wandering" the Dom communicated his name and habits to his fellow-emigrants?

The marked musical talent characteristic of the Slavonian and other European gypsies appears to link them with the Luri of Persia. These are distinctly gypsies; that is to say, they are wanderers, thieves, fortune-tellers, and minstrels. The Shah-Nameh of Firdusi tells us that about the year 420 A. D. Shankal, the Maharajah of India, sent to Behram Gour, a ruler of the Sassanian dynasty in Persia, ten thousand minstrels, male and female, called *Luri*. Though lands were allotted to them, with corn and cattle, they became from the beginning irreclaimable vagabonds. Of their descendants, as they now exist, Sir Henry Pottinger says: —

"They bear a marked affinity to the gypsies of Europe.[1] They speak a dialect peculiar to themselves, have a king to each troupe, and are notorious for kidnapping and pilfering. Their principal pastimes are drinking, dancing, and music. . . . They are invariably attended by half a dozen of bears and

[1] *Travels in Beloochistan and Scinde*, p. 153.

monkeys that are broke in to perform all manner of grotesque tricks. In each company there are always two or three members who profess . . . modes of divining, which procure them a ready admission into every society."

This account, especially with the mention of trained bears and monkeys, identifies them with the Ričinari, or bear-leading gypsies of Syria (also called Nuri), Turkey, and Roumania. A party of these lately came to England. We have seen these Syrian Ričinari in Egypt. They are unquestionably gypsies, and it is probable that many of them accompanied the early migration of Jāts and Doms.

The Nāts or Nuts are Indian wanderers, who, as Dr. J. Forbes Watson declares, in "The People of India," "correspond to the European gypsy tribes," and were in their origin probably identical with the Luri. They are musicians, dancers, conjurers, acrobats, fortune-tellers, blacksmiths, robbers, and dwellers in tents. They eat everything, except garlic. There are also in India the Banjari, who are spoken of by travelers as "gypsies." They are traveling merchants or ped-dlers. Among all these wanderers there is a current slang of the roads, as in England. This slang extends even into Persia. Each tribe has its own, but the name for the generally spoken *lingua franca* is *Rom*.

It has never been pointed out, however, by any writer, that there is in Northern and Central India a distinct tribe, which is regarded, even by the Nāts and Doms and Jāts themselves, as peculiarly and dis-tinctly gypsy. There are, however, such wanderers, and the manner in which I became aware of their existence was, to say the least, remarkable. I was going one day along the Marylebone Road when I

met a very dark man, poorly clad, whom I took for a
gypsy; and no wonder, as his eyes had the very expression of the purest blood of the oldest families.
To him I said, —

" *Rakessa tu Romanes ?* " (Can you talk gypsy?)

" I know what you mean," he answered in English.
" You ask me if I can talk gypsy. I know what
those people are. But I 'm a Mahometan Hindu
from Calcutta. I get my living by making curry
powder. Here is my card." Saying this he handed
me a piece of paper, with his name written on it:
John Nano.

" When I say to you, ' *Rakessa tu Romanes ?* ' what
does it mean ? "

" It means, ' Can you talk Rom ? ' But *rakessa* is
not a Hindu word. It 's Panjabī."

I met John Nano several times afterwards and
visited him in his lodgings, and had him carefully
examined and cross-questioned and pumped by Professor Palmer of Cambridge, who is proficient in Eastern tongues. He conversed with John in Hindustani,
and the result of our examination was that John declared he had in his youth lived a very loose life,
and belonged to a tribe of wanderers who were to
all the other wanderers on the roads in India what
regular gypsies are to the English Gorgio hawkers
and tramps. These people were, he declared, " the
real gypsies of India, and just like the gypsies here.
People in India called them Trablūs, which means
Syrians, but they were full-blood Hindus, and not
Syrians." And here I may observe that this word
Trablūs which is thus applied to Syria, is derived
from Tripoli. John was very sure that his gypsies
were Indian. They had a peculiar language, consist-

ing of words which were not generally intelligible. " Could he remember any of these words?" Yes. One of them was *manro*, which meant bread. Now *manro* is all over Europe the gypsy word for bread. John Nano, who spoke several tongues, said that he did not know it in any Indian dialect except in that of his gypsies. These gypsies called themselves and their language *Rom*. Rom meant in India a real gypsy. And Rom was the general slang of the road, and it came from the Roms or Trablūs. Once he had written all his autobiography in a book. This is generally done by intelligent Mahometans. This manuscript had unfortunately been burned by his English wife, who told us that she had done so " because she was tired of seeing a book lying about which she could not read."

Reader, think of losing such a life! The autobiography of an Indian gypsy, — an abyss of adventure and darksome mysteries, illuminated, it may be, with vivid flashes of Dacoitee, while in the distance rumbled the thunder of Thuggism! Lost, lost, irreparably lost forever! And in this book John had embodied a vocabulary of the real Indian Romany dialect. Nothing was wanting to complete our woe. John thought at first that he had lent it to a friend who had never returned it. But his wife remembered burning it. Of one thing John was positive: Rom was as distinctively gypsy talk in India as in England, and the Trablūs are the true Romanys of India.

What here suggests itself is, how these Indian gypsies came to be called *Syrian*. The gypsies which roam over Syria are evidently of Indian origin; their language and physiognomy both declare it plainly. I offer as an hypothesis that bands of gypsies who have roamed from India to Syria have, after returning, been called Trablūs, or Syrians, just as I have known Germans, after returning from the father-land to America, to be called Americans. One thing, however, is at least certain. The Rom are the very gypsies of gypsies in India. They are thieves, fortune-tellers, and vagrants. But whether they have or had any connection with the migration to the West we cannot establish. Their language and their name would seem to indicate it; but then it must be borne in mind that the word *rom*, like *dom*, is one of wide dissemination, *dūm* being a Syrian gypsy word for the race. And the very great majority of even English gypsy words are Hindi, with an admixture of Persian, and do not belong to a slang of any kind. As in India, *churi* is a knife, *nāk* the nose, *balia* hairs, and so on, with others which would be among the first to be furnished with slang equivalents. And yet these very gypsies are *Rom*, and the wife is a *Romni*, and they use words which are not Hindu in common with European gypsies. It is therefore not improbable that in these Trablūs, so called through popular ignorance, as they are called Tartars in Egypt and Germany, we have a portion at least of the real stock. It is to be desired that some resident in India would investigate the Trablūs. It will probably be found that they are Hindus who have roamed from India to Syria and back again, here and there, until they are regarded as foreigners in both countries.

Next to the word *rom* itself, the most interesting in Romany is *zingan*, or *tchenkan*, which is used in twenty or thirty different forms by the people of every country, except England, to indicate the gypsy. An incredible amount of far-fetched erudition has

been wasted in pursuing this philological *ignis fatuus*.
That there are leather-working and saddle-working
gypsies in Persia who call themselves Zingan is a fair
basis for an origin of the word; but then there are
Tchangar gypsies of Jāt affinity in the Punjāb. Wonderful it is that in this war of words no philologist
has paid any attention to what the gypsies themselves
say about it. What they do say is sufficiently interesting, as it is told in the form of a legend which is
intrinsically curious and probably ancient. It is given
as follows in "The People of Turkey," by a Con-
sul's Daughter and Wife, edited by Mr. Stanley Lane
Poole, London, 1878: " Although the gypsies are not
persecuted in Turkey, the antipathy and disdain felt
for them evinces itself in many ways, and appears to
be founded upon a strange legend current in the country. This legend says that when the gypsy nation
were driven out of their country (India), and arrived
at Mekran, they constructed a wonderful machine to
which a wheel was attached." From the context of
this imperfectly told story, it would appear as if the
gypsies could not travel farther until this wheel
should revolve : —

"Nobody appeared to be able to turn it, till in the
midst of their vain efforts some evil spirit presented
himself under the disguise of a sage, and informed
the chief, whose name was Chen, that the wheel
would be made to turn only when he had married his
sister Guin. The chief accepted the advice, the wheel
turned round, and the name of the tribe after this
incident became that of the combined names of the
brother and sister, Chenguin, the appellation of all
the gypsies of Turkey at the present day."

The legend goes on to state that in consequence of

this unnatural marriage the gypsies were cursed and condemned by a Mahometan saint to wander forever on the face of the earth. The real meaning of the myth — for myth it is — is very apparent. *Chen* is a Romany word, generally pronounced *chone*, meaning the moon ;[1] while *guin* is almost universally given as *gan* or *kan*. That is to say, Chen-gan or -kan, or Zin-kan, is much commoner than Chen-guin. Now *kan* is a common gypsy word for the sun. George Borrow gives it as such, and I myself have heard Romanys call the sun *kan*, though *kam* is commoner, and is usually assumed to be right. Chen-kan means, therefore, moon-sun. And it may be remarked in this connection, that the neighboring Roumanian gypsies, who are nearly allied to the Turkish, have a wild legend stating that the sun was a youth who, having fallen in love with his own sister, was condemned as the sun to wander forever in pursuit of her, after she was turned into the moon. A similar legend exists in Greenland [2] and in the island of Borneo, and it was known to the old Irish. It is in fact a spontaneous myth, or one of the kind which grow up from causes common to all races. It would be natural, to any imaginative savage, to regard the sun and moon as brother and sister. The next step would be to think of the one as regularly pursuing the other over the heavens, and to this chase an erotic cause would naturally be assigned. And as the pursuit is interminable, the pursuer never attaining his aim, it would be in time regarded as a penance. Hence it comes that in the most distant and differ-

[1] English gypsies also call the moon *shul* and *shone*.
[2] *Tales and Traditions of the Eskimo*, by Dr. Henry Rink. London, 1875, p. 236.

ent lands we have the same old story of the brother
and the sister, just as the Wild Hunter pursues his
bride.

It was very natural that the gypsies, observing that
the sun and moon were always apparently wandering,
should have identified their own nomadic life with
that of these luminaries. That they have a tendency
to assimilate the idea of a wanderer and pilgrim to
that of the Romany, or to *Romanipen*, is shown by
the assertion once made to me by an English gypsy
that his people regarded Christ as one of themselves,
because he was always poor, and went wandering
about on a donkey, and was persecuted by the Gorgios. It may be very rationally objected by those to
whom the term "solar myth" is as a red rag, that
the story, to prove anything, must first be proved
itself. This will probably not be far to seek. Everything about it indicates an Indian origin, and if it
can be found among any of the wanderers in India,
it may well be accepted as the possible origin of the
greatly disputed word *zingan*. It is quite as plausible
as Dr. Miklosich's very far-fetched derivation from
the Acingani, — 'Ατσίγαιοι, — an unclean, heretical
Christian sect, who dwelt in Phrygia and Lycaonia
from the seventh till the eleventh century. The
mention of Mekran indicates clearly that the moon
story came from India before the Romany could have
obtained any Greek name. And if gypsies call themselves or are called Jen-gan, or Chenkan, or Zingan,
in the East, especially if they were so called by
Persian poets, it is extremely unlikely that they ever
received such a name from the Gorgios of Europe. It
is really extraordinary that all the philologists who
have toiled to derive the word *zingan* from a Greek

or Western source have never reflected that if it was
applied to the race at an early time in India or Persia all their speculations must fall to the ground.

One last word of John Nano, who was so called
from two similar Indian words, meaning "the pet of
his grandfather." I have in my possession a strange
Hindu knife, with an enormously broad blade, perhaps five or six inches broad towards the end, with a
long handle richly mounted in the purest bronze
with a little silver. I never could ascertain till I
knew him what it had been used for. Even the old
ex-king of Oude, when he examined it, went wrong
on it. Not so John Nano.

"I know well enough what that knife is. I have
seen it before, — years ago. It is very old, and it was
long in use; it was the knife used by the public ex-
ecutioner in Bhotan. It is Bhotanī."

By the knife hangs the ivory-handled court-dagger
which belonged to Francis II. of France, the first
husband of Mary Queen of Scots. I wonder which
could tell the strangest story of the past!

"It has cut off many a head," said John Nano;
"and I have seen it before!"

I do not think that I have gone too far in attaching
importance to the gypsy legend of the origin of the
word *chen-kan* or *zingan*. It is their own, and
therefore entitled to preference over the theories of
mere scholars; it is Indian and ancient, and there
is much to confirm it. When I read the substance of
this chapter before the Philological Society of London, Prince Lucien Bonaparte, — who is beyond question a great philologist, and one distinguished for
vast research, — who was in the chair, seemed, in his
comments on my paper, to consider this sun and

moon legend as frivolous. And it is true enough that German symbolizers have given us the sun myth to such an extent that the mere mention of it in philology causes a recoil. Then, again, there is the law of humanity that the pioneer, the gatherer of raw material, who is seldom collector and critic together, is always assailed. Columbus always gets the chains and Amerigo Vespucci the glory. But the legend itself is undeniably of the gypsies and Indian.

It is remarkable that there are certain catch-words, or test-words, among old gypsies with which they try new acquaintances. One of these is *kekkávi*, a kettle; another, *chinamangrī*, a bill-hook, or chopper (also a letter), for which there is also another word. But I have found several very deep mothers in sorcery who have given me the word for sun, *kam*, as a precious secret, but little known. Now the word really is very well known, but the mystery attached to it, as to *chone* or *shule*, the moon, would seem to indicate that at one time these words had a peculiar significance. Once the darkest-colored English gypsy I ever met, wishing to sound the depth of my Romany, asked me for the words for sun and moon, making more account of my knowledge of them than of many more far less known.

As it will interest the reader, I will here give the ballad of the sun and the moon, which exists both in Romany and Roumani, or Roumanian, in the translation which I take from "A Winter in the City of Pleasure" (that is Bucharest), by Florence K. Berger, — a most agreeable book, and one containing two chapters on the Tzigane, or gypsies.

THE SUN AND THE MOON.

Brother, one day the Sun resolved to marry. During nine years, drawn by nine fiery horses, he had rolled by heaven and earth as fast as the wind or a flying arrow.

But it was in vain that he fatigued his horses. Nowhere could he find a love worthy of him. Nowhere in the universe was one who equaled in beauty his sister Helen, the beautiful Helen with silver tresses.

The Sun went to meet her, and thus addressed her: "My dear little sister Helen, Helen of the silver tresses, let us be betrothed, for we are made for one another.

"We are alike not only in our hair and our features, but also in our beauty. I have locks of gold, and thou hast locks of silver. My face is shining and splendid, and thine is soft and radiant."

"O my brother, light of the world, thou who art pure of all stain, one has never seen a brother and sister married together, because it would be a shameful sin."

At this rebuke the Sun hid himself, and mounted up higher to the throne of God, bent before Him, and spoke : —

"Lord our Father, the time has arrived for me to wed. But, alas! I cannot find a love in the world worthy of me except the beautiful Helen, Helen of the silver hair!"

God heard him, and, taking him by the hand, led him into hell to affright his heart, and then into paradise to enchant his soul.

Then He spake to him, and while He was speaking

the Sun began to shine brightly and the clouds passed over : —

"Radiant Sun ! Thou who art free from all stain, thou hast been through hell and hast entered paradise. Choose between the two."

The Sun replied, recklessly, " I choose hell, if I may have, for a life, Helen, Helen of the shining silver hair."

The Sun descended from the high heaven to his sister Helen, and ordered preparation for his wedding. He put on her forehead the waving gold chaplet of the bride, he put on her head a royal crown, he put on her body a transparent robe all embroidered with fine pearls, and they all went into the church together.

But woe to him, and woe to her ! During the service the lights were extinguished, the bells cracked while ringing, the seats turned themselves upside down, the tower shook to its base, the priests lost their voices, and the sacred robes were torn off their backs.

The bride was convulsed with fear. For suddenly, woe to her! an invisible hand grasped her up, and, having borne her on high, threw her into the sea, where she was at once changed into a beautiful silver fish.

The Sun grew pale and rose into the heaven. Then descending to the west, he plunged into the sea to search for his sister Helen, Helen of the shining silver hair.

However, the Lord God (sanctified in heaven and upon the earth) took the fish in his hand, cast it forth into the sky, and changed it anew into the moon.

Then He spoke. And while God was speaking the entire universe trembled, the peaks of the mountains bowed down, and men shivered with fear.

" Thou, Helen of the long silver tresses, and thou resplendent Sun, who are both free from all stain, I condemn you for eternity to follow each other with your eyes through space, without being ever able to meet or to reach each other upon the road of heaven. Pursue one another for all time in traveling around the skies and lighting up the world."

Fallen from a high estate by sin, wicked, and therefore wandering : it was with such a story of being penitent pilgrims, doomed for a certain space to walk the earth, that the gypsies entered Europe from India, into Islam and into Christendom, each time modifying the story to suit the religion of the country which they invaded. Now I think that this sun and moon legend is far from being frivolous, and that it conforms wonderfully well with the famous story which they told to the Emperor Sigismund and the Pope and all Europe, that they were destined to wander because they had sinned. When they first entered Europe, the gypsies were full of these legends ; they told them to everybody ; but they had previously told them to themselves in the form of the Indian sun and moon story. This was the root whence other stories grew. As the tale of the Wandering Jew typifies the Hebrew, so does this of the sun and moon the Romany.

A GYPSY MAGIC SPELL.

THERE is a meaningless rhyme, very common among children. It is repeated while counting off those who are taking part in a game, and allotting to each a place. It is as follows: —

> " Ekkeri akkery u-kery an
> Fillisi', follasy, Nicolas John
> Queebee-quäbee — Irishman.
> Stingle 'em — stangle 'em — buck ! "

With a very little alteration in sounds, and not more than children make of these verses in different places, this may be read as follows: —

> " 'Ekkeri, akai-ri, you kair — án.
> Filissin follasy. Nakelas jä'n.
> Kīvi, kavi. Irishman.
> Stini — stani — buck ! "

This is nonsense, of course, but it is Romany, or gypsy, and may be translated : —

> " First — here — you begin.
> Castle — gloves. You don't play. Go on !
> *Kivi* — kettle. How are you ?
> *Stini* — buck — buck."

The common version of the rhyme begins with : —

> " *One* 'eri — two-ery, ékkeri — án."

But one-ry is the *exact* translation of ékkeri ; ek or yek being one. And it is remarkable that in

> "*Hickory* dickory dock,
> The rat ran up the clock;
> The clock struck *one*,
> And down he run,
> *Hickory* dickory dock."

We have hickory or ekkeri again, followed by a significant *one*. It may be observed that while, the first verses abound in Romany words, I can find no trace of any in other child-rhymes of the kind. It is also clear that if we take from the fourth line the *ingle 'em, angle 'em*, evidently added for mere jingle, there remains *stan* or *stani*, "a buck," followed by the very same word in English.

With the mournful examples of Mr. Bellenden Kerr's efforts to show that all our old proverbs and tavern signs are Dutch, and Sir William Betham's Etruscan-Irish, I should be justly regarded as one of the too frequent seekers for mystery in moonshine if I declared that I positively believed this to be Romany. Yet it is possible that it contains gypsy words, especially " fillissi,' follasy," which mean exactly *château* and gloves, and I think it not improbable that it was once a sham charm used by some Romany fortune-teller to bewilder Gorgios. Let the reader imagine the burnt-sienna wild-cat eyed old sorceress performing before a credulous farm-wife and her children the great ceremony of *hākk'ni pānki*, which Mr. Borrow calls *hokkani boro*, but for which there is a far deeper name, — that of *the great secret*, — which even my best friends among the Romany tried to conceal from me. This feat is performed by inducing some woman of largely magnified faith to believe that there is hidden in her house a magic treasure, which can only be made to come to hand by depositing in the cellar another treasure, to which it will come by

natural affinity and attraction. "For gold, as you sees,
my deari, draws gold, and so if you ties up all your
money in a pocket-handkercher and leaves it, you'll
find it doubled. An' was n't there the Squire's lady.
and did n't she draw two hundred old gold guineas
out of the ground where they 'd laid in a old grave, —
and only one guinea she gave me for all my trouble;
an' I hope you 'll do better by the poor old gypsy,
my deari — — ."

The gold and all the spoons are tied up, — for, as
the enchantress observes, there may be silver too, —
and she solemnly repeats over it magical rhymes, while
the children, standing around in awe, listen to every
word. It is a good subject for a picture. Sometimes
the windows are closed, and candles give the only
light. The next day the gypsy comes and sees how
the charm is working. Could any one look under
her cloak he might find another bundle precisely
resembling the one containing the treasure. She
looks at the precious deposit, repeats her rhyme
again, and departs, after carefully charging the house-
wife that the bundle must not be touched or spoken
of for three weeks. "Every word you tell about it,
my-deari will be a guinea gone away." Sometimes
she exacts an oath on the Bible that nothing shall
be said.

Back to the farmer's wife never again. After three
weeks another Extraordinary instance of gross credu-
lity appears in the country paper, and is perhaps repeated in a colossal London daily, with a reference to
the absence of the school-master. There is wailing
and shame in the house, — perhaps great suffering,
for it may be that the savings of years have been
swept away. The charm has worked.

But the little sharp-eared children remember it and sing it, and the more meaningless it is in their ears the more mysterious does it sound. And they never talk about the bundle, which when opened was found to contain only sticks, stones, and rags, without repeating it. So it goes from mouth to mouth, until, all mutilated, it passes current for even worse nonsense than it was at first. It may be observed, however, — and the remark will be fully substantiated by any one who knows the language, — that there is a Romany *turn* to even the roughest corners of these rhymes. *Kivi, stingli, stangli,* are all gypsyish. But, as I have already intimated, this does not appear in any other nonsense verses of the kind. There is nothing of it in

"Intery, mintery, cutery corn" —

or in anything else in Mother Goose. It is alone in its sounds and sense, — or nonsense. But there is not a wanderer of the roads who on hearing it would not explain, " Rya, there's a great deal of Romanes in that ere."

I should also say that the word *na-kelas* or *né-kelas,* which I here translate differently, was once explained to me at some length by a gypsy as signifying "not speaking," or "keeping quiet."

Now the mystery of mysteries of which I have spoken in the Romany tongue is this. The *hokkani boro,* or great trick, consists of three parts. Firstly, the telling of a fortune, and this is to *pen dukkerin* or *pen durkerin.* The second part is the conveying away of the property, which is to *lel dūdikabin,* or to take lightning, possibly connected with the very old English slang term of *bien lightment.* There is evidently a great confusion of words here. And the third is to

"*chiv o manzin apré láti*," or to put the oath upon
her, which explains itself. When all the deceived are
under oath not to utter a word about the trick, the
gypsy mother has "a safe thing of it."

The *hokkani boro*, or great trick, was brought by
the gypsies from the East. It has been practiced by
them all over the world, it is still played every day
somewhere. This chapter was written long ago in
England. I am now in Philadelphia, and here I read
in the "Press" of this city that a Mrs. Brown,
whom I sadly and reluctantly believe is the wife of
an acquaintance of mine, who walks before the world
in other names, was arrested for the same old game
of fortune-telling and persuading a simple dame that
there was treasure in the house, and all the rest of
the grand deception. And Mrs. Brown, good old
Mrs. Brown, went to prison, where she will linger
until a bribed alderman, or a purchased pardon, or
some one of the numerous devices by which justice is
evaded in Pennsylvania, delivers her.

Yet it is not a good country, on the whole, for
hokkani boro, since the people here, especially in
the rural districts, have a rough-and-ready way of in-
flicting justice which interferes sadly with the profits
of aldermen and other politicians. Some years ago,
in Tennessee, a gypsy woman robbed a farmer by the
great trick of all he was worth. Now it is no slander
to say that the rural folk of Tennessee greatly resem-
ble Indians in certain respects, and when I saw thousands of them, during the war, mustered out in Nash-
ville, I often thought, as I studied their dark brown
faces, high cheek bones, and long straight black hair,
that the American is indeed reverting to the abo-
riginal type. The Tennessee farmer and his neigh-

bors, at any rate, reverted very strongly indeed to the original type when robbed by the gypsies, for they turned out all together, hunted them down, and, having secured the sorceress, burned her alive at the stake. And thus in a single crime and its punishment we have curiously combined a world-old Oriental offense, an European Middle-Age penalty for witchcraft, and the fierce torture of the red Indians.

23

SHELTA, THE TINKERS' TALK.

"So good a proficient in one quarter of an hour that I can drink with any tinker in his own language during my life." — *King Henry the Fourth.*

ONE summer day, in the year 1876, I was returning from a long walk in the beautiful country which lies around Bath, when, on the road near the town, I met with a man who had evidently grown up from child-hood into middle age as a beggar and a tramp. I have learned by long experience that there is not a so-called "traveler" of England or of the world, be he beggar, tinker, gypsy, or hawker, from whom something cannot be learned, if one only knows how to use the test-glasses and proper reagents. Most in-quirers are chiefly interested in the morals — or im-morals — of these nomads. My own researches as regards them are chiefly philological. Therefore, after I had invested twopence in his prospective beer, I addressed him in Romany. Of course he knew a little of it; was there ever an old "traveler" who did not?

"But we are givin' Romanes up very fast, — all of us is," he remarked. "It is a gettin' to be too blown. Everybody knows some Romanes now. But there *is* a jib that ain't blown," he remarked reflectively. "Back slang an' cantin' an' rhymin' is grown vulgar, and Italian always *was* the lowest of the lot ; thieves *kennick* is genteel alongside of organ-grinder's lingo, you know. Do *you* know anythin' of Italian, sir ? "

" I can *rakker* it pretty *flick* " (talk it tolerably), was my reply.

" Well I should never a *penned* [thought] sitch a swell gent as you had been down so low in the slums. Now *Romanes* is genteel. I heard there 's actilly a book about Romanes to learn it out of. But as for this other jib, its wery hard to talk. It is most all Old Irish, and they calls it Shelter."

This was all that I could learn at that time. It did not impress me much, as I supposed that the man merely meant Old Irish. A year went by, and I found myself at Aberystwith, the beautiful sea-town in Wales, with my friend Professor Palmer — a palmer who has truly been a pilgrim *outre-mer*, even by Galilee's wave, and dwelt as an Arab in the desert. One afternoon we were walking together on that end of the beach which is the antithesis of the old Norman castle ; that is, at the other extremity of the town, and by the rocks. And here there was a little crowd, chiefly of young ladies, knitting and novel-reading in the sun, or watching children play-ing on the sand. All at once there was an alarm, and the whole party fled like partridges, skurrying along and hiding under the lee of the rocks. For a great rock right over our heads was about to be blasted. So the professor and I went on and away, but as we went we observed an eccentric and most miserable figure crouching in a hollow like a little cave to avoid the anticipated falling stones.

" *Dikk o' dovo mush adoi a gavverin lester kokero !* " (Look at that man there, hiding himself !) said the

professor in Romanes. He wished to call attention
to the grotesque figure without hurting the poor fellow's feelings.

" *Yuv's atrash o'ye baryia* " (He is afraid of the
stones), I replied.

The man looked up. " I know what you 're saying, gentlemen. That 's Romany."

" Jump up, then, and come along with us."

He followed. We walked from rock to rock, and
over the sand by the sea, to a secluded nook under a
cliff. Then, seated around a stone table, we began
our conversation, while the ocean, like an importunate beggar, surfed and foamed away, filling up the
intervals with its mighty roaring language, which
poets only understand or translate : —

> " Thus far, and then no more : "
> Such language speaks the sounding sea
> To the waves upon the shore.

Our new acquaintance was ragged and disreputable. Yet he held in his hand a shilling copy of
" Helen's Babies," in which were pressed some fern
leaves.

" What do you do for a living?" I asked.

" *Shelkin gallopas* just now," he replied.

" And what is that ? "

" Selling ferns. Don't you understand? That 's
what we call it in *Minklers Thari*. That 's tinkers'
language. I thought as you knew Romanes you
might understand it. The right name for it is *Shelter*
or *Shelta*."

Out came our note-books and pencils. So this was
the *Shelter* of which I had heard. He was promptly
asked to explain what sort of a language it was.

" Well, gentlemen, you must know that I have no

great gift for languages. I never could learn even French properly. I can conjugate the verb *être*, — that is all. I'm an ignorant fellow, and very low. I've been kicked out of the lowest slums in Whitechapel because I was too much of a blackguard for 'em. But I know rhyming slang. Do you know Lord John Russell ? "

" Well, I know a little of rhyming, but not that."

" Why, it rhymes to *bustle*."

" I see. *Bustle* is to pick pockets."

" Yes, or anything like it, such as ringing the changes."

Here the professor was " in his plate." He knows perfectly how to ring the changes. It is effected by going into a shop, asking for change for a sovereign, purchasing some trifling article, then, by ostensibly changing your mind as to having the change, so bewilder the shopman as to cheat him out of ten shillings. It is easily done by one who understands it. The professor does not practice this art for the lucre of gain, but he understands it in detail. And of this he gave such proofs to the tramp that the latter was astonished.

" A tinker would like to have a wife who knows as much of that as you do," he remarked. " No woman is fit to be a tinker's wife who can't make ten shillings a day by *glantherin*. *Glantherin* or *glad'herin* is the correct word in Shelter for ringing the changes. As for the language, I believe it's mostly Gaelic, but it's mixed up with Romanes and canting or thieves' slang. Once it was the common language of all the old tinkers. But of late years the old tinkers' families are mostly broken up, and the language is perishing."

Then he proceeded to give us the words in Shelta, or Minklers Thari. They were as follows : —

Shelkin gallopas,	Selling ferns.
Soobli, } Soobri, }	Brother, friend — a man.
Bewr,	Woman.
Gothlin or goch'thlin,	Child.
Young bewr,	Girl.
Durra, or derra,	Bread.
Pani,	Water (Romany).
Stiff,	A warrant (common cant).
Yack,	A watch (cant, *i. e.* bull's eye. *Yack*, an eye in Romany).
Mush-faker,	Umbrella mender.
Mithani (mithni),	Policeman.
Ghesterman (ghesti),	Magistrate.
Needi-mizzler,	A tramp.
Dinnessy,	Cat.
Stall,	Go, travel.
Biyèghin,	Stealing.
Biyêg,	To steal.
Biyêg th'eenik,	To steal the thing.
Crack,	A stick.
Monkery,	Country.
Prat,	Stop, stay, lodge.
Nêd askan,	Lodging.
Glantherin (glad'herin),	Money, swindling.

This word has a very peculiar pronunciation.

Sauni or sonni,	See.
Strépuck (reepuck),	A harlot.
Strépuck lusk, } Luthrum's gothlin, }	Son of a harlot.
Kurrb yer pee,	Punch your head **or face.**
Pee,	Face.
Borers and jumpers,	Tinkers' tools.
Borers,	Gimlets.

Jumpers,	Cranks.
Ogles,	Eyes (common slang).
Nyock,	Head.
Nyock,	A penny.
Odd,	Two.
Midgic,	A shilling.
Nyö(d)ghee,	A pound.
Sai, sy,	Sixpence.
Charrshom, Cherrshom, Tusheroon,	A crown.
Tré-nyock,	Threepence.
Trípo-rauniel,	A pot of beer.
Thari, Bug,	Talk.

Can you thari Shelter? Can you bug Shelta? Can you talk tinkers' language?

| Shelter, shelta, | Tinker's slang. |
| Lárkin, | Girl. |

Curious as perhaps indicating an affinity between the Hindustani *larki*, a girl, and the gypsy *rakli*.

Snips,	Scissors (slang).
Dingle fakir,	A bell-hanger.
Dunnovans,	Potatoes.
Fay (*vulgarly* fee),	Meat.

Our informant declared that there are vulgar forms of certain words.

| Gladdher, | Ring the changes (cheat in change). |

"No minkler would have a bewr who couldn't gladdher."

| Reesbin, | Prison. |
| Tré-moon, | Three months, a 'drag.' |

Rauniel, ⎱ Runuiel, ⎰	Beer.
Max,	Spirits (slang).
Chiv,	Knife. (Romany, a pointed knife, *i. e. tongue.*)
Thari,	To speak or tell.

" I tharied the soobri I sonnied him."   (I told the man I saw him.)

Mushgraw.

Our informant did not know whether this word, of Romany origin, meant, in Shelta, policeman or magistrate.

| Scri, scree, | To write. |

Our informant suggested *scribe* as the origin of this word.

| Reader, | A writ. |

" You 're readered soobri."   (You are put in the " Police Gazette," friend.)

Our informant could give only a single specimen of the Shelta literature.   It was as follows : —

> " My name is Barney Mucafee,
>   With my borers and jumpers down to my thee (thigh),
>   An' it 's forty miles I 've come to kerrb yer pee."

This vocabulary is, as he declared, an extremely imperfect specimen of the language. He did not claim to speak it well. In its purity it is not mingled with Romany or thieves' slang. Perhaps some student of English dialects may yet succeed in recovering it all. The pronunciation of many of the words is singular, and very different from English or Romany.

Just as the last word was written down, there came up a woman, a female tramp of the most hardened

kind. It seldom happens that gentlemen sit down in
familiar friendly converse with vagabonds. When
they do they are almost always religious people, anxious to talk with the poor for the good of their souls.
The talk generally ends with a charitable gift. Such
was the view (as the vagabond afterwards told us)
which she took of our party. I also infer that she
thought we must be very verdant and an easy prey.
Almost without preliminary greeting she told us that
she was in great straits, — suffering terribly, — and
appealed to the man for confirmation, adding that if
we would kindly lend her a sovereign it should be
faithfully repaid in the morning.

The professor burst out laughing. But the fern-
collector gazed at her in wrath and amazement.

"I say, old woman," he cried; "do you know who
you're *rakkerin* [speaking] to? This here gentleman
is one of the deepest Romany ryes [gypsy gentlemen]
a-going. And that there one could *gladdher* you out
of your eye-teeth."

She gave one look of dismay, — I shall never forget
that look, — and ran away. The witch had chanced
upon Arbaces. I think that the tramp had been in
his time a man in better position. He was possibly
a lawyer's clerk who had fallen into evil ways. He
spoke English correctly when not addressing the beggar woman. There was in Aberystwith at the same
time another fern-seller, an elderly man, as wretched
and as ragged a creature as I ever met. Yet he
also spoke English purely, and could give in Latin
the names of all the plants which he sold. I have always supposed that the tinkers' language spoken of
by Shakespeare was Romany; but I now incline to
think it may have been Shelta.

Time passed, and "the levis grene" had fallen

thrice from the trees, and I had crossed the sea and was in my native city of Philadelphia. It was a great change after eleven years of Europe, during ten of which I had " homed," as gypsies say, in England. The houses and the roads were old-new to me; there was something familiar-foreign in the voices and ways of those who had been my earliest friends; the very air as it blew hummed tunes which had lost tones in them that made me marvel. Yet even here I soon found traces of something which is the same all the world over, which goes ever on " as of ever," and that was the wanderer of the road. Near the city are three distinct gypsyries, where in summer-time the wagon and the tent may be found; and ever and anon, in my walks about town, I found interesting varieties of vagabonds from every part of Europe. Italians of the most Bohemian type, who once had been like angels, — and truly only in this, that their visits of old were few and far between, — now swarmed as fruit dealers and boot-blacks in every lane; Germans were of course at home; Czechs, or Slavs, supposed to be Germans, gave unlimited facilities for Slavonian practice; while tinkers, almost unknown in 1860, had in 1880 become marvelously common, and strange to say were nearly all Austrians of different kinds. And yet not quite all, and it was lucky for me they were not. For one morning, as I went into the large garden which lies around the house wherein I wone, I heard by the honeysuckle and grape-vine a familiar sound, — suggestive of the road and Romanys and London, and all that is most traveler-esque. It was the tap, tap, tap of a hammer and the clang of tin, and I knew by the smoke that so gracefully curled at the end of the garden a tinker was near. And I advanced to him, and as he glanced up and

greeted, I read in his Irish face long rambles on the
roads.

"Good-morning!"

"Good-mornin', sorr!"

"You 're an old traveler?"

"I am, sorr."

"Can you rakker Romanes?"

"I can, sorr!"

"*Pen yer nav.*"   (Tell your name.)

"Owen ——, sorr."

A brief conversation ensued, during which we ascertained that we had many friends in common in the
puro tem or Ould Country.   All at once a thought
struck me, and I exclaimed, —

"Do you know any other languages?"

"Yes, sorr: Ould Irish an' Welsh, an' a little
Gaelic."

"That 's all?"

"Yes, sorr, all av thim."

"All but one?"

"An' what 's that wan, sorr?"

"Can you *thari shelta, subli?*"

No tinker was ever yet astonished at anything.   If
he could be he would not be a tinker.   If the coals
in his stove were to turn to lumps of gold in a twinkle,
he would proceed with leisurely action to rake them
out and prepare them for sale, and never indicate by
a word or a wink that anything remarkable had occurred.   But Owen the tinker looked steadily at me
for an instant, as if to see what manner of man I
might be, and then said, —

"*Shelta*, is it?   An' I can talk it.   An' there 's not
six min livin' as can talk it as I do."

"Do you know, I think it 's very remarkable that
you can talk Shelta."

"An' begorra, I think it's very remarkable, sorr, that ye should know there is such a language." ·

"Will you give me a lesson?"

"Troth I will."

I went into the house and brought out a note-book. One of the servants brought me a chair. Owen went on soldering a tin dish, and I proceeded to take down from him the following list of words in *Shelta:*

Théddy,	Fire (*theinne.* Irish).
Strawn,	Tin.
Blyhunka,	Horse.
Leicheen,	Girl.
Soobli,	Male, man.
Binny soobli,	Boy.
Binny,	Small,
Chimmel,	Stick.
Gh'ratha, grata,	Hat.
Griffin, or gruffin,	Coat.
Réspes,	Trousers.
Gullemnocks,	Shoes.
Grascot,	Waistcoat.
Skoich, or skoi,	Button.
Numpa,	Sovereign, one **pound.**
Gorhead, or godhed,	Money.
Merrih,	Nose (?).
Nyock,	Head.
Graigh,	Hair.
Kainé, or kyni,	Ears (Romany, *kan*).
Mélthog,	Inner shirt.
Médthel,	Black.
Cunnels,	Potatoes.
Faihé, or feyé,	Meat (*féoil.* Gaelic).
Muogh,	Pig (*muck.* Irish).
Miesli, misli,	To go (origin of "mizzle"?)
Mailyas, or moillhas,	Fingers (*meirleach*, stealers. Gaelic).

Shaidyog,	'Policeman.
Réspun,	To steal.
Shoich,	Water, blood, liquid.
Alemnoch,	Milk.
Räglan, or réglan,	Hammer.
Goppa,	Furnace, smith (*gobha*, a smith. Gaelic).
Têrry,	A heating-iron.
Khoi,	Pincers.
Chimmes (compare *chimmel*),	Wood or stick.
Mailyas,	Arms.
Koras,	Legs (*cos*, leg. Gaelic).
Skoihōpa,	Whisky.
Bulla (*ull* as in *gull*),	A letter.
Thari,	Word, language.
Mush,	Umbrella (slang).
Lyesken cherps,	Telling fortunes.
Loshools,	Flowers (*lus*, herb or flower? Gaelic).
Dainoch,	To lose.
Chaldroch,	Knife (*caldock*, sharply pointed. Gaelic).
Bog,	To get.
Masheen,	Cat.
Cāmbra,	Dog.
Laprogh,	Goose, duck.
Kaldthog,	Hen.
Rumogh,	Egg.
Kîéna,	House (*ken*, old gypsy and modern cant).
Rawg,	Wagon.
Gullemnoch,	Shoes.
Anālt,	To sweep, to broom.
Anālken,	To wash.
D'erri,	Bread.
R'ghoglin (gogh'leen),	To laugh.

Krädyin,	To stop, stay, sit, lodge, remain.
Oura,	Town.
Lashool,	Nice (*lachool*. Irish).
Moïnni, or moryeni,	Good (*min*, pleasant. Gaelic).
Moryenni yook,	Good man.
Gyami,	Bad (*cam*. Gaelic).

Probably the origin of the common canting term *gammy*, bad.

Ishkimmisk,	Drunk (*misgeach*. Gaelic).
Roglan,	A four-wheeled vehicle.
Lorch,	A two-wheeled vehicle.
Smuggle,	Anvil.
Granya,	Nail.
Riaglon,	Iron.
Gūshūk,	Vessel of any kind.
Tédhi, thédi,	Coal; fuel of any kind.
Grawder,	Solder.
Tanyok,	Halfpenny.

(Query *tāni*, little, Romany, and *nyok*, a head.)

Chlorhin,	To hear.
Sūnain,	To see.
Salkaneoch,	To taste, take.
Mailyen,	To feel (*cumail*, to hold. Gaelic).
Crowder,	String.
Sobyé,	(?)
Mislain,	Raining (mizzle ?).
Goo-ope, gūop,	Cold.
Skoichen,	Rain.
Thomyok,	Magistrate.
Shadyog,	Police.
Bladhunk,	Prison.
Bogh,	To get.

Salt,	Arrested, taken.
Straihmed,	A year.
Gotherna, guttema,	Policeman.
[A very rare old word.]	
Dyūkās, or Jukas,	Gorgio, Gentile ; one not of the class.
Misli,	Coming, to come, to send.
To my-deal,	To me.
Lychyen,	People.
Grannis,	Know.
Skolaia,	To write.
Skolaiyami,	A good scholar.
Nyok,	Head.
Lurk,	Eye.
Menoch,	Nose.
Glorhoch,	Ear.
Koris,	Feet.
Tashi shingomai,	To read the newspaper.
Gorheid,	Money.
Tomgarheid (*i. e.* big money),	Gold.
Skawfer, skawper,	Silver.
Tomnumpa,	Bank-note.
Terri,	Coal.
Ghoi,	Put.
Nyadas,	Table.
Kradyin,	Being, lying.
Tarryin,	Rope.
Kor'heh,	Box.
Miseli,	Quick.
Krad'hyī,	Slow.
Th-mddusk,	Door.
Khaihed,	Chair (*khahir*. Irish).
Bord,	Table.
Grainyog,	Window.
Rūmog,	Egg.
Aidh,	Butter.

Okonneh,	A priest.

Thus explained in a very Irish manner: " *Okonneh,* or *Koony,* is a *sacred* man, and *kunī* in Romany means secret. An' sacret and sacred, sure, are all the same."

Shliéma,	Smoke, pipe.
Munches,	Tobacco.
Khadyogs,	Stones.
Yiesk,	Fish (*iasg.* Gaelic).
Cāb,	Cabbage.
Cherpin,	Book.

This appears to be vulgar. *Llyower* was on second thought declared to be the right word. (*Leabhar,* Gaelic.)

Misli dainoch.	To write a letter; to write; that is, send or go.
Misli to my bewr,	Write to my woman.
Gritche,	Dinner.
Gruppa,	Supper.
Goihed,	To leave, lay down.
Lūrks,	Eyes.
Ainoch,	Thing.
Clisp,	To fall, let fall.
Clishpen,	To break by letting **fall.**
Guth, gūt,	Black.
Gothni, gachlin,	Child.
Styémon,	Rat.
Krépoch,	Cat.
Grannien,	With child.
Loshūn,	Sweet.
Shum,	To own.
L'yogh,	To lose.
Crīmūm,	Sheep.
Khadyog,	Stone.
Nglou,	Nail.

Gial,	Yellow, red.
Talosk,	Weather.
Laprogh,	Bird.
Madel,	Tail.
Carob,	To cut.
Lūbran, luber,	To hit.
Thom,	Violently.
Mish it thom,	Hit it hard.
Subli, or soobli,	Man (*siublach*, a vagrant. Gaelic).

There you are, readers! Make good cheer of it, as Panurge said of what was beyond him. For what this language really is passeth me and mine. Of Celtic origin it surely is, for Owen gave me every syllable so garnished with gutturals that I, being even less of one of the Celtes than a Chinaman, have not succeeded in writing a single word according to his pronunciation of it. Thus even Minklers sounds more like *minkias*, or *pikias*, as he gave it.

To the foregoing I add the numerals and a few phrases : —

Hain, or heen,	One.
Do,	Two.
Tri,	Three.
Ch'air, or k'hair,	Four.
Cood,	Five.
Shé, or shay,	Six.
Schaacht, or schach',	Seven.
Ocht,	Eight.
Ayen, or nai,	Nine.
Dy'ai, djai, or dai,	Ten.
Hiuniadh,	Eleven.
Do yed'h,	Twelve.
Trin yedh,	Thirteen.
K'hair yedh, etc.,	Fourteen, etc.

24

Tat 'th chesin ogomsa,	That belongs to me.
Grannis to my deal,	It belongs to me.
Dioch man krady in in this nadas,	I am staying here.
Tash émilesh,	He is staying there.
Boghin the brass,	Cooking the food.
My deal is mislin,	I am going.
The nidias of the kiéna, don't granny what we're a tharyin,	The people of the house don't know what we're saying.

This was said within hearing of and in reference to a bevy of servants, of every hue save white, who were in full view in the kitchen, and who were manifestly deeply interested and delighted in our interview, as well as in the constant use of my note-book, and our conference in an unknown tongue, since Owen and I spoke frequently in Romany.

That bhoghd out yer mailya,	You let that fall from your hand.

I also obtained a verse of a ballad, which I may not literally render into pure English : —

> " Cosson kailyah corrum me morro sari,
>   Me gul ogalyach mir ;
>   Rähet mänent trasha moroch
>   Me tu sosti mo diéle."

> " Coming from Galway, tired and weary,
>   I met a woman ;
>   I 'll go bail by this time to-morrow,
>   You 'll have had enough of me."

Me tu sosti, " Thou shalt be (of) me," is Romany, which is freely used in Shelta.

The question which I cannot solve is, On which of the Celtic languages is this jargon based ? My informant declares that it is quite independent of Old

Irish, Welsh, or Gaelic. In pronunciation it appears
to be almost identical with the latter; but while there
are Gaelic words in it, it is certain that much examination and inquiry have failed to show that it is con-
tained in that language. That it is "the talk of the
ould Picts — thim that built the stone houses like bee-
hives" — is, I confess, too conjectural for a philologist. I have no doubt that when the Picts were
suppressed thousands of them must have become
wandering outlaws, like the Romany, and that their
language in time became a secret tongue of vagabonds
on the roads. This is the history of many such lin-
goes; but unfortunately Owen's opinion, even if it
be legendary, will not prove that the Painted People
spoke the Shelta tongue. I must call attention, however, to one or two curious points. I have spoken of
Shelta as a jargon; but it is, in fact, a language, for
it can be spoken grammatically and without using
English or Romany. And again, there is a corrupt
method of pronouncing it, according to English,
while correctly enunciated it is purely Celtic in
sound. More than this I have naught to say.

Shelta is perhaps the last Old British dialect as
yet existing which has thus far remained undiscov-
ered. There is no hint of it in John Camden Hotten's Slang Dictionary, nor has it been recognized by
the Dialect Society. Mr. Simson, had he known the
"Tinklers" better, would have found that not Romany, but Shelta, was the really secret language which
they employed, although Romany is also more or less
familiar to them all. To me there is in it something
very weird and strange. I cannot well say why; it
seems as if it might be spoken by witches and talking toads, and uttered by the Druid stones, which are

fabled to come down by moonlight to the water-side to drink, and who will, if surprised during their walk, answer any questions. Anent which I would fain ask my Spiritualist friends one which I have long yearned ˙ to put. Since you, my dear ghost-raisers, can call spirits from the vasty deep of the outside-most beyond, will you not — having many millions from which to call — raise up one of the Pictish race, and, having· brought it in from the *Ewigkeit*, take down a vocabulary of the language? Let it be a lady *par préference*, — the fair being by far the more fluent in words. Moreover, it is probable that as the Picts were a painted race, woman among them must have been very much to the fore, and that Madame Rachels occupied a high position with rouge, enamels, and other appliances to make them young and beautiful forever. According to Southey, the British blue-stocking is descended from these woad-stained ancestresses, which assertion dimly hints at their having been literary. In which case, *voilà notre affaire!* for then the business would be promptly done. Wizards of the secret spells, I adjure ye, raise me a Pictess for the˙ sake of philology — and the picturesque!

You may also enjoy ...

Wandering Between Two Worlds: Essays on Faith and Art
Anita Mathias
Benediction Books, 2007
152 pages
ISBN: 0955373700

Available from www.amazon.com, www.amazon.co.uk
www.wanderingbetweentwoworlds.com

     In these wide-ranging lyrical essays, Anita Mathias writes, in lush, lovely prose, of her naughty Catholic childhood in Jamshedpur, India; her large, eccentric family in Mangalore, a sea-coast town converted by the Portuguese in the sixteenth century; her rebellion and atheism as a teenager in her Himalayan boarding school, run by German missionary nuns, St. Mary's Convent, Nainital; and her abrupt religious conversion after which she entered Mother Teresa's convent in Calcutta as a novice. Later rich, elegant essays explore the dualities of her life as a writer, mother, and Christian in the United States-- Domesticity and Art, Writing and Prayer, and the experience of being "an alien and stranger" as an immigrant in America, sensing the need for roots.

About the Author

Anita Mathias was born in India, has a B.A. and M.A. in English from Somerville College, Oxford University and an M.A. in Creative Writing from the Ohio State University. Her essays have been published in The Washington Post, The London Magazine, The Virginia Quarterly Review, Commonweal, Notre Dame Magazine, America, The Christian Century, Religion Online, The Southwest Review, Contemporary Literary Criticism, New Letters, The Journal, and two of HarperSanFrancisco's The Best Spiritual Writing anthologies. Her non-fiction has won fellowships from The National Endowment for the Arts; The Minnesota State Arts Board; The Jerome Foundation, The Vermont Studio Center; The Virginia Centre for the Creative Arts, and the First Prize for the Best General Interest Article from the Catholic Press Association of the United States and Canada. Anita has taught Creative Writing at the College of William and Mary, and now lives and writes in Oxford, England.
Website: www.anitamathias.com/
Blog: wanderingbetweentwoworlds.blogspot.com/

www.ingramcontent.com/pod-product-compliance
Lightning Source LLC
Chambersburg PA
CBHW021537260326
41914CB00001B/59

9781849028271